# Generational
# Patterns
# Using Astrology

# Generational Patterns Using Astrology

Edwin Rose

BOOKS

Winchester, UK
Washington, USA

First published by O-Books, 2011
O Books is an imprint of John Hunt Publishing Ltd., The Bothy, Deershot Lodge, Park Lane, Ropley,
Hants, SO24 0BE, UK
office1@o-books.net
www.o-books.com

For distributor details and how to order please visit the 'Ordering' section on our website.

Text copyright Edwin Rose 2010

ISBN: 978 1 84694 446 8

A CIP catalogue record for this book is available from the British Library.

Design: Stuart Davies

Printed in the UK by CPI Antony Rowe, Chippenham, Wiltshire
Printed in the USA by Offset Paperback Mfrs, Inc

We operate a distinctive and ethical publishing philosophy in all
areas of its business, from its global network of authors to
production and worldwide distribution.

# CONTENTS

# Introduction

## Brief Introduction to Astrology

There are four parts to an astrology chart: signs, planets, aspects, and houses. These form the basis of the chart.

There are 12 signs (Aries, Taurus, etc.) that are arranged along the circle of the zodiac. Each sign is exactly one-twelfth of the 360 degrees of the whole zodiac – therefore each sign is 30 degrees. The Sun, Moon, and planets all move along this zodiacal circle (in astrology, the Sun and Moon are also called 'planets'). As they move, each planet 'transits' the signs.

So, at the spring equinox, the Sun moves into the sign Aries, a month later the Sun is in Taurus, and a month after that it is in Gemini, etc. Likewise the Moon, Mercury, Venus, Mars, Jupiter, Saturn, Uranus, Neptune, and Pluto move through the signs. Whereas the Sun takes a month per sign and a year to circle the zodiac, the Moon takes two and a half days per sign and a month to circle the whole zodiac. The slowest-moving planet, Pluto, takes 246 years to circle the zodiac and averages 21 years per sign.

As the planets move through the zodiac, they form angular relationships, called 'aspects', to each other. When two planets are at the same part of the zodiac (when they are right next to each other in the sky), they are said to be 'conjunct'. At the new Moon, the Sun and Moon are conjunct. When they are at opposite sides of the zodiac, 180 degrees apart, they are said to be 'in opposition'. At the Full Moon, the Sun and Moon are in opposition; when the Sun sets at the western horizon, the Moon is rising in the east. Another way of saying this is that 'the Sun opposes the Moon'.

Conjuncts merge the energy of the two planets and start a cycle. The cycle completes when the faster-moving planet comes back around to conjunct the slower-moving planet. On a clock, the hour and minute hand are conjunct at noon. They conjunct again at about 1:06 pm when the faster-moving minute hand catches up to the slower-moving hour hand. At around 12:33 pm the hands are in opposition.

The longest cycle is that of Neptune and Pluto. This cycle takes 493 years (two cycles of Pluto and three of Neptune). For more information, see the Aspects section below.

The houses are in individual people's charts – there are 12 houses, which start with the ascendent or eastern horizon. These are areas of life. Each house is numbered, starting with the first house and ending with the twelfth house. So, for example, the fourth house, like the fourth sign of Cancer, is the area of the home and family.

Each planet is both in a sign and in a house. For example, you may have Pluto in Leo in the tenth house.

To have your chart – your natal horoscope – drawn for you, go to any chart calculation service or a friend with a computer and an astrology program.

## Historical Cycles

*Those who ignore history are doomed to repeat it.*
George Santayana

Are there cycles in history? Of course there are. These cycles can help you to understand the generation into which you and those close to you were born. The ability to predict what people will be like in the future is based on the cycles repeating. Just as a weather forecaster can see a storm approaching and compares it to other, similar storms, so we can see what each cycle has meant in the past and use it to predict the future.

The cycles used in this book are based on astrology, specifically the cycles of the outer planets: Jupiter through Pluto. The outer planets of each person are in a specific pattern of sign and aspect at birth, but after that, the planets continue their movements – the 'transits' – and go to other signs and form different aspects.

This book focuses on the cycles of the outer planets in the signs and how the generations born with them will act. This is the 'nature' of each person – his or her birth or 'natal' pattern. But you are also shaped by how you fit into the cycles of your country, so there is a section on the generational patterns of the United States and Europe.

Before we examine the cycles, we need to understand the outer planets and the signs of the zodiac. We will focus here on the broader meaning of the outer planets and the broader, impersonal qualities of the signs.

## The Planets

Astrology has slower-moving planets that define broad social change and generational patterns, and inner planets that rule more individual qualities. For our purposes, the following planets are useful for viewing long-term social change:

- Jupiter – one year per sign or 12 years for the zodiac
- Saturn – two and a half years per sign or 29 years for the zodiac
- Uranus – seven years per sign or 84 years for the zodiac
- Neptune – 14 years per sign or 164 years for the zodiac
- Pluto – 12 to 32 years per sign (it has an erratic orbit); average of 21 years per sign with 246 years for the zodiac

The planets can be thought of as an onion. The slowest-moving planets form the deepest layers and have the broadest effects. The outer planets fall into two camps. Uranus, Neptune, and Pluto fall into one camp of transcendental planets, while Jupiter and Saturn fall into the other camp of planets with broad social, political, and material stability.

The transcendental planets in the sky rule change and transformation. They break out of the limits of 'normalcy' characterized by Saturn and Jupiter. However, in an individual's chart,
they define that person's (often unquestioned) wisdom, faith, and
reality.

Each person is born with a planet in a sign and house, which
becomes part of who he or she 'is' and of that individual's generational footprint. Then throughout the person's lifetime, each
planet visits other signs and houses.

As an example, if you have Jupiter in Aries, for you Jupiter
would always represent the need to kick open doors, to plan
aggressively, etc. As Jupiter spends a year in each sign, this
aggressive Jupiter would find itself in different circumstances.
When Jupiter goes through Pisces, you would need to be more
compassionate and helpful to the downtrodden, but your
tendency would be to try to help by angrily telling them to better
themselves!

## Jupiter

Jupiter takes one year per sign. When you were in school, most of
your classmates were in the same Jupiter sign. This explains why
each different grade in school has a different quality.

Jupiter is your sense of humor, your optimism, your need for
growth, how you expand into new possibilities, and your plans.
Images for Jupiter are a rotund politician or jovial businessman.
Jupiterians, due to their magnetism, tend to be lucky, and oftentimes wealthy. Each generation of Jupiterians has a different
sense of humor and different plans to improve their lives. This is
the rational and reasonable planet.

Sometimes Jupiter can be rational and reasonable when the
situation calls for immediate change or action. Jupiter can smooth
over what really needs to be addressed. For example, if you
discover you have been underpaid and overworked relative to
your co-workers, and you have turned down better offers, a

reasonable and rational explanation from your smiling boss really won't cut it.

Jupiter's downfall is greed, over-reaching, and snobbishness. These are the classic sins of hubris.

Each Jupiter generation's particular sense of superiority or inferiority is based on Jupiter. The generation with Jupiter in Scorpio feels superior because they are more intense, while the generation with Jupiter in Virgo feels superior because they know more facts, are neater, and are more efficient.

## Saturn

Saturn is, in many ways, the opposite of Jupiter. Jupiter is humorous; Saturn is serious. Jupiter is expansive; Saturn contractive. Jupiter is optimistic; Saturn is pessimistic. Jupiter is limitless; Saturn limits. Jupiter is liberal; Saturn is conservative. Jupiter looks forward to the future; Saturn looks back to the past. Jupiter can be greedy and superior; Saturn can be just the opposite: miserly and inferior. Yet they are both social planets.

Jupiter bonds people through a common goal, while Saturn bonds people through organization, especially hierarchical organization.

Saturn is where you feel you must 'get it together'. All your fears and your sense of inadequacy come up in the natal sign of Saturn, and you sense you must accomplish something lasting within that realm.

The way people view authority and the types of leaders they follow tend to be a function of Saturn. For example, Saturn in Gemini represents intellectual authority, Saturn in Sagittarius represents political and religious authority, and so on.

While Jupiter is middle age, Saturn is old age. The sign where Saturn is placed in your chart indicates where you are conservative and serious.

In political astrology, Saturn represents the infrastructure, the government, the corporations, and the 'establishment'. When people talk about 'going through channels', they are talking about Saturn. The best tactic with Saturn is delay – stretch it out for years until all the fire and immediacy have left the issue. Saturn is time. 'One step at a time' is the Saturn mantra.

Aspects to Saturn involve the relationship to government and to those in established positions of control. In a natal chart, Saturn represents how you view authority – either your own authority, or, if projected, another's authority.

Jupiter is liberal and optimistic; Saturn is conservative and pessimistic. Jupiter believes people are basically good, that they need to be given the means to be productive and they will improve the situation. Saturn believes just the opposite; it believes people will take advantage of others, are basically evil and, given the chance, will rob others blind. Jupiter, therefore, believes in giving more to the poor, and Saturn believes in giving less to the 'thieving' poor. Jupiter believes in being caring and nurturing, like a mother or a caring father, while Saturn believes in blind 'justice' and stern father figures. Negative Saturn is the scrooge archetype.

Saturn is the planet of fear and difficulties. What you fear and how you handle fear come from Saturn. How you approach difficult situations can be predicted by your Saturn placement.

## Uranus

Uranus is the start of the outer planet trio of Uranus, Neptune, and Pluto. Saturn is the last 'traditional' planet and the capstone on 'normal' reality. The outer planets break you out of normal routine and awaken you to alternative ways of living.

Uranus is like a brief jolt that breaks you out of your normal life. Uranus is electrical excitement, the flash of recognition, the winds of change and revolution, and the wisdom that pierces through blocks. Uranus is unfettered joy and flashes of inventiveness. Uranus can also be weird, eccentric, and unsettling.

What excites each generation is Uranus. The Uranus-in-

Gemini generation gets excited about books and ideas. Uranus in Cancer feels the joy of cooking and the excitement of home and family. In Leo, Uranus gets excited and joyful through drama and romance.

People try to become free of the sign in which Uranus was when they were born – they rebel. With Uranus in Gemini, people try to free themselves of the mind; with Uranus in Cancer, they try to free themselves from their family and from having a family dependent on them.

Uranus is the planet of freedom. People find freedom through the sign Uranus occupies. People with Uranus in Leo find freedom through fun and games. People with Uranus in Gemini get their freedom through curiosity, thought, and writing.

But Uranus also rules people's ideals – the goals toward which they strive and what they 'hope' will happen. For example, people with Uranus in Cancer try to rebel against their upbringing while simultaneously striving for their ideal home life and family. Uranus in Cancer hopes people will be more caring; Uranus in Libra hopes for greater harmony and justice between people.

How people deal with their causes or ideals is Uranus. Uranus in Aries fights for ideals; Uranus in Gemini talks about ideals; and Uranus in Cancer cares about ideals.

Uranus is like the ascendant of the generation. Uranus is the way people perceive the world and the way the generation comes across (i.e. the equivalent of viewpoint and personality ruled by the ascendant in a person's chart). For example, Uranus in Aries views life as the survival of the fittest; Uranus in Gemini sees life as a mental challenge; and Uranus in Scorpio sees life as sexual, magnetic, and intensely intriguing.

Each generation tries to come across as the sign its Uranus occupies. Uranus in Aries tries to come across as forceful and commanding; Uranus in Scorpio tries to come across as intense, magnetic, and sexy; Uranus in Cancer tries to come across as caring; and Uranus in Gemini tries to come across as intellectual.

Among the primary spiritual qualities of joy, love, and peace, Uranus is the aspect of joy.

## Neptune

Neptune is your image. Each generation's image is filtered through the sign in which Neptune was at their birth. This image pervades the TV programs, advertising, movies, novels, and general culture of the time. What each generation dreams about, what confuses them, where their illusions are, and what appearances they maintain are all Neptune. People's compassion and faith come through this planet. Neptune takes 14 years to transit a sign.

For example, the Neptune-in-Virgo generation, which came of age in the 1950s, tries to maintain the illusion of being clean-cut, polite, organized, and of service to others. However, because image is everything, they may actually have all the clutter hidden in a closet. The Neptune-in-Libra generation, which came of age in the 1960s, idealizes relationships, music, and art. This generation wants to appear harmonious. This is the 'flower child' generation. The Neptune-in-Scorpio generation that followed is into Kiss, Black Sabbath, piercings, and punk.

Neptune is like the Moon of a person's chart, only for each generation. It's the emotionality, the glamour, and the comfortable images of each generation.

But the most important aspect of Neptune is faith – not just religious faith, but faith in self, faith in society, faith in government, faith in the economy, and even faith in science. When faith in institutions or self is disrupted, major consequences follow.

Whereas Uranus is joy, Neptune is love or compassion. Neptune is the glue that holds people together and also the grease that allows hard situations to be tolerated. When Pluto shows an unpleasant reality, Neptune covers it over with an illusion or tries to escape it.

The downfalls of Neptune are guilt, hypocrisy, illusions, false glamour, and disenchantment. On a broad scale, when the faith and image of a whole society are being transformed, as during a Neptune-Pluto conjunct or opposition, the times will be trying. Those with Neptune conjunct Pluto in their chart will live in trying times.

The spirit of the times is Neptune. Another word for this spirit is 'culture' – the cultural milieu is Neptunian. Each generation's culture comes through Neptune. Neptune in Libra has a culture of music and art; Neptune in Scorpio has a culture of cynicism and sexuality.

Here also are drugs and dreams. How each generation relates to their dreams and what they use drugs to achieve, or to escape from, is through Neptune. Neptune in Libra uses drugs and dreams to relate to others – communal drugs and dream circles are part of this generation's legacy. Neptune in Scorpio use drugs for sexual enhancement (Viagra) and to improve their sense of power. Neptune in Sagittarius use drugs to expand their awareness and to travel to other realms.

## Pluto

This planet uncovers the depths. Pluto exposes the underlying reality and power issues. Whereas Neptune veils, Pluto unveils. Pluto is the planet of revelation. What each generation assumes to be 'real' is Pluto. The destiny, or fate, of each generation is Pluto; people feel they must do Plutonian things. Each generation's 'all or nothing' is Pluto. It reveals their primal dualities. For example, the Pluto-in-Virgo generation has both people who are 'slackers' and others who are workaholics; in other words, they are all or nothing about work. The Pluto-in-Leo generation includes people who must have fun, who must follow life paths with that have 'heart', and must be creative, and it also includes others who can be totally self-centered egotists (the 'me' generation) and against all bosses (ruled by Leo).

Pluto rules whoever has the power, and how that is decided for each generation. With Pluto in Virgo, for example, the most technical people, the ones in command of the most facts, and the best workers, have the power within that generation. With Pluto in Leo, the best performers and the people with the most heart have the power – but so do those who operate the best in risky situations (gambling is Leo).

Pluto takes between 12 and 32 years to transit a sign. Pluto has the most erratic orbit of all the planets. When it is near Scorpio, it takes 12 years; when it is near Taurus, it takes 32 years. So the Pluto-in-Scorpio generation takes place over less than half the time of the Pluto-in-Taurus generation – many of the Pluto-in-Taurus generation had parents with the same Pluto; none of the Pluto-in-Scorpio generation have parents with Pluto in that sign.

In fact, for a while when near Scorpio, Pluto actually goes inside the orbit of Neptune. People of this generation can be less grounded in reality because they live more on faith or image. In the most recent generation, they spend more time playing computer simulations (Neptune) than actually going out into the 'real' world.

Pluto is like the Sun of each generation. The core reality, the bedrock stability, of people is their Pluto. Just as the Sun is people's fundamental way of acting, so Pluto is a generation's reality that forms the basis of their actions.

Your sense of survival is tied up with Pluto, also. It is life or death, psychically, when Pluto is involved. Sometimes it is death and then life – in other words, rebirth. When Pluto transits, something dies, but something else may be born. When Pluto transited Scorpio, sex (ruled by Scorpio) became a life-and-death issue due to AIDS. Children are often born with Pluto making strong aspects to the parents' charts, which means the child will awaken the parents to whatever is indicated by Pluto as the child grows up.

When the veil of illusion of Neptune is drawn back, you get the revelation of Pluto. At that point, there is no denying what is going on; there is no vagueness. So, the sign of Pluto is how each generation is brought face-to-face with reality.

Pluto can be the peacefulness of the depths or the violent agitation of the surface. Pluto also represents the quiet before the storm or the eye of the hurricane.

People in undifferentiated masses are represented by Pluto. For example, the Saturn-Pluto cycle involves the masses versus the establishment (Saturn). How each generation bonds into a social mass is through Pluto. For example, Pluto in Leo bonds through fun and entertainment, while Pluto in Virgo bonds through technology, work, and service.

In transit, Pluto is wherever power lies. As Pluto goes from Cancer to Capricorn, power becomes based in committees and legislatures. As it goes from Capricorn to Cancer, power becomes focused on individuals. When Pluto is on the bottom of the chart, power is in individuals or families; that is, power is personal. When Pluto is on the top half, power is impersonal.

Often, that power associated with Pluto is perceived as alien or alienating. Compulsions are forces that seem to come from outside you, that are alien. Any action you are forced to do under compulsion, either from another or from yourself, is Plutonian. Each generation's compulsions are through their Pluto.

**Aspects**

Aspects are relationships between planets. The more important aspects are based on the planets being a set number of signs apart.

If two planets are conjunct, they are within eight degrees of each other. When two planets are in the same sign of the zodiac, the effects are like a conjunct, but weaker. When planets are conjunct, their energies merge and amplify each other. As with all aspects, each planet's energy modifies or acts on the other planet.

In a cycle of aspects, a conjunct represents the start and end of the cycle. So the results of the old cycle are completed and a new birth of energy is initiated.

For example, when Saturn is conjunct Pluto, the Saturnine need to limit acts on Pluto, the planet of power, in order to limit power. By contrast, Pluto, which represents the breakthrough of reality, tries to blast any limits not based on reality. Working together, the Saturn-Pluto conjunct tries to focus and institution-alize power. Because Pluto is the mass of the people and Saturn is the government and institutions, when these two are conjunct the government tends to be close to and aligned with the masses. The conjuncts of outer planets, and their ability to define generations, are explored in the Conjunct Generations chapter.

An opposition is when two planets are six signs, or 180 degrees, apart on the zodiac. They oppose each other, and their signs reflect the quality of the opposition. Each planet sees the other as distant, as different, which can cause conflict or separation between the energies. Psychologically, this can result in what is called 'projection'; each planet sees the other as like it, but opposing it, even when there is no true similarity and often no real opposition at the root.

In a cycle of aspects, the opposition is the peak of the cycle. The faster-moving planet holds sway between the conjunct and opposition, the period known as the 'waxing', while the slower-moving planet has sway from the opposition to the conjunct, known as the 'waning'.

Going back to Saturn and Pluto, when these planets are in opposition, the government and institutions (i.e. the estab-lishment) are far from the masses of the people and the destiny and reality (also Pluto) of the country. This often creates ignorance of the real needs of the masses in the political estab-lishment and hostility of the masses toward the government and institutions, which seem to be ignoring them.

For a generation with Saturn opposition Pluto, they will find that their attempts to establish a practical stability (Saturn) will be challenged by realities (Pluto) that keep unsettling their attempts to solidify their position. Any fears (Saturn) will be made more graphic by the realities that they are facing (Pluto).

Although the conjunct and the opposition are the main aspects used in this book, there are other major aspects that are sometimes used. The 'square' is when planets are three signs or 90 degrees apart. Squares, like oppositions, are difficult or tense. However, with squares there is a dynamic tension – there is a tendency to flip back and forth between the two planets, with neither side being satisfactory.

There are also smooth or easy aspects: the 'trine', which is four signs or 120 degrees apart, and the 'sextile', which is two signs or 60 degrees apart. When two planets are trine, they create a positive, supportive relationship. The sextile is more dynamic; the two signs have a bantering, back-and-forth relationship. The sextile involves fellow travelers. For example, Leo and Libra are love and marriage because these two signs are sextile each other. Virgo and Scorpio are servant and master – they, too, are sextile.

## Signs of the Zodiac

The zodiac has 12 signs. These represent ways of acting. For example, since Aries is a forceful, direct way of acting, Jupiter in Aries would act forcefully. The image is of a person kicking open the door of opportunity.

The signs show different qualities in a birth chart than they do when considering large generational patterns. The Sun is in Taurus for a month; Pluto is in Taurus for 32 years. The implications of Taurus that come out in a 32-year transit that affects the whole world are more profound than those that reflect how an individual acts who has a Taurus sun sign.

The solar ruler is the planet that shows the manner in which a sign acts, and the lunar ruler is the way that sign reacts.

Capricorn, for example, acts seriously and conservatively (solar ruler: Saturn), and reacts spontaneously to unsettling situations (lunar ruler: Uranus). In fact, Capricorn is most at ease when everything is chaotic around it (Uranus) because a chaotic environment is created when patience and the ability to get it together (Saturn) win out. Another example is that Libra creates beauty and relationships (solar ruler: Venus), while Taurus reacts to and appreciates beauty (lunar ruler: Venus).

'Exaltation' refers to the planet that has the qualities that a sign looks up to. A 'fall' is when a sign is in opposition to another sign that has an exaltation, and tends to denigrate or pull down the qualities of that planet. For example, Saturn is the wisdom and stability of old age, and it is looked up to by Libra, but slighted and pulled down by Aries. You want a Libran judge to be older and experienced; you want the seriousness of Saturn to solidify the dilettante quality of Libra. Old, conservative people (Saturn) are not what vibrant, confrontative pioneers (Aries) need. In fact, they put down those sorts.

## Aries (solar ruler: Pluto; lunar ruler: Mars; exalted: Sun; fall: Saturn)

This is the start of the zodiac. New entities come into being here. Here is the pioneer, the leader in a dangerous adventure. Aries must be direct, forceful, and confrontational. When Neptune and Pluto went through Aries, it was the age of the captains of industry, whose motto was 'The public be damned'. Aries doesn't care what others think; Aries has its own destiny or cause. Neptune in Aries gave birth to new countries and new cultural entities, as arbitrary divisions were swept away. Aries must keep in constant movement and renounce anything that would tie it down.

Although we have listed Pluto as the solar ruler and Mars as the lunar ruler, Mars is the more apparent ruler. Danger, aggression, and directness are all Martian traits. Pluto is the sense of destiny that drives Aries.

## Taurus (lunar ruler: Venus; exalted: Moon)

Taurus finds a spot and stays there. At first, this spot is a break with the past, but it soon becomes part of the accepted way of being. If Aries is the pioneer, Taurus is the homesteader.

This sign loves the senses and sensuality. It is the connoisseur of the zodiac. During the 3,000 years of Neptune-Pluto conjuncts and oppositions in Taurus, humanity needed physical prophets – actual people who represented God. Many religions spoke about getting beyond the senses and considered sensuality to be evil.

Taurus is associated with large tomes written after years of research. Both Sigmund Freud and Karl Marx were Tauruses. Capital accumulation and building-up of personal wealth also come under this sign. Ownership ('this is *mine*') is Taurus. When outer planets go through Taurus, ownership of land and resources are causes of fighting.

## Gemini (lunar ruler: Mercury)

Gemini rules communication, travel over short distances, dexterity, speediness, and intellectual pursuits. This sign is immensely curious. Journalism is a prime Gemini career because it involves all these qualities. Another Gemini career is sales. If there were a Geminian animal, it would be the monkey.

When outer planets transit Gemini, transportation and communication are often affected. New mental capacities or intellectual theories are introduced. Gemini is the sign of amusement. When Neptune and Pluto went through Gemini, amusement parks, bicycles, and automobiles were introduced. New intellectual concepts for seeing the world, such as radio and movies, also were introduced (see the Neptune-Pluto conjunct section for more details). The next couple of thousand years are under Gemini because of the Neptune-Pluto conjunct. Since this conjunct went into Gemini, the world has sped up and become more interconnected.

### Cancer (lunar ruler: Moon; exalted: Jupiter; fall: Mars)

Home and family are Cancer. A person's personal structure is under this sign. The focus is on caring when planets cross Cancer. Cancer is the sign of awareness and sensitivity. Dependence on others (e.g. a child on its mother) is the focus of the sign. Issues about maternal femininity or the feminine come up with transits here. For example, witch hunts occurred when outer planets were here. Because Cancer is the base of the chart, sometimes outer planets here shake up the base.

For example, people born with Uranus in Cancer want to be free (Uranus) of dependency on others, or others depending on them. They want to be free of ruts and of habitual ways of acting; ruts and habits are also Cancerian.

### Leo (solar ruler: Sun; exalted: Neptune)

Leo is the sign of royalty. It rules creativity, fun, and children. Leos love to bluff and take risks. When outer planets transit Leo, the focus is on humanity's rulers, but also on having a good time. Leo likes to be intensely alive. However, this can also be the sign of being overbearing. When Pluto first entered Leo in 1939, Hitler screamed of the need for 'room to live' and overran the rest of Europe. It is not surprising that Germany is in the center of Europe. Another example of Leo is Neptune in Leo in the 1920s, also called the 'Roaring Twenties', with hot jazz babies, speakeasies, and glamorous movies.

The Leo-Virgo cusp is associated with over-expansion, or overheating, leading to illness or a crash. A prime example is Neptune crossing the cusp in 1929, leading to the stock market crash. Other examples are given throughout the book.

### Virgo (solar ruler: Mercury; exalted: Mercury)

After the Leo party comes the clean-up. Virgo is the servant and the hard worker. This is also the sign of the military, bureaucracies, and technology. When outer planets transit here, technology becomes important. For example, when Pluto entered Virgo, the USSR's Sputnik spacecraft was sent into orbit and the USA put its emphasis on technology and science education for the space race. People born with Pluto in Virgo are in the forefront of the computer and Internet revolutions with their technical knowledge. The focus of the Virgo club is on work – 'What is your job?'

## Libra (solar ruler: Venus; exalted: Saturn; fall: Sun)

Librans are the harmonizers of the zodiac. Love, harmony, and beauty are the qualities of Libra. Whereas Taurus appreciates beauty, Libra wants to create beauty. Librans' focus is partnership, whether in marriage or business. However, it should be remembered that open enmity was associated with Libra in the older astrology books. Any one-on-one close interaction with others is Libran.

The fads of society, and society itself, are both Libran. Librans have a broad, sometimes encyclopedic, knowledge, but they can also be 'on the surface', or dilettantes.

## Scorpio (solar ruler: Mars; lunar ruler: Pluto; fall: Moon)

As with Aries, the lunar ruler Pluto is more apparent as the ruler. Scorpio is intense, sexual, dark, and secretive. Scorpios often have poker faces; they try to discover everything about others and show nothing about themselves. Typical Scorpio activities involve subtle use of force, such as is done by a surgeon, detective, or psychologist.

When outer planets go through Scorpio, social transformation is often brought about by the masses (ruled by Pluto) demanding more power (also Pluto). Sometimes, changes in sexual mores occur. For example, Pluto in Scorpio brought the life-and-death quality of Pluto to the sexuality of Scorpio through the AIDS epidemic.

### Sagittarius (solar ruler: Jupiter; lunar ruler: Neptune)

Sagittarius rules politics, philosophy, and religion, all of which are expounded from a raised platform. Universities and professors also come under Sagittarius. Because politics and religion often result in heated debate, Sagittarius is adept at smoothing things over. Sagittarians are planners and architects. They also cheerlead and inspire others. Without enthusiasm, Sagittarius is lost. Philosophers, religious leaders, and politicians are important when an outer planet transits this sign.

This sign is the visionary. It concerns itself with the future, as does its Jupiter ruler. Sagittarius aspires – goals are Sagittarian. However, this sign is also the clown, the sign of humor and pratfalls.

One downfall to Sagittarius is the need to proselytize, to bring others on board to one's beliefs. When outer planets transit Sagittarius, this proselytizing, especially for religion, can go overboard.

### Capricorn (solar ruler: Saturn; lunar ruler: Uranus; exaltation: Mars; fall: Jupiter)

The symbol for Capricorn is the mountain goat. Capricorns climb the hierarchical pyramids of government and industry. They use time (Saturn) to bring themselves to and maintain themselves at the top of the heap. They outlast others. When outer planets transit Capricorn, the government and ruling establishments come under stress.

Capricorns are serious, hard-working, career-oriented individuals. A career is a long-term working goal, and so careers are under Capricorn. Capricorns like to achieve. A person's accomplishments and responsibilities are both Capricornian. Capricorns often come into their own in later life, especially if they have accomplished their goals. Like Saturn, old age is their time to shine.

One of the key words for Capricorn is 'independence'. Outer

planets in Capricorn often result in splits due to independence movements. Prime examples are the American and Protestant revolutions, when Pluto transited Capricorn.

However, also like Saturn, Capricorns can run into trouble when they try to exercise too much control over themselves and others. This is especially true when they try to force obedience and become moralistic.

## Aquarius (solar ruler: Uranus; lunar ruler: Saturn; fall: Sun)

If Sagittarius is aspiration, Aquarius is inspiration. Aquarians want to be unique individuals, but work best when part of a group. Whereas Capricorns focus on organized hierarchies, Aquarians focus on clubs where they can meet friends ('friends' is a big Aquarian word). Some call everyone they meet, 'my friend'. Trust and friendship are important, always.

Aquarians prize freedom. They are free spirits, especially when younger. When older, they want to be free to act in their eccentric ways. Aquarians can often be spotted by the flashing electricity in their eyes.

Aquarians are humanitarian and theoretical. Aquarians can think about an idea for years, to come up with their theory of what is happening.

Aquarians are often out of step with time. They often live in the future or the past in an idealized world. If you wish upon a star, you are probably an Aquarian.

However, with a Saturn lunar ruler, fear is the downfall of Aquarius. Pluto in Aquarius resulted in the *Grande Peur*, or 'Great Fear', before the French Revolution. Uranus in Aquarius saw the 'Red Scare' in 1919. In Aquarian individuals, this may come out as hypochondria. Franklin Delano Roosevelt, an Aquarian, said, 'The only thing to fear is fear itself', stating a primary lesson of Aquarius.

## Pisces (solar ruler: Neptune; lunar ruler: Jupiter; exaltation: Venus; fall: Mercury)

Pisces is the end of the zodiac. As the zodiac progresses, it becomes less individualistic. Pisces, therefore, is the least individualistic sign. Pisces gives in to others; 'Whatever!' is a key expression.

Here are institutions of confinement and places where people are on the fringes of society: hospitals, insane asylums, prisons, ghettoes, and monasteries. If success is Sagittarian, failure is Piscean in the sense that you must come to grips with those parts of yourself that cause failure or with ways to deal with failure. Often Pisces seems like a closed loop; it seems impossible to get out of the ghetto.

However, the lunar ruler of Jupiter brings humor and a sense of the unconfined to Pisces, as well. Pisces rules the ocean and compassion (from the Neptune ruler). Many large, humorous comedians are Piscean. Pisces people often run on intuition.

During Pisces transits, greater compassion is shown for the poor and the lower classes. Charity increases and institutions to help others are founded. However, due to fuzzy boundaries, countries can be invaded by outsiders or by other nations.

### Nature versus Nurture

In astrology, nature is the natal positions of the planets, while nurture is the transiting planets. Planets act differently when you are living *through* certain times than they do when you were born *in* the times. For example, the Uranus-Pluto conjunct in the 1960s was a time of great change and transformation, yet people born in the 1960s are not as revolutionary as the times. Perhaps this is because the people born during that decade embody the changes, while the people living through the decade were awakening to what needed to be changed.

The people coming of age in the 1960s were those born after World War II, a relatively conservative period. And yet these were the people who rebelled against the ways embodied by their parents. Often, a given period will have three or four Neptune-Pluto generations and ten or more Uranus generations reacting to what is going on. Furthermore, each of these generations can be sub-classified by the Jupiter-Saturn combinations going on. The generational planets are the planets of your birth.

## Planet Cycles

There are two planetary cycles: the place of each outer planet within the zodiac and the cycle of aspects between outer planets. The zodiacal cycle is straightforward. Each planet starts the cycle at Aries and completes it when it comes around to Aries again. Of course, both people and places have planetary returns. For example, the USA has its Sun in Cancer. You could do transit cycles for the USA that start and end at the Sun's position in the USA chart.

The other cycles involve the planets relative to each other. When two outer planets conjunct, they start a cycle. It is as though the slower-moving planet is on the ascendant (wherever it is), while the faster-moving planet goes through the houses of the cycle. For example, when the faster-moving planet conjuncts the slower-moving one, it is like crossing the ascendant. When the faster-moving planet reaches 30 degrees in front of the slower-moving one, it enters the second house. When the two planets oppose each other, the faster planet is entering the seventh house. To get a feel for the cycle, watch what happens at the major aspect points.

Also, from the conjunct to the opposition (the first six houses) is the period when the faster-moving planet holds sway (the waxing of the faster planet), while the remaining six houses that occur from the opposition back to the conjunct are the waning of the faster planet and the domination of the slower-moving planet.

For example, the Jupiter-Saturn cycle takes 20 years and starts with the even decades (e.g. 1900, 1920, 1940, 1960, 1980, 2000). For the first decade (the even decade), the times are more liberal and Jupiterian. During the second decade, the odd decade (e.g. 1950, 1970, 1990), the times are more conservative, more Saturnine.

In fact, each pair of outer planets has a meaning:

- Jupiter-Saturn (20 years) = growth versus consolidation: the largest planetary cycle known to the ancients, and the basis of the economy (often, by element)
- Jupiter-Uranus (17 years) = steady, continuous growth versus abrupt change; when conjunct, a breakthrough in what is possible
- Jupiter-Neptune (15 years) = mundane versus spiritual growth, compassion, economic growth
- Jupiter-Pluto (15 years) = continuous, reasonable growth versus total breaks with the past; transformation of the economic 'rules'
- Saturn-Uranus (39 years) = stability versus revolutionary flux; break in administrations; perhaps the most difficult aspect pair
- Saturn-Neptune (35 years) = practical limits and experience versus dreams; dreams are tested against practical reality; bringing dreams down to practical reality
- Saturn-Pluto (33 years) = what has been done in the past versus what must be done now; limits on power; establishment versus masses/reality; stock market and the political cycle
- Uranus-Neptune (160 years) = people's faith is shaken up; a new faith is born or old faiths revitalized
- Uranus-Pluto (112 years) = a cataclysmic change in outlook; the avant-garde has a new vision; what constitutes the avant-garde changes; spontaneous revolutionary outbreaks
- Neptune-Pluto (493 years) = people's image/faith/beliefs

versus the underlying reality; major paradigm shift (Dark Ages, Middle Ages, Renaissance, modernity)

If a person has any of these planets conjunct or in major aspect in his or her natal chart, the person is part of a generation that is changing the world. For example, the middle-aged men and women born in the 1890s with Neptune conjunct Pluto lived through two world wars and the Depression between. This generation was part of a 500-year paradigm shift from the Renaissance to modernity. Of course, the conjunct is the most powerful aspect because it initiates the whole cycle.

## Making It Personal

In your chart you have the five outer planets in a sign and a house – as an example, Uranus in Cancer in the twelfth house. The planets make aspects between themselves and with the other personal planets in your chart. The most personal planets are Sun, Moon, Mercury, Venus, and Mars.

Briefly, the Sun is your sense of self, your life's path – as in 'How's your life going?' When an outer planet is conjunct the Sun, you identify with that energy. For example, Sun conjunct Pluto in Sagittarius would mean you identify with the drive to fight for the cause of truth. If this were in the third house, the world of the third sign Gemini, you would fight for truth in advertising or perhaps become a crusading journalist. You would bring the higher principles in an intense way down into the more mundane world of convenience. People would find that you were not into convenient ways of resolving intellectual issues. If you have this placement, you should read about Plutonian generations with Pluto in Sagittarius.

Mercury, Venus, and Moon are your thoughts, feelings, and emotions, respectively. Mars is your drive, anger, aggression, and desires – your masculine qualities. Venus, by contrast, is relationships, beauty, and harmony – your feminine qualities. In a man's chart, Venus represents the qualities he wants in a woman, while in a woman's chart, Mars represents the qualities she wants in a man. So, if an outer planet is conjunct Venus in a man's chart, he will want a woman who represents that outer planet's energies.

For example, if Uranus is conjunct a man's Venus, he will want a woman who is a free spirit, who is different every day, who is a unique individual. His relationships will emphasize freedom. In younger life, he will want to be free of entanglements. If Neptune is conjunct his Venus, he will want a dreamer, though he has to watch out for co-dependency, of course.

In transit, the outer planets have major effects. Pluto takes 248 years to circle the zodiac, so perhaps only a third of all people have Pluto conjunct their Sun in their lifetime. When Pluto conjuncts the Sun (often three times due to direct and retrograde motion), you go through a transformation of identity. Your reality comes up, whether positive or negative, and must be addressed. Often, what you are experiencing ties in with the social transformations this book describes.

If Pluto conjuncts another inner planet, that same transformation will affect that planet's working. Pluto conjunct Venus will transform relationships, and often this conjunct will result in an intense, Plutonian type coming into your life. Pluto conjunct Mercury will transform the way you think and speak, etc.

Where your planets were when you were born (your natal planets) determines their normal mode of operating (by sign, house, and aspect). As the planets transit other places in your chart, it is as though they are visiting those other places, but retaining the qualities they had at birth.

The outer planets have a generational impact because of this. For example, those born with Pluto in Leo will always believe fun and creativity are central to their reality. As Pluto transits Virgo, it is as if Pluto-in-Leo party people came into the workplace or the army (both ruled by Virgo); their tour of these new 'places' didn't go smoothly, if you remember the 1960s.

Now, let's see how to go through the sections to make this book personal. It would be a good idea to have your astrology chart ready.

Start by finding your generational pattern. Read the sections on generational Pluto, Neptune, Uranus, Saturn, and Jupiter in the signs from your astrology chart. Look on your chart to see what houses and aspects these planets make to other planets. This explains how these generational energies tie into your chart (the aspects) and in what areas of life they appear (the houses). See if you have any outer planet conjuncts and read the appropriate section(s).

Finally, see what American or European generation you were part of and how that generation fared as different parts of the American and European cycle unfolded.

Now do that for your parents and friends. You may have more sympathy for the different challenges of your parents!

*Chapter 1*

# Jupiter Generations

Jupiter is the largest planet, by far. If the Sun represents the king, Jupiter represents the nobles. Jupiter in the birth chart shows how you are 'better' than other people. This is because Jupiter is a social planet – it is always comparing itself with others.

When you ask a person, 'What makes you great, what makes you superior to others, what makes you better?', expect to hear a series of words describing the qualities of the sign and house in which Jupiter is placed.

If you look at the famous people who have Jupiter in a particular sign, you will notice they are often great based on the sign of their Jupiter. They are uniquely better than others for the qualities of the sign of Jupiter.

When you compare yourself with others, you often feel you are superior based on the sign of Jupiter. For example, if you have Jupiter in Virgo, you feel others don't really have the grasp of details or don't work as hard as you do. Or if you have Jupiter in Libra, they aren't as social, harmonious, or fair. If you have Jupiter in Scorpio, you think they aren't as intense or probing as you are – they are living life on the surface.

Because Jupiter rules growth, it also rules personal growth (how you grow and explore the world). With Jupiter in Cancer, you explore emotions, caring for others, and dependency issues. With Jupiter in Aries, you explore aggression and the spirit of newness. With Jupiter in Sagittarius, you explore new ways to tell a joke; you explore philosophy, religion, and the world.

People often overdo the sign in which Jupiter is placed. Jupiter in Scorpio can be overly sexual. Jupiter in Cancer can care too much (but often will not show it). Jupiter in Gemini can have a big mouth and be outspoken.

Finding one's purpose, often a big part of personal growth, comes through Jupiter. Jupiter in Scorpio investigates one's purpose. Jupiter in Cancer feels one's purpose is to care for others. In Leo, the purpose is to have fun, to be creative, to be happy. In Sagittarius, life can be a joke.

Jupiter is the reasonable planet. There is a reason for everything, even though that reason may not have much to do with the real purpose.

Of course, Jupiter is your sense of humor, what you find funny. Jupiter in Scorpio finds humor in pain and in subtle interactions that no one else notices. Jupiter in Capricorn finds humor in disasters, in serious situations; there is a bluesy quality to Jupiter in Capricorn. Jupiter in Aries finds humor in a challenge.

## Jupiterian Qualities

- Greatness, what makes one excel
- Superiority
- Exploration (i.e. exploring the qualities of the sign)
- Outpouring of feeling, highly expressive
- Exaggerated tendencies (e.g. Jupiter in Cancer can be overly sensitive)
- Focused on purpose, on knowing the reasons
- Sense of humor
- Growth
- Luck comes through … (fill in quality of sign here). Example: Jupiter in Gemini – luck through selling, communicating

## Jupiter Generation Dates

Aries: Mar 1, 1904 – Aug 8, 1904; Aug 31, 1904 – Mar 7, 1905

Taurus: Aug 8, 1904 – Aug 31 1904; Mar 7, 1905 – Jul 21, 1905; Dec 4, 1905 – May 9, 1906

Gemini: Jul 21, 1905 – Dec 4, 1905; Mar 9, 1906 – Jul 30, 1906

Cancer: Jul 30, 1906 – Aug 18, 1907
Leo: Aug 18, 1907 – Sep 12, 1908
Virgo: Sept 12, 1908 – Oct 11, 1909
Libra: Oct 11, 1909 – Nov 11, 1910
Scorpio: Nov 11, 1910 – Dec 10, 1911
Sagittarius: Dec 10, 1911 – Jan 2, 1913
Capricorn: Dec 10, 1911 – Jan 2, 1913
Aquarius: Jan 2, 1913- Feb 4, 1915
Pisces: Feb 4, 1915 – Feb 12, 1916

Aries: Feb 12, 1916 – Jun 26, 1916; Oct 26, 1916 – Feb 12, 1917
Taurus: Jun 26, 1916 – Oct 26, 1916; Feb 12, 1917 – Jun 29, 1917
Gemini: Jun 29, 1917 – Jul 13, 1918
Cancer: Jul 13, 1918 – Aug 2, 1919
Leo: Aug 2, 1919 – Aug 27, 1920
Virgo: Aug 27, 1920 – Sept 26, 1921
Libra: Oct 7, 1921 – Oct 26, 1922
Scorpio: Oct 26, 1922 to Nov 24, 1923
Sagittarius: Nov 24, 1923 – Dec 18, 1924
Capricorn: Dec 18, 1924 – Jan 8, 1926
Aquarius: Jan 8, 1926 – Jan 18, 1927
Pisces: Jan 18, 1927 – Jun 6, 1927; Sep 11, 1927 – Jan 23, 1928

Aries: Jun 6, 1927 – Sep 11, 1927; Jan 23, 1928 – Jun 4, 1928
Taurus: Jun 4, 1928 – Jun 12, 1929
Gemini: Jun 12, 1929 – Jun 26, 1930
Cancer: Jun 26, 1930 – Jul 17, 1931
Leo: Jul 17, 1931 – Aug 11, 1932
Virgo: Aug 11, 1932 – Sept 10, 1933
Libra: Sep 11, 1933 – Oct 12, 1934
Scorpio: Oct 12, 1934 to Nov 10, 1935
Sagittarius: Nov 9, 1935 – Dec 2, 1936
Capricorn: Dec 2, 1936 – Dec 20, 1937
Aquarius: Dec 20, 1937 – May 14, 1938; Aug 30, 1938 – Dec 29,

1938

Pisces: May 14, 1938 – Jul 30, 1938; Dec 29, 1938 – May 11, 1939;
Oct 30, 1939 – Dec 20, 1939

Aries: May 11, 1939 – Oct 30, 1939; Dec 20, 1939 – May 16, 1940

Taurus: May 16, 1940 – May 26, 1941

Gemini: May 26, 1941 – Jun 10, 1942

Cancer: Jun 10, 1942 – Jun 30, 1943

Leo: Jun 30, 1943 – Jul 26, 1944

Virgo: Jul 26, 1944 – Aug 25, 1945

Libra: Aug 26, 1945 – Sep 26, 1946

Scorpio: Sep 26, 1946 – Oct 25, 1947

Sagittarius: Oct 24, 1947 – Nov 15, 1948

Capricorn: Nov 15, 1948 – Apr 12, 1949; Jun 27, 1949 – Nov 30,
1949

Aquarius: Nov 30, 1949 – Apr 15, 1950; Sep 15, 1950 – Dec 1, 1950

Pisces: Apr 15, 1950 – Sep 15, 1950; Dec 1, 1950 – Apr 21, 1951

Aries: Apr 21, 1951 – Apr 28 1952

Taurus: Apr 28 1952 – May 9, 1953

Gemini: May 9, 1953 – May 24, 1954

Cancer: May 24, 1954 – Jun 13, 1955

Leo: Jun 13, 1955 – Nov 17, 1955; Jan 18, 1956 – Jul 7, 1956

Virgo: Nov 18, 1955 – Jan 19, 1956; Jul 8, 1956 – Dec 14, 1956; Feb
20, 1957 – Aug 7, 1957

Libra: Dec 14, 1956 – Feb 21, 1957; Aug 8, 1957 – Jan 14, 1958; Mar
21, 1958 – Sep 8, 1958

Scorpio: Jan 13, 1958 to Mar 20, 1958; Sep 7, 1958 to Feb 10, 1959;
Apr 24, 1959 to Oct 5, 1959

Sagittarius: Feb 10, 1959 – Apr 24, 1959; Oct 5, 1959 – Mar 1, 1960

Capricorn: Mar 1, 1960 – Jun 10, 1960; Oct 26, 1960 – Mar 15, 1961;
Aug 12, 1961 – Nov 4, 1961

Aquarius: Mar 15, 1961 – Aug 12, 1961; Nov 4, 1961 – Mar 25,
1962

Pisces: Mar 25, 1962 – Apr 4, 1963

Aries: Apr 4, 1963 – Apr 12, 1964

Taurus: Apr 12, 1964 – Apr 22, 1965

Gemini: Apr 22, 1965 – Sep 21, 1965

Cancer: Sep 21, 1965 – Nov 17, 1965; May 5, 1966 – Sep 27, 1966; Jan 16, 1967 – May 23, 1967

Leo: Sep 27, 1966 – Jan 16, 1967; May 23, 1967 – Oct 19, 1967; Feb 27, 1968 – Jun 15, 1968

Virgo: Oct 20, 1967 – Feb 28, 1968; Jun 16, 1968 – Nov 16, 1968; Mar 31, 1969 – Jul 16, 1969

Libra: Nov 16, 1968 – Mar 31, 1969; Jul 16, 1969 – Dec 17, 1969; Apr 30, 1970 – Aug 16, 1970

Scorpio: Dec 17, 1969 to Apr 30, 1970; Aug 16, 1970 to Jan 15, 1971; Jun 6, 1971 to Sep 12, 1971

Sagittarius: Jan 14, 1971 – Jun 5, 1971; Sep 11, 1971 – Feb 6, 1972; Jul 24, 1972 – Sep 25, 1972

Capricorn: Feb 6, 1972 – Jul 24, 1972; Sep 25, 1972 – Feb 20, 1973

Aquarius: Feb 23, 1973 – Mar 8, 1974

Pisces: Mar 8, 1974 – Mar 18, 1975


Aries: Mar 18, 1975 – Mar 26, 1976

Taurus: Mar 26, 1976 – Aug 23, 1976; Oct 16, 1976 – Apr 3, 1977

Gemini: Aug 23, 76 – Oct 16, 1976; Apr 3, 1977 – Aug 20, 1977; Dec 30, 1977 – Apr 12, 1988

Cancer: Aug 20, 1977 – Dec 30, 1977; Apr 12, 1978 – Sep 5, 1978; Feb 28, 1979 – Apr 20, 1979

Leo: Sep 5, 1978 – Feb 28, 1979; Apr 20, 1979 – Sep 29, 1979

Virgo: Sept 30, 1979 – Oct 28, 1980

Libra: Oct 27, 1980 – Nov 28, 1981

Scorpio: Nov 28, 1981 to Dec 27, 1982

Sagittarius: Dec 26, 1982 – Jan 19, 1984

Capricorn: Jan 1, 1984 – Feb 6, 1985

Aquarius: Feb 6, 1985 – Feb 20, 1986

Pisces: Feb 20, 1986 – Mar 2, 1987

Aries: Mar 2, 1987 – Mar 8, 1988
Taurus: Mar 8, 1988 – Jul 22, 1988; Nov 30, 1988 – Mar 11, 1989
Gemini: Jul 22, 1988 – Nov 30, 1988; Mar 11, 1989 – Jul 30, 1989
Cancer: Jul 30, 1989 – Aug 18, 1990
Leo: Aug 18, 1990 – Sep 12, 1991
Virgo: Sep 12, 1991 – Oct 10, 1992
Libra: Oct 10, 1992 – Nov 10, 1993
Scorpio: Nov 10, 1993 to Dec 9, 1994
Sagittarius: Dec 9, 1994 – Jan 13, 1996
Capricorn: Jan 3, 1996 – Jan 21, 1997
Aquarius: Jan 21, 1997 – Feb 4, 1998
Pisces: Feb 4, 1998 – Feb 3, 1999

Aries: Feb 13, 1999 – Jun 28, 1999; Oct 23, 1999 – Feb 14, 2000
Taurus: Jun 28, 1999 – Oct 23, 1999; Feb 14, 2000 – Jun 30, 2000
Gemini: Jun 30, 2000 – Jul 13, 2001
Cancer: Jul 13, 2001 – Aug 1, 2002
Leo: Aug 1, 2002 – Aug 27, 2003
Virgo: Aug 27, 2003 – Sep 25, 2004
Libra: Sep 25, 2004 – Oct 25, 2005
Scorpio: Oct 26, 2005 – Nov 24, 2006
Sagittarius: Nov 24, 2006 – Dec 16, 2007
Capricorn: Dec 17, 2007 – Jan 5, 2009
Aquarius: Jan 5, 2009 – Jan 18, 2010
Pisces: Jan 18, 2010 – Jun 6, 2010; Sep 9, 2010 – Jan 22, 2011

## Jupiter in Aries
## Qualities
- All 'out there'
- So open, it's funny (Mae West, Conan O'Brien)
- Heroic dimensions
- Known for their competitive drive
- Can be overly aggressive or pushy
- Sense of humor about their pushiness and aggression

(John Cleese, Lily Tomlin, Mae West)
- Famous athletes
- Caustic wits (George Bernard Shaw, Oscar Wilde)

People famous for either their competitive spirit or their wide-eyed openness have this placement. Many men famous for race car driving or pro wrestling are here: Mario Andretti, Al Unser, Jesse Ventura, and Paul Hogan. Practitioners of both these sports are unabashedly aggressive.

Actors with Jupiter in Aries have a steely quality: Chuck Norris, Rosie Perez, Brad Pitt, Steven Seagal, and Johnny Depp. Chuck Norris and Steven Seagal started their careers as karate experts and moved to the screen.

Robin Williams is known for pushing his humor – he constantly wants to be out there. Mae West was humorous through her pushy sexuality. John Cleese in *Fawlty Towers* lost his temper constantly, which was the main point to the humor of that show.

The athletes are known for their competitive spirit, which is why they became athletes in the first place. Billy Martin, Tiger Woods, Jack Nicklaus, and Bonnie Blair are examples.

People with Jupiter in Aries believe sufficient drive will open any door. If not, they feel like kicking open the door. They want others to stay as open to possibilities as they are.

This generation can have a biting wit. They simply say it like it is. Sometimes they can be aggressive about it.

When this group feels superior, it is because they are stronger, more aggressive, more pushy, more competitive, or more forthright than others.

## Jupiter in Taurus
## Qualities
- Great expression of feelings
- Great orators (John F. Kennedy, Martin Luther King)
- Great productions (Cecil B. DeMille)

- Great singers
- Outpouring of gentle, solid, but powerful needs
- Soft-spoken
- Earthy sense of humor, often tied to everyday people and events, can be gross or slapstick (Roseanne, Jack Benny, Terry Gilliam, Andy Warhol)

These are down-to-earth people, many with sympathy for ordinary people and their needs. Many have a quiet, solid presence and give the sense they will be there for you. Joan Baez, Bob Dylan, John F. Kennedy, Martin Luther King, Franklin D. Roosevelt, Frank Zappa, and Jesse Jackson all fought for the common person. Some, such as Dean Martin, Sandra Bullock, and Henry Fonda, have an image as just ordinary people who made good. Norman Rockwell made an art form of glorifying everyday events.

Roseanne, for example, expresses the humor of lower-middle-class life. Terry Gilliam made gruesome but hilarious cartoons for *Monty Python's Flying Circus*. Jack Benny had a dry wit and perfect timing; one of his funniest skits was about his own bank vault (he was notoriously cheap). Richard Pryor's humor was earthy. All of these are Taurean ways to be funny.

Production is Taurean, and Cecil B. DeMille became famous for his lavish sets and productions. Others, such as Christopher Reeve and Keanu Reeves, specialize in roles of soft-spoken super heroes.

There are a number of orators in this group: Jesse Jackson, Martin Luther King, and John F. Kennedy. These are people who can bring lofty concepts down to practical terms and also look at the practical problems of people and see the underlying issues that are broader than each individual.

Jupiter in Taurus can feel superior for being more productive, having more possessions, or being more solid or more stubborn than others.

## Jupiter in Gemini
## Qualities

- Big mouth, outspoken
- Famous writers and song writers
- Very animated, sometimes bouncy
- Quick wit

Two of the great technologists involved in communications were Alexander Graham Bell, who invented the telephone, and Thomas Edison, who invented the phonograph and movie projector. Both had Jupiter in Gemini, the sign of communication and transportation.

Hazrat Inayat Khan brought the Sufi message to the West. His focus was on the great communication he carried with him.

Authors include Jane Austen, Charles Dickens, Sir Arthur Conan Doyle, Kahlil Gibran, Aldous Huxley, John Irving, Erica Jong, Carole King, Jessica Mitford, Anne Rice, and Arthur Schlesinger.

Muhammad Ali, Ed Asner, Phyllis Diller, Nikita Khrushchev, Courtney Love, and Carry Nation all were very outspoken. While Jupiter in Taurus is soft-spoken, these people have megaphone mouths. Even when people in this group are talking low, they have something important to say and it is worthwhile to listen to them.

There aren't many comics in this group, perhaps because they aren't into frivolous talking. Tim Allen's humor centers on his self-importance and how his important utterances are completely wrong most of the time. Gracie Allen's humor centered on her hoof-in-mouth problem, often a problem with Jupiter. Both had humor that centered on being deflated. Phyllis Diller is, well, loud.

This group are quick on their feet, like Muhammad Ali, or quick with a quip, like Barbara Walters, Dick Clark, or Bob Newhart. Barbara Walters excels at asking questions, a talent that

Gemini, with its constant curiosity, brings.

Jupiter here can feel superior because they are smarter, quicker, and more adaptable than others.

## Jupiter in Cancer
## Qualities

- Great emotionality
- Can be overly sensitive
- Emotionally open, sometimes pained as a result
- Care in a large way
- Make institutions where people feel at home

Cancer is the sign of emotional comfort and security, and of home, family, and tradition. Many in this group are famous for expressing emotions; singers, actors, and artists make up the majority. While the Jupiter in Gemini group are loud with words, this group are loud with their emotions: James Belushi, James Dean, Frida Kahlo, Jimi Hendrix, and especially, Janis Joplin.

Some furrow their brow in a concerned and caring way: Kirstie Alley, Debra Winger, Art Carney, Sean Connery, Kevin Costner, John Cusack, Bruce Willis, Gene Hackman, Harrison Ford, and Kelsey Grammer. Emotionally, they are open, although some men in particular have a tough exterior with a sensitive underside – Sean Connery, Gene Hackman, and Harrison Ford – how like Cancer!

Mark Twain was a great American writer, while Marcel Proust was a great French one. They both talked about the emotions associated with past events. Proust's work, in fact, is titled *In Search of Lost Time* (*Remembrance of Things Past* is an earlier translation of the title).

Many of this group could be seen as being good in a traditional way. Think Kevin Costner, Annette Funicello, Patrick Swayze, and Harrison Ford.

This group feel superior because they care more than others, because they're more nurturing and more emotional.

### Jupiter in Leo
### Qualities
- Very theatrical and dramatic
- Lots of fun
- Larger than life
- Party! (F. Scott Fitzgerald, Hedda Hopper)
- Have fun doing what they are doing
- Large, warm presence

Some in this group have a large, warm presence and aren't into performing as much; others are larger than life and simply exude fun, creative energy. The latter want to be the life of the party or have a life of partying – F. Scott Fitzgerald, for example.

It is hard to imagine being too much Leo because, by definition, Leo is the sign of excessive fiery fun, creativity, and entertainment, but the Jupiter in Leo crowd manages it.

Think of the bluster of Howard Cosell (bluster is Leo), James Bond's partying (invented by Ian Fleming), Mick Jagger (still rocking in his sixties), and Whoopi Goldberg (having a good time). Whoopi has that warm presence characteristic of this group, as do Bill Maher, Arsenio Hall, Penny Marshall, Jim Morrison, and Dan Rather.

We would expect famous and great performers in this group, and of course there are, starting with Annie Oakley and continuing to Ethel Merman (who first played her on Broadway), through Peggy Lee, Celine Dion, and Mick Jagger.

Becoming fabulously wealthy can happen with this placement – think Bill Gates. Bill Gates ran Microsoft, which prospered by taking over other companies, and did so at its very start with a huge bluff (Leo). However, most of the famous people here became well known through their performances, which later brought them money.

Jupiter in Leo feel superior because they are more fun, more creative, more lively, and more theatrical than others.

## Jupiter in Virgo
## Qualities
- Great at details
- Great technicians, or simply have great technique
- Can have the Virgo dry, raspy voice
- Can have a humorous 'aw shucks' quality
- Famous for sleight of hand, magicians

This group are magical. By doing the small things extremely well, they put together incredible execution. Magicians David Copperfield and Harry Houdini both have Jupiter here.

Virgo is not only the sign of health but of physical shape. Halle Berry, Yasmine Bleeth, Jane Russell, Bo Derek, Ellen Burstyn, and Jayne Mansfield are famous, in part, for their voluptuous figures.

Because Jupiter rules humor, we would expect a dry sense of humor with Jupiter here. Among those who use humor are Victor Borge, Michael Caine, Joan Collins, Spike Lee, Rob Reiner, and Danny DeVito – all have that dry sense of humor.

The athletes, musicians, and actors are supreme technicians: Victor Borge, Eric Clapton, Amelia Earhart, Meadowlark Lemon, and Martina Navratilova.

As with any placement in Virgo, the voice can have a certain hoarseness. Think Rod Stewart, Burl Ives, Molly Ringwald, Joan Rivers, Al Jolson, and even Carrie Fisher, Paul Reiser, Macaulay Culkin, and Julia Roberts.

Although Virgo is usually associated with a clean-cut look, surprisingly, this group is almost the opposite. They often are rough-hewn. Even Tom Hanks played some sleazy characters, such as the coach in *A League of Their Own*. The rough-hewn look is most obvious in Wallace Beery, James Brown, Danny DeVito,

Dennis Franz, and Spike Lee.

Jupiter in Virgo feel superior because they have better technique, are better technicians, know more facts, and can handle details better than can others.

## Jupiter in Libra
### Qualities
- Great smile
- Strong need for justice
- Try to maintain a great personal appearance
- Can be great airheads (in a humorous way)
- Fashion greats

When any planet is in Libra, look for a wide, happy smile. With Jupiter, the smile is bigger and wider than with other planets here. Examples are Brigitte Bardot, Annette Bening, Cher, Bill Clinton, Judy Garland, Doris Day, Ronald Reagan, and Diane Keaton.

Because Libra is the sign of balance, it demands justice and fairness. Helen Gurley Brown, Bill Moyers, Ralph Nader, Gloria Steinem, Oliver Stone, and Mother Teresa are examples.

Fashion is Libran. Famous fashionistas with Jupiter in Libra include Georgio Armani, Bill Blass, Naomi Campbell, and Pierre Cardin. Art, too, is Libran. Famous artists are Cézanne and Chagall. William Randolph Hearst was a great art collector and created Hearst Castle, which is a work of art in itself.

Goldie Hawn has a sense of humor that is based on being an airhead. So do Gilda Radner, Betty White, Barbara Eden, and to an extent Diane Keaton.

Finally, this group have great poise. They can keep composed through any difficulty. Winston Churchill showed this capacity during World War II.

Jupiter in Libra feel superior because they smile wider, wear better clothes, and can relate better than others. They are better at keeping up with the latest trends.

## Jupiter in Scorpio
## Qualities
- Great at intense roles (if actors)
- Sarcasm with a smile
- Can be overly sexual or have other excesses
- Deep thinkers, want to research the purpose of everything
- Explore the depths
- Explore intense situations

Perhaps the quintessence of Jupiter in Scorpio is Alfred Hitchcock, with his macabre sense of humor and his suspenseful movies. This group laughs at intense situations, sometimes inappropriately.

This group is famous for their depth and intensity. Think of the stories of Kurt Vonnegut, Stephen King, Jack London, and Jules Verne or the movies of Steven Spielberg and Alfred Hitchcock.

While Jupiter in Virgo can be voluptuous, Jupiter in Scorpio is darker and more magnetically sexual: Jean Harlow, Glenn Close, Jamie Lee Curtis, Farrah Fawcett, Mata Hari, Queen Latifah, Susan Sarandon, and Britney Spears. Many of these women have played seductresses or women in thriller movies or both. Glenn Close in *Fatal Attraction* comes to mind.

Among men, Elvis Presley was known for his swinging hips. When Presley was on TV, Ed Sullivan told the camera crew to take only upper body shots of him! Rodin was famous for the sensuality of his sculptures.

The only comedians in the group are two women: Lucille Ball and Ellen DeGeneres. In *I Love Lucy*, Lucille Ball is constantly scheming, but her scheming always goes horribly and hilariously awry. Ellen DeGeneres is open about her lesbian sexuality; in fact, she opened the door for more openly lesbian and gay people to have TV series. Both have a large slapstick element to their humor.

Many of this group must find (Scorpio) the reason (Jupiter) for life and the universe. As a result, many have a spiritual nature. Both Kareem Abdul-Jabbar and Eldridge Cleaver explored Islam. The Dalai Lama is known for his spirituality. Carl Sagan had a sense of wonder about the cosmos.

Both Charles Manson and David Koresh are examples of people with great magnetism, but they used it to create a culture of violence. Aleister Crowley made a name for his negativity among members of the Golden Dawn. Other violent people among this group include Al Capone, and more positively, Rocky Marciano, the boxer. Charlton Heston promoted the American National Rifle Association.

Jupiterians here feel superior because they are more intense, more sexual, deeper, and more knowledgeable of the inner workings than are their peers.

## Jupiter in Sagittarius
### Qualities
- Great at foreign affairs
- Internationalists
- Explore humor (often as comedians)
- Big at jokes
- Great sense of humor

This group is loaded with comedians. And why not? Jupiter is in the sign it rules, Sagittarius, and both Jupiter and Sagittarius are into humor. The humor can range from the sarcastic (sarcasm is based on exaggeration, after all) to over-the-top humor, to self-deprecating humor. All these are Sagittarian.

Those who use comedy in their work are Charles Addams, Woody Allen, Billy Crystal, Ted Danson, Cameron Diaz, Phil Hartman, Benny Hill, Don Knotts, John Larroquette, David Hyde

Pierce, Burt Reynolds, and Danny Thomas. Others who weren't primarily comedians had a comedic side to their performances; for example, Alan Alda often smiles at some private joke in his roles.

Sagittarius can have a certain nobility to it. Some people in this group have made that nobility humorous (David Hyde Pierce), while others embody it in a large way (Jeremy Irons, Gloria Vanderbilt).

Sagittarians often have a sense of wonder, an understanding of the larger possibilities. Many of these are famous for opening people to a more global outlook. For example, Copernicus, who discovered the earth went around the Sun, or Al Gore with his crusade on global warming and his legislative work on the Internet.

Jupiter in Sagittarius is known for the large gesture, for the smooth, laughing, open grandness of it all. Think of the large enthusiasm of John Madden or that other John: John McEnroe. What about the absurdity of Benny Hill?

When Jupiter in Sagittarius feel superior, it's because they feel more noble, grand, lucky, or funny than others. It is good for Jupiter in Sagittarius to remember that the 'little' people are important, as well.

## Jupiter in Capricorn
### Qualities
- Serious, but reliable
- Bluesy
- Humor coming out of disaster or the downbeat
- Try to find humor in the serious

When Jupiter in Capricorn are comedians, they are seriously into comedy or they joke about serious or depressing subjects. Of course, they also poke fun at establishment types. One thing that brings this all together is forbidden words. Both Lenny Bruce and George Carlin have Jupiter here.

Many of the comedians have a hang-dog look as part of their repertoire: Charlie Chaplin, Jack Lemmon, Peter Sellers, Red Skelton, and Tom Smothers. These comedians can make you laugh at disastrous experiences.

Musically, Capricorn rules the blues, or at least songs of loss or sadness. Louis Armstrong, Waylon Jennings, Tom Paxton, Roberta Flack, Bruce Springsteen, and Bonnie Raitt aren't famous for upbeat music; their music is more serious and substantial.

The actors tend to play more serious or mature roles. Richard Burton, David Carradine, Gary Cooper, Jack Nicholson, Bill Cosby, Morgan Freeman, Jane Wyman, Loretta Young, Mary Tyler Moore, and Shelley Long are examples of the energy.

Jupiter in Capricorn tend to feel superior because they are more together, have more patience, can deal with adversity better, and have more experience than others.

## Jupiter in Aquarius
## Qualities
- Outrageous, weird, unique
- Very friendly
- Revolutionary
- Try to improve people's life through change

Aquarians can be found by the twinkle in their eye and their need to be different. With Jupiter in Aquarius, many glory in their uniqueness, and some in their oddness. Think of the twinkle and oddness of Groucho Marx, Allen Ginsberg, Jim Carrey, Jerry Lewis, and Dennis Rodman.

These also are very friendly people. Elizabeth Arden, Jeff Bridges, Matthew Broderick, and Jane Pauley are examples.

Some are revolutionary: Susan B. Anthony, Chuck Berry, Fidel Castro, Marie Curie, Albert Einstein, Jane Fonda, Evel Kneivel, and Hugh Hefner. These people made a break with the past.

Each of these people has a strong and unique individuality. Many are stars. Marilyn Monroe could turn on the electricity and simply shine. So could Groucho Marx, but in a completely different way.

Many of these people are archetypical. Hugh Hefner is the archetype of a playboy. Princess Diana was the image of a princess. Fidel Castro was the quintessential revolutionary.

Jupiter in Aquarius can feel superior for their friendliness, uniqueness, freedom, and oddness.

## Jupiter in Pisces
## Qualities

- Visionary
- Great at projecting a dream
- Have a dreamy image
- Explore dreams and the subconscious
- Great storytellers

This group project an image, a dream. Many have that wide-eyed look of innocence. Because Jupiter subrules Pisces, Jupiter is at home in this sign. However, the humor of Pisces is based on humorous reactions. Many of the comedians are straight men, the people who set up the jokes, such as Tom Poston or Dick Smothers.

Pisces is very emotional, but oceanic in their emotion, rather than intensely emotional like Scorpio. Think of the open sympathy of Paula Abdul or Judy Collins.

Pisces can invent entire imaginary worlds: J.R.R. Tolkien and Edgar Allan Poe created their own worlds. Other people created whole new paradigms: Fritjof Capra, Cesar Chavez, Charles Darwin, Sigmund Freud, Johannes Kepler, Sir Isaac Newton, George Orwell, and Orson Welles. Each of these moved his art or science to a new level.

Abraham Lincoln succeeded (Jupiter) by losing (Pisces). He

kept losing political races, but each time in a bigger arena.

This group has dreams of a different way life could be, and they sell it to their fellows. An example is Cesar Chavez, who dreamt of justice for farm workers, and succeeded in bringing them together into a union.

When Jupiter in Pisces are feeling superior, which is less often for this placement than for other Jupiter signs, it's because they feel more compassionate, more intuitive, and more tuned in.

## Chapter 2

# Saturn Generations

Saturn represents old age, when you are limited. Saturn also is control and taking things one step at a time. What each generation fears, and then how they try to 'get it together' to overcome their fears, are represented by Saturn. Often people try to feel accomplished and together, while simultaneously fearing they aren't.

Because Saturn takes about two and a half years per sign, these generations are longer than the one-year generations of Jupiter. So you often have a span of grades in school with the same Saturn.

How the members of this generation bond and what enables them to get organized are Saturn. What they consider authority and what type of authority figures – and hence what type of organizational structures they form – are through Saturn.

The coming of difficulties or difficult people into your life and the way you deal with them are through Saturn. How you deal with hard times, blockages, and limits are all Saturn.

Saturn is time, the past, and your accomplishments. How you relate to your accomplishments and what enabled you to achieve them are both Saturn.

Perhaps one of the most important sides of Saturn is that it represents the establishment or established ways of acting. How people react to or feel identified with the establishment are through Saturn.

## Saturnine Qualities
- Control
- Structure

- Fears
- Authority
- Organization
- Accomplishment
- How to relate to accomplishments
- Trust
- The past
- Limits
- Relationship to the establishment and established ways of acting
- Way of dealing with difficulties

## Saturn Generation Dates

Capricorn: Jan 21, 1900 – Jul 18, 1900; Oct 17, 1900 – Jan 19, 1903
Aquarius: Jan 19, 1903 – Apr 13, 1905; Aug 17, 1905 – Jan 8, 1906
Pisces: Jan 8, 1906 – Mar 19, 1908


Aries: Mar 19, 1908 – May 17, 1910; Dec 14, 1910 – Jan 20, 1911
Taurus: May 17, 1910 – Dec 14, 1910; Jan 20, 1911 – Jul 7, 1912; Nov 30, 1912 – Mar 26, 1913
Gemini: Jul 7, 1912 – Nov 30, 1912; Mar 26, 1913 – Aug 24, 1914; Dec 7, 1914 – May 11, 1915
Cancer: May 11, 1915 – Oct 17, 1916; Dec 7, 1916 – Jun 24, 1917
Leo: Oct 17, 1916 – Dec 1916; Jun 24, 1917 – Aug 12, 1919
Virgo: Aug 12, 1919 – Oct 7, 1921
Libra: Oct 7, 1921 – Dec 20, 1923; Apr 6, 1924 – Sep 13, 1924
Scorpio: Dec 20, 1923 – Apr 6, 1924; Sep 13, 1924 – Dec 2, 1926
Sagittarius: Dec 2, 1926 – Mar 15, 1929; May 5, 1929 – Nov 30, 1929
Capricorn: Mar 15, 1929 – May 5, 1929; Nov 30, 1929 – Feb 24, 1932; Aug 13, 1932 – Nov 20, 1932
Aquarius: Feb 24, 1932 – Aug 13, 1932; Nov 20, 1932– Feb 14, 1935
Pisces: Feb 15, 1935 – Jan 15, 1938

Aries: Apr 25, 1937 – Oct 18, 1937; Jan 14, 1938 – Jul 6, 1939; Sep
    22, 1939 – Mar 20, 1940
Taurus: Jul 6, 1939 – Sep 22, 1939; Mar 20, 1940 – May 8, 1942
Gemini: May 8, 1942 – Jun 20, 1944
Cancer: Jun 20, 1944 – Aug 2, 1946
Leo: Aug 2, 1946 – Sep 19, 1948; Apr 3, 1949 – May 29, 1949
Virgo: Sep 19, 1948 – Apr 3, 1949; May 29, 1949 – Nov 20, 1950;
    Mar 7, 1951 – Aug 13, 1951
Libra: Nov 20, 1950 – Mar 7, 1951; Aug 13, 1951 – Oct 22, 1953
Scorpio: Oct 22, 1953 – Jan 12, 1956; May 14, 1956 – Oct 10, 1956
Sagittarius: Jan 12, 1956 – May 14, 1956; Oct 10, 1956 – Jan 5, 1959
Capricorn: Jan 5, 1959 – Jan 3, 1962
Aquarius: Jan 3, 1962 – Mar 24, 1964; Sep 16, 1964 –Dec 16, 1964
Pisces: Dec 17, 1964 – Mar 4, 1967

Aries: Mar 3, 1967 – Apr 29, 1969
Taurus: Apr 29, 1969 – Jun 18, 1971; Jan 10, 1972 – Feb 21, 1972
Gemini: Jun 18, 1971 – Jan 10, 1972; Feb 21, 1972 – Aug 1, 1973
Cancer: Aug 1, 1973 – Jun 7, 1974; Apr 18, 1974 – Sep 17, 1975; Jan
    14, 1976 – Jun 5, 1976
Leo: Sep 17, 1975 – Jan 14, 1976; Jun 5, 1976 – Nov 17, 1977; Jan 5,
    1978 – Jul 26, 1978
Virgo: Nov 17, 1977 – Jan 5, 1978; Jul 26, 1978 – Sept 21, 1980
Libra: Sept 21, 1980 – Nov 29, 1982; May 6, 1983 – Aug 24, 1983
Scorpio: Nov 29, 1982 – May 6, 1983; Aug 24, 1983 – Nov 17, 1985
Sagittarius: Nov 17, 1985 – Feb 13, 1988; Jun 10, 1988 – Nov 12,
    1988
Capricorn: Feb 13, 1988 – Jun 10, 1988; Nov 12, 1988 – Feb 6, 1991
Aquarius: Feb 6, 1991 – May 21, 1993; Jun 30, 1993 –Jan 28, 1994
Pisces: Jan 28, 1994 – Apr 7, 1998

Aries: Apr 7, 1996 – Jun 9, 1998; Oct 25, 1998 – Mar 1, 1999
Taurus: Jun 9, 1998 – Oct 25, 1998; Mar 1, 1999 – Aug 10, 2000; Oct
    16, 2000 – Apr 20, 2001

Gemini: Aug 10, 2000 – Oct 16, 2000; Apr 20, 2001 – Jun 4, 2003

Cancer: Jun 4, 2003 – Jul 16, 2005

Leo: Jul 16, 2005 – Sep 2, 2007

Virgo: Sep 2, 2007 – Oct 29, 2009; Apr 7, 2010 – Jul 21, 2010

Libra: Oct 29, 2009 – Apr 7, 2010; Jul 21, 2010 – Oct 5, 2012

Scorpio: Oct 5, 2012 – Dec 23, 2014; Jun 15, 2015 – Sep 18, 2015

Sagittarius: Dec 23, 2014 – Jun 15, 2015; Sep 18, 2015 – Dec 20, 2017

Capricorn: Dec 20, 2017 – Mar 22, 2020; Jul 1, 2020 – Dec 17, 2020

Aquarius: Mar 22, 2020 – Jul 1, 2020; Dec 17, 2020 – Mar 7, 2023

Pisces: Mar 7, 2023 – May 25, 2025; Sep 1, 2025 – Feb 14, 2026

## Saturn in Aries
## Qualities

- Serious competitors
- Aggressively conservative
- Fight against difficulties, limits, old ways, the establishment
- Demand authority

Members of this group fight either against or for the established way and create accomplishment by fighting to get it. Therefore, some are aggressively conservative and others fight the established order. Yet others maintain authority by their competitive or forceful nature.

If you ask them, 'How did you accomplish what you did?', they will answer, 'I fought for every inch of it.' Think Johnnie Cochran as he defended O.J. Simpson, Evel Knievel as he jumped huge precipices on his motorcycle, Paul Hogan as he fought wrestling matches, and Mario Andretti, Richard Petty, Al Unser, and Cale Yarborough as they raced cars. All these people made a career of competitiveness.

If these people encounter difficulties, they typically get angry and will invariably fight back. They try to push their way through difficulties, often by themselves.

George Carlin's humor is often about the difficulties, obstacles, and ignorance he encountered from other people that made him mad. John Cleese was hilarious as a man who continually lost his temper in a sputtering, ineffectual way as a manager in *Fawlty Towers* (usually in front of his more competent wife).

Joseph Stalin and Saddam Hussein made a name for themselves as imperious dictators who killed anyone who stood against them. Stalin killed millions of peasants.

Jim Bakker, Pat Buchanan, and Barry Goldwater are examples of the aggressively conservative nature of Saturn in Aries. They, too, wanted to fight for the conservative ideal.

Women with this placement tend to want to have an important say in and make a lasting imprint on what is happening around them. Think Clara Barton, Halle Berry, Bette Davis, Jean Houston, Ashley Judd, Helen Keller, Nicole Kidman, Florence Nightingale, Molly Ringwald, and Grace Slick. These are not weak or retiring women.

'Damn the torpedoes – full speed ahead!' yells Aries in the face of Saturnine difficulties. If you have Saturn in Aries, this could be your motto.

These people command authority, and if not, demand it. They make themselves be recognized. Sometimes they push their accomplishments.

## Saturn in Taurus
### Qualities
- Comfortable with or outlasting the establishment
- Organic structures (Antoni Gaudi – conjunct Uranus Pluto)
- Quiet, earthy authority
- Many singers (Taurus rules the throat and singing)
- In tune with the common person's difficulties

- Solid sense of timing
- Steadfast in the face of difficulties

Members of this group inspire solid trust. They know how to handle difficulties with ease and quiet control. 'This too shall pass' is their motto. It's hard to imagine any of them throwing a tantrum, or even raising their voice, in difficult circumstances. They all exhibit a competent air, even if they aren't feeling it.

Because Taurus rules the throat and singing, many make a career of singing (in every imaginable style). Ann-Margret, Joan Baez, David Crosby, Neil Diamond, Placido Domingo, Bob Dylan, Cass Elliot, Aretha Franklin, Roy Rogers, James Joyce (famous as a singer as well as a writer), John Lennon, Jesse Colin Young, Frank Zappa, and Barbra Streisand are some examples.

Taurus also is the sign of nature. Jacques Cousteau and Antoni Gaudi were both interested in how people fit into the natural world.

Not only are this group aware of nature, but they are aware of the nature of people, particularly the earthy men and women who make up the working class. Examples are Hubert Humphrey, Bob Dylan, Jesse Jackson, Franklin D. Roosevelt, and John Lennon (he wrote the song 'A Working Class Hero').

Even when they are young, they seem mature. Many have a solid sensuality and intimate awareness of that world. Think Erica Jong and Jean Harlow.

The mystics and spiritual people in this group are aware of the suffering of the common person, the beauty of nature, and what transcends time and endures: Kahlil Gibran, Hazrat Inayat Khan, Mother Teresa, Teilhard de Chardin.

## Saturn in Gemini
### Qualities
- Writers and directors
- Fit into establishment through writing or communication

- Intellectual structures
- Write about the establishment or serve as a spokesperson for it
- Get through difficulties by speed or talking
- Talk about fears or problems
- Serious talk

Some of these are serious thinkers, and some are serious talkers. Many have a furrowed brow when they talk. Even if they aren't being so serious, they are talking about weighty subjects.

Many have structured minds or have talked about the structures of the mind. Nicolaus Copernicus, Thomas Merton, Dante, Bobby Fischer, and Sigmund Freud are examples.

Many deal with difficulties by talking about them or thinking them through. Some attack the difficulties of the established way of thought. Angela Davis, Thomas Paine, Jerry Garcia, Vance Packard, and Oscar Wilde spoke their minds.

Hedda Hopper talked (Gemini) about the establishment (Saturn). Many talked with authority (Saturn) and structured (Saturn) communications (Gemini). These directors are George Lucas, Penny Marshall, Frank Oz, Martin Scorsese, and Orson Welles.

Joni Mitchell sang about failed relationships, Mick Jagger has a strong blues side, Jimi Hendrix talked about dark topics, and so did Jim Morrison. The latter two died as Saturn was approaching its return. Musicians whose music addresses sadness or the blues are John Cage, Janis Joplin, and Muddy Waters.

Other musicians with a solid sense of timing, and hence beat, include John Philip Sousa and Jimmy Page.

Cameron Diaz, Gwyneth Paltrow, and Ben Affleck all do low-budget, serious works, so they have something important to say. Julia Child may cut herself as she cooks, but she will just talk through it.

The serious actors include Ben Affleck, Robert De Niro,

Harrison Ford, Christopher Walken, and Joe Pesci. They play heavy roles in which they make heavy comments with a furrowed brow.

There aren't any pure comedians in this group, except for Red Skelton, whose impressions of various people who were either mentally or financially challenged proved that talking about difficulties can be very funny.

## Saturn in Cancer
## Qualities
- Darkly emotional
- Strong character
- Emotionally connected with the past
- Accomplished at emotional expression
- Can get depressed
- Seriously care, especially in difficult situations

Cancer is the sign of emotional comfort and security, and of home, family, and tradition. Cancers have lots of character. This is an emotional sign.

Saturn in Cancer can cause a slowing down of the Cancerian emotions and can cause a toughness to come into the caring of Cancer. This can result in depression or in being hard when you should be soft. However, on the upside, this group can take some serious problems and come through them emotionally intact due to their tough shell. They often feel good about being survivors. Thor Heyerdahl and John F. Kennedy both courageously survived shipwrecks, for example.

'Tough' is a word that can be used proudly by some of the women in this group: Loni Anderson, Mia Farrow, Goldie Hawn, Naomi Judd, Bette Midler, Diane Keaton, Hayley Mills, Sophie Tucker, and Gilda Radner.

Some of this group have a dark emotionality. The Marquis de Sade, Dennis Franz, Al Jolson, Ingrid Bergman, Danny DeVito,

Kirk Douglas, Frank Sinatra, Tom Selleck, and Sylvester Stallone show the depth of this group's emotionality.

This depth of emotionality can result in memorable personal expression in art and on stage. Michelangelo, Richard Boone, Anthony Burgess, Eric Clapton, Clarence Darrow, John Fogarty, and Bob Marley all had the ability to express emotions in a deep way.

## Saturn in Leo
## Qualities

- Limits on responding to or expressing affection
- Insecurity about affection
- 'I am better than my limitations' – tend to 'Leo' their way through difficulties
- Seriously dramatic
- Solid showmanship
- May have a sad look
- Dramatic show of authority
- Can brag about accomplishments

James Barrie wrote *Peter Pan*, a play about a boy who never grew old (Saturn) and continued to have childlike fun (Leo). In some ways, all people with Saturn in Leo see themselves as perpetual (Saturn) children (Leo). Some have a dramatic (Leo) sadness (Saturn) – a sad look, or a tragic look; after all, a drama with a serious ending is a tragedy.

The humorists can be sad characters who make you laugh at their overly serious nature: think Norton (Art Carney) in *The Honeymooners*, Billy Crystal, Stan Laurel, and Phyllis Diller.

When Sally Field, at the Academy Awards, said in surprise, 'You like me. You really like me!' she was talking about a difficulty people with Saturn in Leo have: they don't know how to give or receive affection. Often, they don't believe people really feel affection or appreciation for them. This is because Saturn blocks the warmth and affection of Leo.

Others feel deep affection for the very few people whom they trust, but have difficulty widening their sphere of affection. It's not that they don't feel affection for others; it's that they feel a block in expression.

This group have no problem with problems. They can see where the problems are and want to dramatize them so that they can be dealt with. Al Gore is currently dramatizing the problem of global warming, for example.

When faced with difficulties, they believe, in their kingly or queenly Leo way, that they will surmount them. 'I am too great to have these difficulties stop me,' they think.

In the worst case (Hitler comes to mind), they think of themselves as superior to those whom they see as blocking them. This can result in their exerting the overbearing side of Leo, with the structure and authority of the establishment to aid them.

When they have it together and have accomplished something, they can brag about it. They can wield authority with childlike fun and exuberance: think Teddy Roosevelt, and to a lesser extent, Bill Clinton.

## Saturn in Virgo
### Qualities

- Command of details, facts, and figures
- Can be very aware of technical difficulties and find a way to overcome them
- 'Just the facts, ma'am'
- Serious in a furrowed-brow, focused way
- Disciplined
- Can be overwhelmed by weighty details and difficulties
- Seriously worried
- Serious loners
- Can be limited by shyness

Many of these are shy people, or at least people with an analytical mind, who must deal with the complexities of social interaction. When Jack Webb's character in *Dragnet*, Sgt Friday, says in his flat, dry voice, 'Just the facts, ma'am', he is talking for many Saturn in Virgos. Let's just limit ourselves (Saturn) to the facts (Virgo) and avoid all the emotions and innuendos and complexities.

Cathy Guisewite's cartoon character is overwhelmed by the sheer weight (Saturn) of all the details (Virgo) that constrict her (Saturn, again). Some of these people are the arbiters of details and rules, including game show hosts, such as Hugh Downs, Howard Cosell, and Groucho Marx.

Howard Cosell was the expert on sports details and had the dry wit of Saturn in Virgo. His catchphrase was 'I'm just telling it like it is.' He brought in analysis (Virgo) and context.

Other people with that same dry wit from this group include Ray Bradbury, Lewis Carroll, Agatha Christie, Gerard Depardieu, Federico Fellini, Richard Gere, Phil Hartman, Olivia Hussey, Anjelica Huston, Jay Leno, Shelley Long, Groucho Marx, Bill Murray, and Randy Quaid, among others.

Because Saturn is the way you deal with difficulties, and Virgo is analysis and details, many of this group are consummate technicians who pick apart the problems that face them into their component parts and then solve the problem. 'Don't get emotional [water] about the problem,' they might say. 'Just solve it based on the facts.' Basil Rathbone played Sherlock Holmes, who had a consummate eye for detail.

Descartes wrote, 'I think, therefore I am.' He placed logic above all else, as do many of this group.

Many of the women have that dry wit mentioned before, often with a dry, sometimes raspy voice: Fanny Brice, Carol Channing, Betty Friedan, Phyllis George, Olivia Hussey, Anjelica Huston, Shelley Long, Bonnie Raitt, Christina Ricci, Jane Russell, Sigourney Weaver, and Mae West, among others.

## Saturn in Libra
## Qualities

- Smile in the face of difficulties
- Have a lightness and humor about the way things are
- Have difficulty taking things seriously
- Put a gracious, smooth surface on the established order
- Deeply aware of social interactions
- Take time to make decisions based on experience, hence good judgment

Saturn is exalted in Libra because each brings up the other. Libran advice and judgment improve with age and time. Judges often are older. On the other hand, old age is improved by the sense of lightness, artistry, poise, peacefulness, and social grace that Libra gives. As outer planets transit Libra, often we have smiling elderly gentlemen in power.

Saturn-in-Libra types try to stay poised and give a big Libran smile when encountering difficulties. Of course, sometimes we must actually deal with difficulties rather than simply smiling and ignoring them, as Britney Spears is learning.

Christopher Reeve had an authoritative (Saturn) smile (Libra) as Superman, but kept his sense of humor and justice after he was paralyzed. John Gray became an authority (Saturn) on relationships (Libra). Kinsey, too, was an authority on relationships, but of a different sort. Henry Kissinger is an authority, but on diplomacy (also Libra). J. Paul Getty used his established position (Saturn) to gather art (Libra).

Roseanne loves to punch holes (Scorpio Sun) in the airy-fairy lightness of the established authorities (Neptune conjunct Saturn in Libra). Roseanne points up how parts of your chart can be projected into the outer world.

Many of these people find humor in difficulties. Examples are Betty White, Carl Reiner, and Leslie Nielsen. Some play bubble heads (a side of Libra) confronted with hard situations that they somehow finesse in a humorous way.

## Saturn in Scorpio
### Qualities
- Sarcastic about the establishment
- Known for breaking barriers to sex and violence (Lenny Bruce, Sam Peckinpah)
- Dark sexuality
- Transform the establishment and break with the past
- Poke fun at the right or normal way
- Seriously into power, especially in intimate settings
- Sexual fears or convinced of how they have it together sexually based on experience – sex is serious
- Authority on sex
- Have difficulty with intimacy because secrets revealed
- Careers based on sex, power, violence, or transformation and the occult

As you would expect with Scorpio, some make a career (Saturn) of sex or the sexually explicit. Lenny Bruce, Hugh Hefner, Benny Hill, Allen Ginsberg, Marilyn Monroe, and Howard Sterns are the most obvious examples, but think of Ellen Barkin, Kim Basinger, Rudolph Valentino, Patrick Swayze, and Marlon Brando, among others, who had sexual magnetism as part of their draw.

Many transform (Scorpio) the established ways of their field (Saturn): Chuck Berry (founder of rock and roll), Marlon Brando (acting), Mel Brooks (dark comedy), Lenny Bruce (stand-up and explicit sexual references), James Cameron (digital techniques in film), Frank Capra (common man in films), Marie Curie (physics of matter) – the list goes on for nearly all of this group!

Sarcasm is a typical Scorpio response, and in this case, the response is to the established order of Saturn. So Saturn in Scorpio can be intensely sarcastic about the establishment.

Examples are Lenny Bruce, Matt Groening, and H.G. Wells. Conversely, this can be a placement of people who maintain the establishment through Scorpionic investigation, such as J. Edgar Hoover.

This group meet problems with passion, intensity, magnetism, and power. They don't ever stop halfway through a problem; they solve it completely or not at all. Unlike Saturn in Aries, they don't get angry at people blocking their path – they get even. With the more highly evolved, that can mean subtly bypassing them, and later, when the offending party needs help, bypassing them again.

This group initially can be unsure about sex, but become sure with lots of Saturn experience. This can make them self-proclaimed experts on the subject. Saturn in any sign goes from fear and uncertainty to control and becoming an authority with experience. Saturn in Scorpio takes this path with sex and passion.

## Saturn in Sagittarius
### Qualities
- Inspire people, often to act in a better way
- Able to get people enthusiastic
- Upbeat
- See humor/positivity in difficulties, in the established order
- Find seriousness/difficulties in positive situations

People with this placement can get up on a lectern or pulpit and inspire people to do better. Martin Luther King, Gandhi, Abraham Lincoln, Cesar Chavez, Che Guevara, and Norman Vincent Peale are prime examples. With Saturn here, uplifting people (Sagittarius) becomes a career, a long-term drive to accomplish something (Saturn). Sometimes, that accomplishment can be like that of Moses: getting a people to move to a new state.

Other times, the pedestrian or limited (Saturn) is lifted to a new awareness (Sagittarius). Think of Andy Warhol with his soup cans or his '15 minutes of fame'. Barbara Walters brings out the best in the people she interviews. Auguste Rodin brought out what was literally encased in stone. Escher took optical illusions to the next level.

Charles Darwin's theory of evolution (Sagittarius) was based on the survival (Saturn) of the fittest (Sagittarius). Lincoln and Darwin were born on the same day. Each used this placement in different ways.

One thing these people have in common is that they hate to be limited. Sometimes this means they take a long time to find their career because everything seems so limiting. The people who made it to this list found their dharma. Others who didn't find it spend their time swatting at limitations rather than realizing they need to move to higher ground.

Some, like Michael Jackson, refuse to be limited by race, gender, or sexual orientation. However, we are all limited by that – we transcend in spirit. Michael Jackson tried to transcend personally and physically.

Bill Maher and Spike Lee poke fun (Sagittarius) at the establishment (Saturn). Even James Garner, Bob Newhart, Irma Bombeck, and Gary Oldman are humorous because they don't follow the rules.

There is a need to lift people's spirits, to cheer them up (Sagittarius) in adversity (Saturn). Annette Bening, Humphrey Bogart, and Geena Davis are examples.

## Saturn in Capricorn
### Qualities
- Have a serious, and sometimes somber, side
- Seen as responsible and authoritative
- Take things seriously
- May be mavericks, but within the structure

- Long careers
- Cult authority figures (Rasputin, Jim Jones, David Koresh, and in a more positive way, Robert Anton Wilson)

These are serious people for whom being part of the established order is not usually a question because Saturn is in its natural sign in Capricorn. Perhaps the only exceptions are Dick Gregory and Richard Alpert. But even these two see themselves as Americans. Dick Gregory sees his race as oppressed here, but he still sees himself as a citizen, while Richard Alpert came from wealth and the established order as a Harvard professor. Even these mavericks stayed within the structure.

Some of these people came to grief through their belief in the establishment. Marie Antoinette didn't fare too well. The cult authority figures tried to set up their own establishment outside of the normal structure. Many of these were killed because their cults hurt people or because their connection to the normal structure broke down.

Quiet dignity and self-containment express the authority many of this group have. Louis Armstrong, Bono, Dick Clark, Walt Disney, Emily Post, Barack Obama, Leonard Nimoy, Dan Rather, and Ed Sullivan are examples.

David Hyde Pierce plays an uptight upper-class snob, one of the downsides of this placement, but brings humor to the role. However, Edward Kennedy, despite having an upper-class background, was noted as a liberal and became the head of the liberal wing in the US Senate through his hard work for the average citizen. Walt Disney, by contrast, was creative and innovative, but became an icon of conservatism.

Some studied the structure of society and gave us insight. Margaret Mead, Charles Dickens, Washington Irving, Kant, Milton, and Bertrand Russell all had a deep understanding of how their fellow humans structured themselves.

Nearly all of this group have long careers. Capricorn rules

career, while Saturn is tenacity and time. After they find something they like doing, they simply stick with it.

When afraid or unsure, they tend to rely on authority or look back on their accomplishments. As with any who have a connection with Capricorn, this group become less conservative and freer as they grow older and have less to prove.

## Saturn in Aquarius
## Qualities

- Friendly twinkle when breaking out of established ways
- Innovators, break the mold
- Reformers
- 'Out there' – odd, brilliant, or both

This group have an airy friendliness that they use to break down resistance to the change they want to see. Perhaps the most obvious and outrageous is Salvador Dali, but Carl Jung revolutionized psychology by emphasizing synchronicity and archetypes. Harry Houdini changed magic with his very public tricks. Elizabeth Montgomery, as Samantha in *Bewitched*, twitched her nose, upsetting the stuffy Darrin and his crowd (and she did it with a gleam and a friendly smile). Others who delight in tweaking the serious and stiff are Jim Carrey, Tim Conway, Shirley MacLaine, and Gene Wilder.

The more friendly but less revolutionary include Paula Abdul, Pat Boone, Matthew Broderick, James Brown, Carol Burnett, Barbara Eden, and Joan Collins. But even these had revolutionary effects. James Brown revolutionized rhythm and blues by introducing synchronized dancing and by bringing spoken word into his performances (which evolved into 'rap' under other artists) – he was called the 'Father of Soul'. Carol Burnett made an implicit statement for women's rights.

Many of the humorists from this group are known for their quirkiness: Edgar Bergen, Matthew Broderick, Jim Carrey, Joan

Collins, Tim Conway, Chris Farley, Joan Cusack, Teri Hatcher, and Rosie O'Donnell. All are light, breezy, and well, a bit odd.

When faced with difficulties, this group make friends with the person causing the problem or move on to other fields in which they don't have to interact. They can treat problems with a detached air.

## Saturn in Pisces
### Qualities
- Many mystics and psychics
- Sympathetic character
- Tendency to self-deprecation
- Image of a generation – concrete and enduring image
- Use drugs or escape to deal with problems
- Universalists
- Boundaries are porous and amorphous

These people either are a rock of sympathetic concern or beg sympathy for their shortcomings. Think of the sympathy shown by Alan Alda's characters or the fuzzy thinking of Gracie Allen, which can't be breached, or the pathetic quality of Woody Allen. Many have made a career of this Piscean emotionality and confusion.

Others have a spiritual side (also Pisces) that they pursue throughout their lives: David Carradine (he may not be spiritual, but he plays such a character in his movies), Keanu Reeves (ditto), Edgar Cayce, the Dalai Lama, Hermann Hesse, and Sir Isaac Newton.

Some have to deal with drugs (also Pisces) and depression (Saturn): Kurt Cobain, Robert Downey Jr, Ken Kesey, and Courtney Love. A problem can arise with this placement when drugs or escape is used to deal with difficulties.

Finally, others are archetypal and enduring images: Wyatt Earp, Wilt Chamberlain, Melvin Belli, Woody Allen, Herb Alpert,

Queen Victoria, Mary Tyler Moore, Jack Nicholson, Sir Laurence Olivier, and so on. These all had a unique and memorable character.

Out of sympathy or imagination, many find ways to break down barriers and structures that impede people: Alexander Graham Bell, the Dalai Lama, Thomas Edison, Abbie Hoffman, Ken Kesey, Karl Marx, Newton, and Whitman, among others.

## Chapter 3

# Uranus Generations

People born with Uranus in a sign act differently than do the actual times created by Uranus when it transits. Uranus in your chart is a 'part' of you for your entire lifetime, so it is more stable.

Uranus is your joy, spontaneity, insight, and freedom, but also your need for excitement, change, and rebellion. The way you express joy represents your Uranus. Uranus in Gemini expresses joy through the mind and curiosity; Uranus in Cancer expresses it through emotional quirkiness and emotional changeability; Uranus in Leo expresses joy dramatically.

The rebellion of each Uranian generation is based on the sign. Uranus in Gemini rebels for freedom of speech and yet tries to be free of the mind; Uranus in Cancer runs away from home and rebels against any form of dependency, especially motherhood; Uranus in Leo rebels either for or against fun and self-expression.

Each generation's ideals are Uranian-based. For example, Uranus in Capricorn has the ideal of accomplishment; Uranus in Libra tries for an ideal relationship with another harmonious person in the arts; Uranus in Aries aims to be a great innovator and force for change.

Each generation tries to be free, and to be free of the area represented by the sign. Uranus in Gemini wants free speech, but wants to be free of the mind; Uranus in Cancer wants to be free to express whatever emotion flashes in the moment, but wants to be free of dependencies (both being dependent on others and having others dependent on them). The Uranus-in-Cancer generations tend to have children later, if at all.

Uranus in Leo gets excited by acting, by being the center of attention, by pampering themselves. Uranus in Virgo is turned on and gets excited by helping others, by health facts, and by new techniques. Uranus in Libra gets turned on by art and relationships – new styles make them ecstatic. Each Uranian sign gets excitement through their sign.

Everybody wants to be a unique individual. How generations want to be unique is shown through the sign of Uranus. Uranus in Sagittarius wants to have unique adventures and philosophical outlooks. Uranus in Capricorn has unique accomplishments. Uranus in Aquarius has unique ideals and unique insights.

The way each generation pursues its ideals is through the sign of Uranus. Uranus in Aries fights for its ideals; Uranus in Gemini talks and writes about its ideals; Uranus in Cancer gets emotional about its ideals; Uranus in Leo acts them out.

People view life through their Uranian lens. Uranus in Libra views life as art and as a series of relationships between people; Uranus in Scorpio views life through the lens of sex, intimacy, and squabbles for power (but also through transformative experiences).

Finally, each Uranian generation comes across as the sign in which Uranus is placed. In this way, Uranus is like a generational rising sign. Uranus in Scorpio wants to come across as intense and sexy; Uranus in Leo wants to come across as being fun and dramatic; Uranus in Gemini wants to come across as intellectual, brilliant, and amusing. If you look at each generation, it does tend to have the qualities of Uranus's sign as its most obvious qualities.

## Uranian Qualities
- Scientific inquiry and progress
- Bohemian, avant-garde
- Eyes of populace/view of humanity
- Has ways to express joy
- Rebels against the ideals of the generation

- Tries to be free of ...
- Excitement through ...
- Uniqueness through ...
- Freedom through/from ...
- Change
- Theories
- Genius
- Wants to turn on to ...
- Hopes for/has the ideal of ... (fill in a sign quality here) about causes. For example, Aries fights for ideals; Gemini talks about ideals
- Life is ... (insert a way to view life). For example, Uranus in Leo sees life as a stage
- Comes across as ... (fill in a sign quality here). For example, Uranus in Scorpio wants to come across as intense, sexual

## Uranus in Aries (1844–1850; 1928–1934)
### Qualities
- If odd, you know it – pushy about oddities!
- Brash, inventor, trend setter
- Fights for causes/ideals/freedom
- Toughness
- Comes across as a fighter, is direct

Aries is pushy and direct. When Uranus, which rules oddness, resides in Aries, Aries pushes the Uranian oddities to the limit. Because Aries rules pioneering, being on the cutting edge, Uranus there insists on being on the cutting edge of science and technology, especially electrical technology. Both Edison (phonograph, motion pictures, electric light) and Alexander Graham Bell (telephone) were born with Uranus in Aries.

Members of this group want to put forward a tough image. They see the world in terms of survival of the fittest, in terms of will. Nietzsche wrote a whole philosophy based on the will (he also had Pluto in Aries). They come across as fighters, as people who want to be direct with you about what they want. When you meet them, they come across as who they are.

Many are fighters for causes, revolutionary warriors. They want to change the world now. They often have a Uranian wisdom about which battles to fight and which to avoid.

Many TV and movie pioneers came from this group, especially TV pioneers because these were the people who became the first stars in the new media in the 1950s. Many of the first child stars, such as Shirley Temple and 'Our Gang' came from this group. Innovators in children's TV and books came from this group. They didn't talk down to the children (Captain Kangaroo, Mr Rogers, and Maurice Sendak).

In fact, all the writers and pundits from this group tend to want to say it as it is. Many are overtly political; there is little doubt where they stand politically.

Neptune in Pisces, Pluto in Aries – images and tales of foreign lands

Neptune in Leo, Pluto in Cancer – passionate fighters for causes

Neptune in Virgo, Pluto in Cancer – more refined than Neptune in Leo, youthful in old age

## Uranus in Taurus (1850–1859, 1934–1942)
### Qualities
- Financial freedom
- Financial theories and investigations
- Physical freedom
- Joy of money
- Farming innovation
- Earthy and slower, 'bull' mellowness
- Sensual rebellion (Elvis!), artistic rebel, but also finds joy in earthy, soft music (mellow or country)
- Lots of singers

- Drawl
- Stubborn about/holds on to causes/ideals/freedom
- Comes across as leisurely, relaxed, solid in manner
- Solidly and quietly *there*

Many in this group come across as quiet, maybe even a little shy. Often they have beautiful or mellow voices. Many singers and songwriters come from this group (especially with Pluto in Leo, which loves to be on stage). Taurus is associated with singing and the voice because it rules the throat.

They are earthy, with a love of nature. Their idealism is a practical idealism, a sensual idealism. Once committed to a course of change, they stick with it. Often they have quick, earthy wits.

Many have a slow, almost drawling, voice, and they come across as leisurely, relaxed, and solid. Their revolution is sensual/sexual – think Elvis (or Freud!). Many of the singers of this generation have a slow, country drawl. Many play or love to listen to country music. When they decide it is time for change, they keep at it their whole lives – these are committed revolutionaries! Their revolution sometimes comes through revolutionary songs or songwriting (Bob Dylan, Buffy St Marie, John Lennon). Singers born in this group have an electrical energy.

In fact, the farmers born in these years wanted to work with nature, rather than conquer it, resulting in a farming revolution. Because nature and farming are Taurus and innovation is Uranus, this is a natural outcome.

This group can be very stubborn (Taurus) about change (Uranus) – they tend to 'stay the course' even when the course may be disastrous. They can change, but have to learn to make it 'natural'.

Pluto in Cancer – clarity and mellow determination, many singers

Pluto in Leo – many singers/songwriters

## Uranus in Gemini (1774–1782; 1858–1866; 1942–1949)
### Qualities

- Freedom from the mind
- Gift with words, joy of talking/thought/variety
- Free speech
- Willing to try all kinds of technology to aid communication
- Wants to change the way people think
- Turns on to ideas
- Hopes for new ideas
- Rebels against mind
- Speedy and sometimes hyper
- Talks about ideals/freedom
- Ideal of writing
- Comes across as high-energy, talkative, intellectual, nervous
- Bright (in both energy and smarts), upbeat

People from this generation have high-energy minds. They are often speedy and sometimes hyperactive. During the 1960s, this group tried to attain spiritual states by negating or rebelling against the mind. Many of the more famous people of this generation are novelists, poets, or songwriters. This was the first computer generation – an electrical way to emulate the mind. Many computer pioneers came from this generation.

Because Gemini rules short journeys, people from this generation love automotive innovation. They express their uniqueness through their cars.

They want to change the way people think, or they want people to think about change. If members of this generation have an ideal, they must tell everyone about it. Words and ideas come to this group through flashes.

Often people in this group come across as intellectual or thoughtful. There is a perennial youthful energy among these people, reflecting the youthful quality of Gemini.

Neptune in Libra, Pluto in Leo – this generation adds dramatic intensity to their quest to change people's minds, although they try to appear harmonious

Neptune in Pisces, Pluto in Taurus – incredible innovators of whole new genres of fiction (Sir Arthur Conan Doyle) and ways to format data (Hollerith)

## Uranus in Cancer (1866–1872; 1949–1956)
## Qualities

- Runaways
- Late to have a family
- Even if has children, often has a full-time job, so not domestic
- Free from the mundane, free from dependency
- Wakes up people, loony
- Hates ruts, breaks out of ruts (the more famous stir emotions, break with past)
- Sudden and abrupt emotional changes (Proust wrote books about emotional flashes)
- Emotional, protective of ideals/freedom
- Ideal of the caring mother
- Comes across as emotional and caring

Cancer is the sign of emotional comfort and security, and of home, family, and tradition. Cancers have lots of character. Uranus in Cancer feels the need to break free of security. These people must break out of traditions, out of ruts. The great fear is that they might be dependent on someone else or that someone else might be dependent on them.

With Cancer ruling caring and nurturing and motherhood, Uranus avoids motherhood until the last moment. Many from this generation avoided parenthood until the last possible moment, or never had children. Yet they want to come across as caring and emotional.

Uranus in Cancer can have sudden and unpredictable mood changes. They 'flash' on emotions. They have emotional genius. They intensely want to be free of the mundane, the ordinary.

Uranus in Cancer wants to wake people up who have fallen asleep, who have become too comfortable. These people are like human alarm clocks that go off when things have gotten too tiresome, too normal. 'Wake up!' they blare. If Cancer has a loony side, Uranus in Cancer can be loony in spades.

When members of this generation were in their teens, many ran away from home. Freedom from the home is how a teenager expresses Uranus in Cancer.

## Uranus in Leo (1872–1878; 1956–1962)
### Qualities

- Free from 'big deals', freedom from too much attention
- Doesn't want to make a big deal of anything, aloof to signs of affection/warmth
- Free of bosses
- Joy in the dramatic, dramatically odd (either very dramatic or very quiet!)
- Dramatic innovation, constant dramatic change
- Freedom to be whoever you want to be
- Rebels, free of silliness and fun
- Innovations in amusement, ways to have fun
- Comes across as larger than life, showman, actor
- Very loving, generous, and affectionate
- Free of or very creative in romance
- Free of children!
- Creative freedom, constantly new and different creativity (Madonna, Isadora Duncan)

The key to understanding this group of people is to realize they must have creative freedom. They can be dramatic in a different way every day, or every minute. Just think of Madonna and Isadora Duncan.

Yet other people of this generation are the antithesis of creativity, affection, children, or fun. They want to be free of any 'big deals', drama, and fun. So some Uranus in Leo people can be killjoys or puritans. This type avoids children, the ultimate form of Leo creativity and expression of fun.

However, the majority of the Uranus in Leo generation wants to come across as larger than life, as the center of the party. Freedom to party and have fun is central to this group.

Many put their oddness at the center of attention – 'See how odd I am!' Others stand out for their warmth and showmanship, although that showmanship often comes with an odd twist or a twinkle in the eye.

This generation explores the science of life, what makes us alive, and why and how we live.

Being childlike or having children are both important to this group. Even the gay people in this group want to have children (Rosie O'Donnell, Melissa Etheridge). Many men have a kingly or fatherly air about them, while the women come across as queenly.

## Uranus in Virgo (1878–1885; 1962–1969)
## Qualities
- Sense of destiny (conjunct Pluto)
- Connection with 'ordinary' people, free of bureaucracy, outside of the box, homespun
- Changes in morals, free of morals
- Odd juxtaposition of details, masses of odd workings
- Tweaks the establishment – dry humor about the establishment
- Freedom in the details – very organized about freedom
- Comes across as quiet or thoughtful, knowing all the details, or prim and proper
- Highly technical, detailed in their ideals; work for their

ideals in a practical or technical way
- Breaks free of technology, anti-technology

People in this generation come across as earthy, even a little crusty. Many of them are 'common people' or really connected with the common people (Harry Truman, Will Rogers, Franklin and Eleanor Roosevelt, and James Joyce in his book *Dubliners*).

They want to break free of categories or boxes (Kafka), or invent fantastic and complex scenarios (Rube Goldberg). Klee's work was innovative in a 'boxy' way, and Picasso was one of the founders of Cubism.

Many have a fear of technology (Mary Shelley invented Frankenstein, a run-amok technological monster). A.A. Milne wrote *Winnie the Pooh*, which features odd small animals to convey humor about the prim and proper (ruled by Virgo).

Uranus in Virgo has a certain quiet, shy, 'hoarse' quality to the voice and demeanor. Look at the list of people born in the 1960s and think about their style and voice. They intend to do a job and do it well, but without being ostentatious. They are usually well groomed and well dressed.

Many of the women have a Virgo librarian look – quiet and prim. Others have the voluptuous side of Virgo (Yasmine Bleeth, Mira Sorvino, Lisa Kudrow, Brooke Shields). Some, such as Sandra Bullock, combine both sides into the voluptuous girl-next-door look.

Neptune in Taurus, Pluto in Gemini – livelier than Pluto in Taurus

Neptune in Scorpio, Pluto in Aquarius – an intense generation

## Uranus in Libra (1885–1891; 1969–1974)
## Qualities
- Free of society and fads
- Focus on art and beauty, very social people
- Artistic breakthroughs

- Charmingly odd, oddness with a smile (Ed Wynn, Stan Laurel)
- Comes across as charming, smiling, or suave; want to come across as fair
- Great perception of social trends (de Tocqueville), watches society (Hedda Hopper)
- Socializes with others to create an ideal society
- Revolution in society

When you meet a person from this generation, you think 'kindly and charming'. Think of Maurice Chevalier and Ed Wynn. Social thinkers with insight into society from this group include Sinclair Lewis, Arnold Toynbee, and De Tocqueville. Eisenhower was the smiling grandfather president who played on the golf course ('I like Ike'). His star rose when Neptune entered Libra in 1942 (he became allied commander) and fell in 1956 when Neptune left Libra (problems with segregation, etc.). So this Libran image was his primary asset.

Often people from this generation have a unique view of beauty and human nature. Some famous visual and written artists in this group include Jean Cocteau with his unique films, Charlie Chaplin with his smiling underdog image and sense of justice, Dumas, Elizabeth Barrett Browning, and Emerson.

More recently, the artistic breakthrough side of Uranus in Libra led to hip-hop/rap artists breaking the musical mold. With Pluto in Libra since 1972, these rappers have exhibited the gangster side of rap – gangster (Pluto) and art (Libra). The earlier part of this generation had Pluto in Virgo and therefore they advanced the technology and technique of hip-hop.

In contrast with this are the 'beautiful people' who want to come across as attractive, well-dressed, and pleasant. These people can party with the best because they want to be part of every scene, every style. Nearly all the stars of *Beverly Hills 90210* come from this group. Often they have brilliant, radiant smiles.

**Uranus in Scorpio (1806–1813; 1890–1898; 1974–1981)**
**Qualities**

- Sexual breakthroughs (Henry Miller, Mae West), rebel against sexual repression
- Comes across as intense, sexual, mysterious
- Dark, secretive, passionate (J. Edgar Hoover, Escher, Dashiell Hammett, Basil Rathbone)
- Joy in being intense, joy in solving mysteries (portrays investigators, lawyers, gangsters, etc.) or posing mysteries (the dark images of Escher, Poe, Dickens)
- Gains power to maintain their ideals/freedom
- Theorizes about the intense, cataclysmic quality of nature (Velikovsky)

If you think about the image of people of this generation, you will see it is intensely Scorpionic. Many are dark and brooding. Think of Basil Rathbone, who played the definitive Sherlock Holmes; Edgar Allan Poe, who wrote murder mysteries and horror tales; and Dashiell Hammett, who wrote *The Maltese Falcon.*

Let's not forget the sexual side of Scorpio, as seen through Henry Miller and his erotic tales; Mae West and her joyful and witty sexuality ('A hard man is good to find'); and Rudolph Valentino, who was an idol for a generation of women with his dark looks in *The Sheik.* More recent examples include Liv Tyler and Christina Ricci, who both have that dark Scorpio look. Think of the dark images of Escher and the humor of Groucho Marx. Dickens wrote about the misery of the working class, the underside of society.

Velikovsky made theories about the cataclysmic nature of the world. J. Edgar Hoover dug into the lives of people via the FBI. All of these people have something intense, dark, and mysterious about them – they are fascinated by Scorpionic subjects.

Neptune and Pluto in Gemini – intense writers (Gemini),

actors, and comedians

## Uranus in Sagittarius (1898–1904; 1981–1988)
### Qualities

- Soaring quality, humorous and philosophical, big smiles
- Comes across as casual, philosophical
- Joy of travel and foreign lands (Hemingway, Hope)
- Artists who push the envelope (Disney, Dr Seuss, Dali)
- New ways of seeing, thinking better of yourself
- Joy of nature, outdoors people (Disney, Hemingway, Thoreau)
- Political rebels
- Opens people up to new, soaring ways of looking at things
- Gathers people philosophically or politically for change
- Come across as jovial, humorous

People born with Uranus in Sagittarius come across as upbeat, humorous, earnest, and exaggerated. Think of Fred Astaire, Walt Disney, Cary Grant, and Johnny Weissmuller.

Sagittarians project into the future; they think about future possibilities. With Uranus as the theorizer, this results in surrealistic possibilities, such as those created by Salvador Dali, Alfred Hitchcock, George Orwell, and Dr Seuss.

Sometimes Sagittarians are the upper crust, the nobility. So Uranus here wants to project an aristocratic air or explore the world of nobility. Charles Boyer, Anthony Trollope, the Brontës, and Queen Victoria exemplify this mode. The joy-of-nature types (Sagittarians love the out-of-doors and can be sportspeople) include Walt Disney, Johnny Weissmuller, and Ernest Hemingway.

Of course, we mustn't forget the humor and clowning of Sagittarius. Joyful practitioners in this group include Emmet Kelly, Zasu Pitts, Bob Hope, and Ray Bolger. This type can sometimes combine a conservative perspective with a smiling, upbeat attitude. Examples include Rudy Vallee, Walt Disney, Guy Lombardo, Ed Sullivan, and Bob Hope. Most people with Uranus in Sagittarius are optimistic and smiling, yet very much part of the established culture.

But those who aren't part of the established culture break strongly with the traditional way of doing things; Marx, Engels, and Dali come to mind. Marx and Engels theorized about wealth, and broke with the wealthy on what was good for society.

Walt Disney was a cartoonist, but also loved the outdoors and nature. He made films, such as *Bambi*, that explored the relationship between people and nature.

Finally, some in this group explore philosophy and religion and theorize about these topics. A prime example is Joseph Campbell.

Neptune and Pluto in Gemini – Neptune in Gemini has excellence and is amusing, bright, light

Neptune in Cancer, Pluto in Gemini – much more emotional than Neptune in Gemini, Neptune in Cancer pushes the envelope; is light, humorous, and emotional; and likes children

Neptune in Sagittarius, Pluto in Pisces (Uranus-Neptune conjunct) – soaring philosophies and ideals

## Uranus in Capricorn (1821–1828; 1905–1912; 1988–1996)
### Qualities

- Serious and heavy generation!
- Loner-style eccentrics
- Come across as heavy
- Straight shooter, conservative
- With Uranus conjunct Neptune, more imaginative, religious, involved with helping others
- Dry, quiet sense of humor
- Willing to work for a long time for ideals
- A real 'character'
- Dignified or strong, silent type; a rugged gentleness

- Distinctive (often raspy) voice

A distinction should be made between people born with Uranus in Capricorn alone and those born with the Uranus-Neptune conjunct in Capricorn (during the 1821–1828 period). There is something heavy and serious about many of the pure Uranus-in-Capricorn generation, although some people in this group are quietly authoritative. Some have an anti-authority gleam and will do what they want in spite of what the so-called authorities say. Examples of the heavy and serious include Dostoevsky, Otto Preminger, and Brezhnev.

In the last couple of hundred years, Neptune has been either conjunct or opposed to Uranus when it has been in Capricorn. When Uranus is conjunct Neptune in Capricorn, the generation tries to found compassionate institutions. When Uranus in Capricorn is opposed to Neptune in Cancer, the generation finds itself between reactionary authoritativeness and compassionate caring. Sometimes true compassion is cloaked in an authoritative style (Dag Hammarskjold wrote mystical poems while leading the UN) and at other times, a reactionary conservatism is combined with a compassionate image (Ronald Reagan).

Uranus and Neptune in Capricorn, Pluto in Pisces – involved with religion and spirituality or the deeper motivations of people (Pluto in Pisces), helps the underdogs in society.

Uranus and Neptune in Capricorn, Pluto in Aries – this group is more warlike, driven, and adventurous than is the Pluto- in-Pisces generation. Grant was a general, politician, and compulsive alcoholic; Pasteur explored microbes and found cures for diseases; Strauss wrote tumultuous symphonies; Jules Verne wrote the first science fiction adventure novels; and Tolstoy wrote great novels about war (*War and Peace*) and relationships. Their lives all had a serious tone.

Neptune in Cancer, Pluto in Gemini – nearly all of these

people had a distinctive twinkle in their eyes. They dreamed of getting out of the limitations of their lives (Jimmy Stewart in *It's a Wonderful Life*), but often were forced back into a caring (Neptune in Cancer), conservative (opposed Uranus in Capricorn) life. Their gleam said, 'I am extraordinary', and each broke out of the limitations of Capricorn in his or her own way. Some, of course, embraced conservatism (Roy Rogers and Dale Evans, Ronald Reagan, Barry Goldwater, and Glenn Miller come to mind). Others were more on the side of compassion then conservatism (Katharine Hepburn, Henry Fonda, Jimmy Stewart, Burl Ives, and Hubert Humphrey).

## Uranus in Aquarius (1828–1836; 1912–1919; 1995–2003)
## Qualities
- Friendly, revolutionary in thinking
- Comes across as odd and friendly
- Thrives on the unpredictable, sees humor in oddness
- Great writers
- Insight into humanity (Goethe, Mark Twain, J.D. Salinger, Ibsen, Lewis Carroll)

There are different sets of people with Uranus in Aquarius. Nearly all are friendly and project friendliness. Some are oddballs with a twinkle in the eye who revel in their oddness, such as Red Skelton, Anthony Quinn, Phyllis Diller, Art Carney, Red Buttons, Martha Raye, and Lewis Carroll. Others are insightful writers with a unique perspective on humanity, such as Goethe, Mark Twain, J.D. Salinger, Ibsen, Emily Dickinson, Louisa May Alcott, Arthur C. Clarke, Ann Landers, Abigail Van Buren, Tennessee Williams, and Lewis Carroll. Many stand for freedom from any social mores or are naturally free of social constraints. This group includes some incredible idealists.

Some of the geniuses of this group are jazz musicians and great movie directors. When it comes to deflating Neptune-in-

Leo egos, this group excels. Often, it is done with a humorous jab.

By contrast, the conservative side of Aquarius comes out in the following people: Gerald R. Ford, Menachem Begin, Billy Graham, and Spiro Agnew. But even the conservatives have an electrical air about them. And there aren't many conservatives in this group.

Neptune in Cancer, Pluto in Gemini – twinkling, good-natured, sense of caring, project friendliness

Neptune and Pluto in Cancer – deeply emotional

Neptune in Leo, Pluto in Cancer – larger than life, caring, warm, friendly (or at least, project friendliness), twinkle in the eye (avuncular), many playboys and party people due to the Neptune-in-Leo love of parties with the Uranus-in-Aquarius freedom from society (Desi Arnaz, Dean Martin, John F. Kennedy, Jackie Gleason)

Neptune in Capricorn, Pluto in Aries – many are driven (Pluto in Aries) loners (Neptune in Capricorn); can see the negative side of humanity, but can also perceive something higher, better (idealism of Uranus in Aquarius)

## Uranus in Pisces (1835–1843; 1920–1928; 2003–2010)
### Qualities

- Kindly (Neptune in Leo) and gentle
- Very versatile (chameleon)
- Odd outsider with self-deprecating humor
- Projects a dream, imaginative – joy and excitement of a dream
- Projects a strong image
- *Stars!*
- Life is a dream – sees the world through dreamy eyes
- Comes across as very compassionate
- Odd failures, freedom from failure
- Spiritual freedom, new viewpoint on mystical experience
- Humor through ineptness, human foibles (Irma Bombeck,

Sid Caesar, Jerry Lewis, Peter Sellers, Jack Lemmon)
- Mellow, rich quality to voices and manner

What a group of dreamers and losers! Yet many of these people are incredibly compassionate. And some are both dreamers and losers. For example, Jerry Lewis has his Sun conjunct Uranus in Pisces. Jerry made his living as a self-deprecating-loser comedian, and yet he also ran television marathons to help cure people.

Many people in this group have a rich, mellow quality to their voices, and that same mellow quality is in all their actions. Pisces is the chameleon. These people are the Renaissance ideal; they have talents in many different areas. Examples of people whose acts consist of characterization, which is a form of the chameleon, include Steve Allen, Sid Caesar, Peter Sellers, Marcel Marceau, Johnny Carson, and Jonathan Winters.

The people in this group project a dream, and often others live their dreams through them. An example is Hugh Hefner, with his dream of the playboy. Other examples include Donna Reed as the archetypical 1950s mom, Judy Garland and *The Wizard of Oz*, and Rod Serling and *The Twilight Zone*. Yet others are masters of fantasy, including Fellini, Timothy Leary, Judy Garland, Charles Schulz, Kurt Vonnegut, Norman Mailer, and Peter Sellers.

Uranus-in-Pisces people think of themselves as compassionate, and they project that. They care for the sick, the disadvantaged, and those who live on the fringes of society.

Ramakrishna, William James, and Allen Ginsberg were focused on the spiritual. These people brought a deeper insight to spirituality.

Artistically, the Impressionists Cézanne, Monet, and Renoir painted the way they saw the world, as a series of Piscean impressions. To them, the world was an unfocused place of dreamy images.

*Chapter 4*

# Neptune Generations

Neptune is the image of each generation. All the advertising, imagery, movies, clothing, hair styles, and photographs of that generation reflect the quality of Neptune's sign at birth.

What people in this generation dream about, what confuses them, where their illusions lie, and what appearances they maintain are all Neptune. You might think of it as the psychic covering, or psychic veil, around everything. People's compassion and faith come through this planet, as well. Neptune represents universal love, but also universal *samsara*, or illusion.

Neptune takes 14 years to transit a sign, so whole generations fall under each sign. Neptune in Virgo is clean-cut, organized, and of service to others. This generation came of age in the 1950s. Because their image is everything, these people may actually keep all their clutter hidden in a closet. Neptune in Libra wears flowery or stylish clothes. These people came of age in the 1960s and idealized relationships, music, and art. Neptune in Scorpio wears black leather and pierces body parts when they are young. They want to maintain a tough, sexy image. Neptune in Sagittarius wears clothes that are loose, sometimes baggy. Neptune in Capricorn wears clothes with prestige value (this may be modified by Uranus conjunct Neptune, whereby prestigious and odd/technological merge). Neptune in Aquarius wears odd clothes, the odder the better. Of course, they may wear technologically advanced clothing instead.

Each generation's faith is ruled by Neptune. For example, the Neptune-in-Libra generation has faith in the power of art and music to heal. Large rock concerts to generate money for charity were spearheaded by Neptune-in-Libra people. If you think of faith as a belief in something you haven't touched, proven, or experienced, then it can be defined as a possibility outside of Saturnine limitations.

How each generation feels about religion is evident through Neptune. For example, the Neptune-in-Gemini generation focuses on religious scriptures (and is also the generation most troubled by intellectualism about religion). For Neptune in Cancer, religion is a family endeavor: 'The family that prays together stays together.' People born with Neptune in Leo see religion and showmanship as one thing; for them, religion should be a good show. Cleanliness (and work) is next to godliness for Neptune in Virgo; this placement has a Puritan quality – good works!

Each Neptunian generation has a different reason for taking drugs. When Neptune is in Scorpio, drugs are used for psychological insights. When Neptune is in Sagittarius, drugs are used to tune in to nature. Neptune in Capricorn means drugs are used to give greater productivity and a sense of control and power, but also to break through walls and limits (ego) that keep one from connecting with others. With Neptune in Aquarius, drugs are used to be free, to think better, and to communicate better with other people.

Neptune is a higher octave of Jupiter. Very broad-scale economic changes are signaled by Neptune. For example, when Neptune went from Leo, with its extravagance, to Virgo, with its focus on illness, in 1929, the Great Depression hit. It wasn't until Neptune entered Libra in 1942 that the cycle really ended.

Everybody has dreams. The common dreams of a generation, and more importantly, what methods the individuals use to achieve those dreams, are ruled by Neptune. People who have Neptune in Aries are driven by their dreams, and have martial dreams. People who have Neptune in Gemini talk about their dreams. They have dreams of writing or communicating in whole new ways.

People in each generation swim in a world of Neptune. In a way, Neptune is the content the generation uses. It is the content, or media programming, with which each generation works. When Neptune is in Aries, people work with strife, and make that their world. By contrast, those born with Neptune in Libra work with relationships, art, and diplomacy. The Neptune-in-Taurus generation works within a world of earthy imagery, of brooding heaviness and sensuality.

How people escape reality or the hardships of life happens through Neptune. Drugs are only part of the means to escape – fudging the truth, daydreaming, traveling, and so on are all used to make life smoother. Like water, Neptune takes the easiest path. Sometimes this means lying, stealing, and glamorizing to avoid actually doing something that involves real accomplishment or hard work.

Some people are primarily Neptunian in nature. The mystics, dreamers, addicts, musicians, and image-conscious are Neptunian. As Neptune changes signs, these folk change their entire image. When Neptune was in Scorpio, they were into transformation and social justice. When Neptune entered Sagittarius, they wanted to live in nature, to get away from the cities. In Capricorn, these same people decided they had to form a business and get it together – then they moved back to the cities!

Just imagine all these people as part of a Neptunian current. When Neptune changes signs, the waters in which they swim change; the image they try to project changes. Their whole self-identity changes at this point.

If Uranus is like the ascendant of a generation, Neptune is like the Moon of that generation. Neptune rules the environment and emotions of the generation, but also the glamour and comfortable images of each generation. Neptune is the universal love of the generation because it is the middle part of the trinity of joy, love, and peace.

## Neptune in Aries (1697–1710; 1861–1874)
## Qualities

- Driven by their dreams
- Tumultuous imagery, aggressive pursuit of compassion
- Compassion in battle, battle imagery
- The image of oneself as a warrior, as fighting for one's vision
- Great storytellers (O. Henry, H.G. Wells, Proust, Stephen Crane)

This group fights for its dreams and its religion. Vivekananda was a pioneer who brought Hinduism to America, and he fought prejudice and ignorance about religion in the USA. Stephen Crane wrote about the American Civil War, but never was involved in a war – he imagined it. D.W. Griffith was a pioneer in films (Neptunian imagery). H.G. Wells wrote science fiction about wars he envisioned in the future (*War of the Worlds* and *The Time Machine*). Gandhi used passive resistance to fight for Indian independence.

People born during these times have vivid imagery based on new ways of seeing. Matisse, Frank Lloyd Wright, Toulouse-Lautrec, and Ravel created new forms of art, architecture, and music.

If Neptune is the image of a generation, then these people see themselves as tough and daring. Rudyard Kipling wrote about British battles. Churchill saw himself and the men and women of his country as tough and courageous. Many of these people have a mission, an intense purpose to their lives that is almost spiritual in nature. Art is a fiery, emotional release for this generation, or it is futuristic and avant-garde.

This group does not suffer the illusions of others well; rather, they are right there with the pin to puncture the balloon. One can image all of them saying, 'Yeah, right'. Churchill fought those who tried to appease Hitler; Vivekananda talked about the illusion of samsara ('We think we will live forever; that, too, is samsara'); Gandhi fought the British non-violently, based on the compassion of the British population; and H.G. Wells saw the predatory nature of capitalism. All of these people dealt with the illusive and compassionate reality of Neptune, as distinct from the brutal and aggressive reality of Aries.

## Neptune in Taurus (1710–1724; 1874–1888)
## Qualities

- Practical dreams and earthy imagery
- Spiritual dimensions of matter (Einstein)
- Super solid demeanor, rock-like
- Sensual (Mata Hari, Isadora Duncan, Picasso)
- Practical compassion (Eleanor Roosevelt)
- Homespun, common-man or -woman image
- Peace important in one's life, peaceful
- Very aware of form (Picasso, Chagall)

Each day's ordinary events become extraordinary for these people. Ordinary people are exalted. Ordinary matter holds incredible energies. These individuals really like others. During World War I, this generation was in its thirties and forties. They lived through the Great Depression and World War II, and they were the generation in power. Herbert Hoover and Franklin and Eleanor Roosevelt had Neptune in Taurus.

Brooding heaviness and sensual imagery are art forms for this generation – think of the writings of Willa Cather, the dance of Isadora Duncan, and the sensual intrigue of Mata Hari; the spiritual writings of Edgar Cayce, Hermann Hesse, and Martin Buber; and the art of Picasso, Chagall, and Klee. When they exhibit humor, it is earthy or slapstick in nature – think of W.C. Fields, Mack Sennett, and Ed Wynn. Some of the humor is of imperturbability in the midst of chaos. Neptune in Taurus keeps the image of rock-like stability in spite of everything.

Will Rogers said he never met a man he didn't like. He had the homespun, down-to-earth practicality of Taurus, and his image resonated with others of his generation. Another example is Harry Truman, who had his Sun conjunct Neptune in Taurus, and so personally embodied this energy. Like Eleanor Roosevelt, he had compassion for the everyday men and women of the United States because he was one of them.

Einstein abstracted (Neptune) the qualities of matter (Taurus is earth). Martin Buber elevated personal love (Venus rules Taurus) into the love of the divine (Neptune). Many of these people had 'gravity' – they had a deep and heavy presence. Boris Karloff, Stokowski, Picasso, and John Foster Dulles are examples.

## Neptune in Gemini (1724–1737; 1887–1901)
### Qualities
- Witty image – many writers and thinkers
- Faith in the written and spoken word
- Twinkling eyes
- Find humor and joy in life
- Mental imagery
- Dreams of communicating, teaching
- Communicates an image
- Debonair, cosmopolitan image
- Light-hearted
- Drugs used tend to be forms of speed rather than depressants

These folks float from one situation to another. Some of the most tyrannical (Hitler, Khrushchev, Al Capone) and most easy-going (Harpo Marx, Henry Miller, Hedda Hopper) people had this placement. Nearly all are quick-witted and have a message (although, of course, Hitler's message isn't good). Each has a unique style, a certain panache. Their being says something –

they are vivid characters. Many have a rueful, yet innocent smile, giving the impression they are simultaneously jaded and open to something new and interesting. They've seen it all and yet... Think of Mae West, Fred Astaire, and Clark Gable.

People in this generation are bright and witty and are interested in gay, amusing times. In fact, amusement is one of their primary ways of dealing with the world. They want to amuse others and see the amusing quality of those around them. They were born, after all, in the Gay Nineties.

These are often mesmerizing people (e.g. Mesmer, who was born with Neptune in Gemini). They constantly discover new ways to fascinate others.

If Neptune is the image of a generation, then this generation's image changes constantly. They don't want to be pinned down to a particular image. If anything, they want to keep up a sharp or intellectual image. Nearly all are quick-witted and make snappy comebacks.

These are the communicators, the messengers. Paul Revere is remembered for delivering the message 'The British are coming!' The most recent generation loves their cars and telephones (both Gemini) and are the first generation to use these innovations extensively.

Examples of people with the cosmopolitan, debonair image of Neptune in Gemini include Maurice Chevalier, Hedda Hopper, Cole Porter, F. Scott Fitzgerald, Charles Boyer, and Clark Gable.

Many have Neptune and Pluto conjunct in Gemini, which makes them prototypic firsts. Henry Miller is the prototypic pornographic writer, and Mae West the prototypic risqué female movie star (both with Uranus in Scorpio). Amelia Earhart, Escher, Laurel and Hardy, Charlie Chaplin, Hitler, and Edward G. Robinson are also in this group. Look at the list of people, at the end of the book, with Neptune in Gemini and find the many 'firsts'.

## Neptune in Cancer (1737–1751; 1901–1914)
## Qualities

- Emotional imagery (Disney, Dr Seuss, Dali)
- Family values (Goldwater)
- Soft, watery façade
- Can be sappy and homespun (Disney, Lawrence Welk, Ozzie Nelson)
- Faith in family, tradition, home country
- Patriotic
- Food issues (lived through Great Depression)
- Emotional dreams about family
- Alcohol and prohibition generation

When the 1950s started, this generation was between the ages of 36 and 49. So these are the people who were coming into power at that time. If you think of the emotionality and patriotism of Disney, Lawrence Welk, and the TV characters Ozzie and Harriet during the 1950s, you have the flavor of this group. Most have Pluto in Gemini, like the prior Neptune generation, but this group is much more caring. These people idealize Mom, apple pie, and small-town living.

Even the more zany members of this group turn the traditional upside down and rebel against it. Dali idealized his wife in the emotional way common to this generation, and Dr Seuss wrote for children.

Their drug of choice was the emotionally effusive alcohol; they used alcohol for emotional sustenance. But this was also the generation that experienced prohibition just as they were coming of age.

With respect to food, this generation lived through the Depression. As a result, they kept their refrigerators stocked with food so they would never have to go hungry again. Food security is an important article of faith.

These people idealize the family. Think of the idealized

families in Disney films and in *The Adventures of Ozzie and Harriet*. This is the world of the 1950s sitcom. This generation tried to create the image of a warm family with no real problems. In some cases, as often happens with Neptune, this warm family is just that: an image.

The Uranus-in-Capricorn sub-generation, many of whom want to come across as conservative, are ultra-patriotic and right-wing. Examples include Barry Goldwater, John Wayne, Ronald Reagan, and Roy Rogers. However, others in this sub-generation are less conservative because they have an emotional connection to families and their roots (Dag Hammarskjold, Burl Ives, Hubert Humphrey, and Lyndon Johnson, for example). Those who are more liberal are more in tune with Neptune in Cancer. Uranus in Capricorn is in opposition to Neptune in Cancer, and so the people of this sub-generation have to choose sides.

Uranus in Sagittarius, Pluto in Gemini – emotional, sometimes sappy, upbeat, philosophical, edgy (Dr Spock, Orwell, Dr Seuss, Joseph Campbell), new ways of seeing things

Uranus in Capricorn, Pluto in Gemini – upright, conservative, but with a twinkle

Uranus in Aquarius, Pluto in Gemini – twinkling, good-natured, sense they care, project friendliness, many comedians (if not, often have a sense of humor)

Uranus in Aquarius, Pluto in Cancer – deeply emotional, with twinkling humor

## Neptune in Leo (1751–1765; 1914–1929)
### Qualities
- Warm, or at least have a warm image
- Faith in 'heart', goodness of people
- Radiate one's dream
- Actors
- Dramatic image
- Dreams of acting, being famous, creative, being a star

- Older parents in 1960s
- Drugs used for 'good times'

Some of the greatest good-time party people are in this generation. Would you like to be at a party with Dean Martin, Desi Arnaz, Betty Grable, Ann Landers, and Abigail Van Buren? What if you were at a party with Hugh Hefner, Liberace, Tony Bennett, Jerry Lewis, Allen Ginsberg, Harry Belafonte, Marlon Brando, Paul Newman, and Jack Lemmon? These are not wallflowers!

Life is indeed a stage for these people, a place to have fun. Drugs, also, are used for fun. Fun is a central Leo goal. Even the more serious of the Neptune-in-Leo people exude a warm, fatherly aura. Think of Walter Cronkite, Jackie Gleason, Jack Paar, Harry Belafonte, and Andy Griffith. Actually, even the serious people have a strong sense of humor.

These people exude warmth, greatness, and generosity (good Leo qualities). Think of the warmth of Dean Martin, Frank Sinatra, Jackie Gleason, Chuck Berry, Pearl Bailey, Johnny Carson, Dick Van Dyke – the list goes on and on. In their personal lives, they may not be as warm as the image they project on stage, but they all project a warm image in their public lives.

This generation uses drugs to have fun, of course. Alcohol consumed at parties is a big favorite. Their way to spirit is through *raja* yoga, the yoga characterized by the kingly quality of God.

The Judy Garland dream of being a star, an admired actor or stage personality, is a central dream (and accomplishment) for many of these people. An incredible number of actors are born with Uranus in Pisces (coming across as a chameleon – easily able to take on parts); Neptune in Leo; or Pluto in Cancer (for that internal emotional power).

The majority of this generation was born in the Roaring Twenties and partook of that wild and playful energy. By the end of that decade, the oldest were 15 years old. These are the parents of many children born in the 1960s. They appreciate the need for the Pluto-in-Leo generation to party, be creative, and follow their hearts. When World War II started, they were between 11 and 25 years old, so they made up the majority of the fighting force. They had just lived through the Great Depression, as well.

Uranus in Aquarius, Pluto in Cancer – larger than life, caring, warm (twinkle in the eyes)

Uranus in Pisces, Pluto in Cancer – incredible number of actors (Uranus in Pisces + Neptune in Leo), many with gruff/raspy voices (men) or husky/wispy voices (women)

Uranus in Aries, Pluto in Cancer – passionate fighters for causes

## Neptune in Virgo (1765–1779; 1928–1943)
## Qualities

- Quiet (sometimes stone-faced)
- Solid feel, stoic
- Men tend to be strong, silent types; women are cool, quiet types
- Sculptured image (Dick Clark, Sean Connery, Jack Lord)
- Faith in hard work
- Help/compassion for people with problems
- Help people through jobs
- Comic/cartoon generation
- Clean-cut image, 'straighter' than Neptune in Leo
- Dream of people working together without regard to upbringing (Pluto in Cancer wipeout of upbringing)
- Younger parents in 1960s
- Few drug problems – stimulants and coffee, and drugs that come from drugstores are their drugs of choice
- Religious service(s)

These people have a chiseled, sometimes craggy, appearance.

They look like they are carved out of stone. They are more serious than the Neptune-in-Leo generation that preceded them (even though that generation included the majority of those who fought in World War II and lived through the Depression). With Sun conjunct Neptune in Virgo, Sean Connery has that craggy look to his face, the self-deprecating quiet demeanor (his jokes are often understated), and the clean-cut image.

Even the rebels of this generation (Jules Feiffer, Richard Alpert, Andy Warhol, and Yoko Ono, for example) stayed within the larger 'scene'. When they stepped outside their role, they still had a real sense of what their role was.

These are relatively quiet people, sometimes shy. They may be out in the public, but when they are, they still have a sense of stillness, of an inner quality.

A few in this group have a drug problem (well, okay, maybe that would be Richard Alpert). Even when they have a drug problem, they overcome it for the sake of their work. Their drugs of choice tend to be those that enable them to work harder and longer hours, such as caffeine, or to live longer, such as legal health drugs.

When they are spiritual, it is a very practical spirituality that benefits them in the here and now. Examples are Dr Martin Luther King, Jr, Ram Dass, and Shirley MacLaine. They connect with spirit through work and service to others. Many have a quiet humility, the high side of Virgo.

During the 1950s, this was the so-called clean-cut generation (they were seven to 22 years old when the 1950s started). They try to portray the image of being hard-working and of punctilious cleanliness. This being Neptune, of course, they sometimes swept the dirt under the rug to keep up appearances.

Uranus in Aries, Pluto in Cancer – more refined than Neptune in Leo (works with ardor for causes)

## Neptune in Libra (1779–1792; 1942–1957)
## Qualities

- Smiling, social, musical
- Dream of ideal mate
- Tries to keep social harmony
- Help/compassion through music and art
- Maintains a beautiful, harmonious image
- Uses drugs to socialize and connect with others
- Artistic imagery – or image as an artist
- Equal before God, sees God in other people
- Faith in beauty, others
- Social justice important

This is the 'flower child' generation. These folks try to keep a harmonious, smiling image. They dream of being musicians or artists, and idealize musicians and artists if they can't become one themselves. They also idealize and spiritualize relationships; many are looking for their soulmate.

Drugs are used either to socially connect to others or to beautify/enhance themselves. Drugs that enable them to better relate to others or to see artistic visions are preferred. As they get older, Botox, wrinkle creams, and Viagra are their drugs of choice.

They have elevated beautiful clothing, beautiful homes, and beautiful surroundings to the level of a religion. When they came of age in the 1960s, they could have been sleeping on the floor in an unfurnished room, but have a stereo system and clothes that cost more than everything else in the room combined. In later life, this fascination with clothes and music continues.

This generation loves to project an artistic appearance. In the 1960s, they experimented with creatively taking on an image, from grandmothers with granny glasses to eighteenth-century gentlemen in stove-pipe hats. This was the generation of psychedelic art, an art form born of Neptune in Libra.

These people could fill a stadium without any rowdiness, with everyone harmonious. They help others through benefit concerts and charity art. Often, they have more faith in others than in themselves. They subscribe to the article of faith that says all are equal. Social justice and the equality of humankind are important touchstones.

This generation doesn't like those who place themselves either above or below others. They tend to be able to see spirit best in other people. They also have the Libran sensitivity to being outcast from groups.

## Neptune in Scorpio (1792–1806; 1955–1970)
### Qualities

- Aware of dark side of humanity (Mary Shelley, Balzac, Hawthorne, Madonna)
- Deep insights into life (Ralph Waldo Emerson, De Tocqueville, Spike Lee)
- Sexual imagery
- Illusions about power, try to maintain an image that is in control or believe they have power when they don't have any power in the situation – can be confused about power
- Sarcastic about religion (and all things Neptunian – faith, compassion, etc.)
- Maintain a powerful, tough, sexy, cool image of being in control
- Pluto, ruler of Scorpio, modifies Neptune (Pluto in Pisces are more spiritual; in Aquarius more focused on technology, inspiration)
- Try to push, hard-sell, or manipulate people into buying an image that is patently not true
- Gushing, often followed by backstabbing
- Don't know where you stand with them
- Masters of spin control

The Neptune-in-Scorpio generation has a tough, intense image. This is the generation that, in their youth, loved piercings, black clothes, and face-painted rock bands, such as Kiss and Black Sabbath. The more mainstream members of this generation still have a dark, sexy image (Cameron Crowe, Michelle Pfeiffer, Gloria Estefan, Pamela Lee Anderson, Victoria Principal, Robert Townsend, Jason Priestley).

Because Scorpio rules power, reality, death, sex, and taxes, this generation can get very confused or self-deluded about these issues (just as the Neptune in Libra generation can be deluded or confused about relationships). I have seen some Neptune-in-Scorpio types believing they are in power in a situation in which they patently are not, while others scheme to get power when they have no ability to do anything useful with it.

Often power is a dream for Neptune in Scorpio, and the reality of power is not something the person can handle. However, sometimes when these people get Scorpionic power, they learn true Neptunian compassion from it. Other times, they are in a power bubble where they have temporary power in a local situation and delude themselves about how powerful they really are.

Because Neptune is the image of the generation and Scorpio is the way the image is transmitted, this generation can try the hard sell on images. They sometimes dramatically (and emotionally) try to sell an image of themselves or their relationships that you soon learn is totally untrue. In the worst cases, this can come across into hypocrisy if they actually believe their own story. The best of this generation can come up with enduring images of power struggles, the deeper nature of humanity, the realities of sex, etc.

This generation, which deals with compassion and spirituality (Neptune) through Scorpio, can consider themselves too tough and realistic to believe in religion or spirituality. If they do have faith, it must be a transformative spirituality with intense practices, and it must allow the practitioner to deal with the realities of death, power, torture, deep psychological problems, etc. When this generation has faith, it is an intense, realistic faith.

Scorpio is transformation, while Neptune is image. Neptune in Scorpio can be a constant transformation of the person's image. Madonna, who changes images practically every week, and Jim Carrey, who changes images practically every few seconds, are examples of this effect. Other Scorpio modes include the self-destructive drama queen – or king! Neptune in Scorpio asks for sympathy for the person who is in an emotional car wreck every day: 'They all are to blame' is the cry of this person.

However, some of the most insightful observations about culture come from the Neptune in Scorpio generation. Examples are Spike Lee, Ralph Waldo Emerson, and de Tocqueville. Here the probing nature of Scorpio dives into the depths of the Neptunian culture to bring back pearls of insight.

## Neptune in Sagittarius (1806–1820; 1970–1984)
## Qualities

- Progress through failure (Lincoln and Darwin)
- Grandiose entertainment (P.T. Barnum, Wagner)
- Want to energize and uplift the common people (Darwin = evolution, Lincoln/Stowe = freed slaves)
- Can see larger picture, grander scheme of things (Darwin)
- People who made up romantic movement in 1840s – grand romantics
- Loose-fitting clothes, hang-loose attitude
- Rap generation (with Pluto in Libra)
- Imagine (Neptune) the future (Sagittarius)
- Truth, crusaders, yearn for something better (all Sagittarius)

This is a smooth generation. Many are upbeat, 'fresh', wholesome, and religious. Now, you may think the rap generation isn't this way, but many do talk about God. When they became teenagers, these people wore loose-fitting clothes, sometimes downright baggy, and a hang-loose attitude. Sagittarians must be unconfined in their clothes.

Unlike the previous generation, which often defined themselves through their sexuality, this group has a hang-loose attitude about sex, too. When they are sexy, they are dramatic about it, yet vulnerable. Madonna and Bo Derek are from the Neptune in Scorpio generation, while Britney Spears and Drew Barrymore are from the Neptune in Sagittarius generation, so you can compare and contrast their respective sexual personas.

Because they envision themselves in a Sagittarian way, they see themselves as crusaders for truth, for a better future, and for ethics. The downside is that they can see themselves as better than others and are constantly dissatisfied with their current situation – they can feel entitled. This can make this generation constantly yearning, striving, and flighty.

This generation had five subsets in the 1970s and 1980s because Uranus was in three signs and Pluto in two. The Pluto in Virgo set are tougher and heavier than the Pluto in Libra set, who are more graceful and social. The Uranus and Pluto in Libra folks have a more romantic, innocent quality, but they are intensely aware of relationships (and many are famous for their relationships). Those with Uranus in Scorpio have more of an edge and are known for their wide-eyed intensity and open sexuality.

If you look back at the last time Neptune went through Sagittarius, you see some outrageous showmen and great philosophers. The writers and artists tend to be melodramatic tellers of tall tales (the Sagittarian tendency to exaggerate). They are concerned with uplifting the common person (the bettering quality of Jupiter). Showmen include P.T. Barnum and Richard Wagner. Philosophers include Darwin (evolution is so Sagittarian), Thoreau, Marx, and Whitman. Tellers of tales include Longfellow, Poe, Stowe, Trollope, Brontë, Dickens, and

Melville. Bettering the common person was a concern of every one except the patrician writers Trollope and Brontë (nobility is Sagittarian, also).

## Neptune in Capricorn (1820–1834; 1984–1998)
### Qualities

- Very aware of how social change affects people (Uranus conjunct Neptune and Neptune in a Uranus-ruled sign) – Clara Barton through her nursing, Dostoevsky through his writing
- Visionaries who came up with a different way to look at the world (Lord Leighton, Dante Rossetti, Burne-Jones, Jules Verne, James Clerk Maxwell, Pasteur); Pre-Raphaelites, scientists, science fiction
- Dream of climbing the social ladder (Horatio Alger, Dumas, Louisa May Alcott)
- Serious demeanor
- Many scientists and social thinkers (think outside or beyond the box)
- Very aware of the inner workings of nature and politics, driven to make social change (Susan B. Anthony, Ibsen, Jean Dumont, Lewis Carroll, Edwin Booth)

People with a serious, sometimes tough, image (when lighter, can be very odd indeed, due to the Uranus sub-ruler of Capricorn)

Imagine a Capricornian image: a serious, status-oriented person who works hard and has it all together. Now, that may not be the reality of this generation, but they will definitely have that image. Even those who aren't overtly serious have a certain gravity to them, and other people tend to take them seriously.

Stonewall Jackson's main image was very Saturnine and Capricornian: a stone wall! Many of the people in this group are loners or stoics.

The world of Neptune in Capricorn is one of structure. Some of these people imagine alternative structures (Jules Verne, Friedrich Engels, Lewis Carroll), some illuminate and rail against the structure (Ibsen), while others find the honorable path within the structure (Alexandre Dumas, Nobel, Horatio Alger). Still others create new structures of compassion (Florence Nightingale, Susan B. Anthony, Mary Baker Eddy, Clara Barton, Jean Dumont). Finally, some create new structures deep within nature, often associated with fields or waves (Neptune): Pasteur, Helmholtz, Lister, Maxwell. Some philanthropists also are in this group (Nobel, Levi Strauss), as well as others who gain wealth the standard way so they have the money to dream (Schliemann).

Clearly, you have to make a distinction between those with Uranus conjunct Neptune in Capricorn and those with just Neptune in Capricorn. Those born with the conjunct break free of social structures and of their serious image, and imagine structures completely different from the ones surrounding them. The people with Uranus conjunct Neptune have more 'juice' than do the ones with just Neptune in Capricorn.

Clara Barton had her Sun conjunct Uranus and Neptune, so she epitomized the conjunct. She worked where there was war, death, poverty, and disaster to improve the situation of those hurt in the disorder. She started the first free public school in New Jersey (she was replaced by a man as head – after all, she was a woman). Then she organized supplies for doctors so they could help wounded soldiers in the Civil War. She spearheaded a struggle to find the relatives of men missing in action. Finally, she founded the American Red Cross.

This is typical Capricorn: out of chaos (lunar Uranus) comes order (solar Saturn). In Clara's case, out of chaos came practical compassion (Neptune) and organizations to help those harmed by the chaos. Clara changed the world (Uranus) by creating organizations on which people in need could rely.

Mary Baker Eddy, the founder of Christian Science, looked

into healing through faith. She also fought against the scribes through the *Christian Science Monitor* newspaper. Interestingly, both of these famous women were born with this conjunction and became healers who founded organizations. In fact, all of the Neptune-in-Capricorn women who were famous were very strong, independent women.

Most of the Pre-Raphaelites were born with Uranus in Aquarius, Neptune in Capricorn, and Pluto in Aries, and the movement was born when Uranus conjuncted Pluto in Aries in 1848. The Pre-Raphaelites produced incredibly realistic and detailed images of mythological worlds to illuminate history and the subconscious.

## Neptune in Aquarius (1834–1848; 1998–2011)
### Qualities

- New imagery, new ways of painting (Homer, Cézanne, Renoir, Monet), seeing
- Great inventors (Bell, Edison – founder of group science in laboratory)
- Storytellers (Twain, James, Harte)

This generation has the artistic and scientific geniuses of its day. While Neptune in Capricorn's generation are scientists, these are more practical inventors. This quality is counterintuitive because usually Capricorn is associated with the experimental end of science and Aquarius with the more theoretical. A possible explanation is that the Uranus-Neptune conjunct in Capricorn creates the time for a paradigm shift and hence is more inner, while the unfolding of the conjunct in Aquarius makes for more action and practical results, even though it is in Aquarius.

If you look at the work of painters from the Neptune in Capricorn period, you see they connected historically or mythically, while the painters of this generation connected with the world through a new, Impressionist light. Impressionism couldn't be more Neptunian: the word itself is Neptunian, and painters use techniques that force the viewer to synthesize the painting out of discrete points or brushstrokes that don't cohere into a painting until one steps back.

This generation got groups of inventors together to invent the telephone, the elevator, the light bulb, the phonograph, and the movie camera. Think of modern life without these inventions!

Even the writers of the day created breakthrough works. Mark Twain leads the pack, but Henry James, Bret Harte, Anatole France, and Emile Zola wrote works that will never be forgotten. Of course, with Aquarius, there must be some questioning of society, and *J'Accuse* by Zola fits that bill.

One consistent theme through the work of many of the writers and artists in this generation is the need to look more closely or differently at the world. Mark Twain had a sparkling, humorous insight into his characters and human nature. Emile Zola looked deep into the legal system and justice. The Impressionists examined our very perceptions.

## Neptune in Pisces (1848–1861; 2011–2025)
### Qualities

- Legends, fluid imagery, great storytellers/writers (especially about childhood)
- Dreamers
- Writers of children's stories – Baum (*Wizard of Oz*), Barrie (*Peter Pan*), Stevenson (*Treasure Island*), Arthur Conan Doyle (*Sherlock Holmes*)
- Creators of school philosophy (Dewey, Steiner)
- Great with imagery (Gauguin, Van Gogh, Barrie, Baum, Grandma Moses, Wharton, Chekhov, Mahler, Doyle)

These people live their dreams, or live in dreams. For example, Van Gogh's paintings had a dreamlike quality to them, while Freud delved into people's subconscious and their dreams.

Seurat's paintings showed the dream in an everyday setting through the illusion of many points of light making up a picture.

Some of the most famous children's writers ever come from this group. After all, aren't children's stories based on vivid imagination? Think of the alternative worlds in the *Wizard of Oz, Peter Pan,* and *Treasure Island.* In general, children figure prominently whenever Pisces is involved.

Other writers become more entranced with dissolution, which is also Piscean: Chekhov, Wilde, Shaw, and, to an extent, Wharton. Still others escape to far-off islands or write about adventures in exotic lands: Gauguin, Joseph Conrad, and Robert Louis Stevenson are examples.

Again, the children's theme comes up again when you consider that the most famous educational philosophers were born in this generation: Dewey and Steiner. Although their philosophies were different, they both advanced new ways at looking at education.

Of course, some people from this generation love to punch holes in the Piscean world, perhaps because they are more aligned with Uranus and Pluto, either conjunct or in the same sign. People who come to mind are George Bernard Shaw (his addition to education: 'Those who can, do; those who can't, teach'), Oscar Wilde, Clarence Darrow, Sir Arthur Conan Doyle, and Chekhov.

Uranus in Aries, Pluto in Aries – adventurers, but dreamers

Uranus in Taurus, Pluto in Aries – adventurers with a more staid outlook, but dreamers

Uranus in Aries, Pluto in Taurus – fights for revolutionary change, dreamer with practicality

Uranus in Taurus, Pluto in Taurus – dreamers with a practical face, punched practical holes in illusions of Neptune in Pisces or saw deeply into dreams (Shaw, Van Gogh, Freud, Baum)

Uranus in Gemini, Pluto in Taurus – writers and thinkers, but dreamers

*Chapter 5*

# Pluto Generations

As Pluto changes signs, people's psychological reality shifts. What had power yesterday doesn't have the same power, the same 'juice', today. What you 'must' do, as part of the generation, is defined by Pluto.

People's primal dualities are under Pluto. For the Pluto in Gemini generation it was publish or perish. This group of people saw their word, their thoughts, as life and death matters. Secret treaties started World War I. But this was also a generation of amusements and bon mots. One of the archetypes was Mickey Mouse with his squeaky voice.

For the Pluto in Cancer generation, family is everything. These are the people who live in security homes in gated communities – security is life and death. With many having lived through the Depression, a well-stocked larder is also a matter of life and death. The world is divided into the familiar and the unfamiliar, the family and outsiders. This is a fiercely emotional group for whom their homeland is worth dying for – they are more patriotic than the generations before or after. This is the 'family values' generation.

However, their generation also lived 'on the road', the negating side of Pluto, who wanted nothing to do with a home or family. This generation has some of the most alienated family members, perhaps because so many power struggles take place among family members – they may decide to have nothing to do with their family.

Power for Pluto in Cancer people is around emotional protection of their community or country. This lies behind their patriotism.

The Pluto in Leo generation were the hippies but also the 'me' generation. The keyword is 'fun'. The most successful people of this generation say that if they are not having fun it isn't worth doing. These people must be creative. Leadership is all or nothing – this group followed leaders blindly or didn't follow anyone! They love to gamble and take risks or can spend their lives avoiding risks.

Power for this generation lies with the creative, the dramatic, the leaders, the people on stage, the people with heart. These people can be totally egoic and overbearing (the worst side of Leo) or they attempt to be egoless and defer to others (dramatically, of course). The best of this generation try to clear out ego while retaining the childlike generosity of Leo.

By now you are getting a sense of how Pluto defines the generations. Each generation of Plutonians is often in an adjacent sign to that of their parents (difficult) and a sextile sign to their grandparents (easy), which is why children often get along better with their grandparents (the same is often true of Neptune placement, as well).

Remember that each generation lives through four or five Pluto signs that follow where it was at birth. So the Pluto in Taurus generation must live through the challenges of Pluto in Gemini, Pluto in Cancer, etc. Of course, the generation tends to work better in signs that are sextile or trine to their native Pluto sign since the current 'reality' is more congenial. When people are born with Pluto near the Taurus side of the zodiac, where Pluto takes 30 years per sign, most people live through two or three signs beyond the one they were born with. When Pluto is near Scorpio and takes 12 to 15 years per sign, these generations may easily live through six to eight signs of Pluto.

## Pluto in Aries (1577–1606; 1822–1853)
## Qualities
- Followed inner guide, destiny

- Seized power through force
- Popular will
- Adventurers
- Stormy
- Pioneers
- Forceful personalities

These were tough, solitary people who followed their own promptings. Some were captains of industry (Carnegie, Rockefeller, J.P. Morgan) while others were inventors (Edison, Bell). These were powerful and turbulent people. Adventure was important; some of the greatest adventure writers – Mark Twain, Stevenson, Bret Harte, Jules Verne – were in this group. The popular will was everything. They had a strong sense of collective destiny (Aries). This generation can be incredibly willful. When the revolutions of 1848 shook Europe and the Gold Rush started, the oldest in this generation were 26! The most famous philosophers of this group (among them Nietzsche) felt that will represents reality and power. The music of Tchaikovsky is stormy, like his generation.

## Pluto in Taurus (1606–1638, 1853–1884)
## Qualities

- In touch with human nature and the common, earthy people
- Producing was their focus
- All or nothing about pleasure
- Nature focus, co-existed with it or conquered it

This group was in touch with human nature and the common person. They remained earthy, practical, and grounded. They were involved in producing things. Psychologically they were heavy, sensuous, and ponderous – just think of the Victorian father of those days. The lighter people of this generation had a dry, peasant humor (W.C. Fields, Will Rogers); however, there aren't a lot of comedians here! Like good Victorians, they were all or nothing about pleasure. This generation could be incredibly stubborn. Reality was based on what they could touch.

There was a strong need to find the reality behind the material. This made for scientists who looked deeply into matter – foremost among them was Einstein.

Many had a strong feel for nature (Hearst, Conrad, Frank Lloyd Wright, Jack London, Teddy Roosevelt). Some were into going beyond nature, conquering nature. Still others wanted to penetrate nature's secrets (Pierre Curie, Einstein, Martin Buber). The phrase 'nature red in tooth and claw' came from Jack London.

This need to understand nature was behind their probing into human nature, physical nature, plant and animal nature. For example, Arthur Conan Doyle invented Sherlock Holmes who was hyperaware of every detail around him – he solved cases by looking at the small details and deducing what was behind those details. Proust delved into what was behind each emotion, each image.

Think of 'natural' and 'nature'. These are our ruts, but also our perfectly normal way of being. Those with Pluto in Taurus peer beneath the normal to find the supernatural or deeper levels of 'nature'. This probing is the same motivation for Einstein, Edgar Cayce, and Carl Jung.

## Pluto in Gemini (1639–1668; 1884–1914)
### Qualities
- High-pitched, lively energy
- Intellectual (part of publish-or-perish generation in academia) – reality intellectualized
- Alternative realities
- Communicators
- Pioneers in media

- Propagandists – the word is reality

There were high-pitched voices among this generation, but also high-pitched, lively energy. Mickey Mouse is an icon for this generation. They are light-hearted or intellectual (sometimes both). With their Mercury quickness, fast dancing was in vogue. They have an airy humor – with a twinkle in their eyes they see humor in life. With Pluto ruling external will and Mercury ruling speech and glib lies, propaganda was part of this group's life.

Words are all or nothing. Many had light, raspy voices (there was a certain quality to their voice!). This generation was incredibly intense about words. They sculpted their reality out of words (treaties, newspapers). The pen was mightier than the sword! They were gallant and knowledgeable about the world. It was this generation who were six to 36 years old during the Roaring Twenties (the people most affected – teenagers and young adults) when Pluto was in Cancer (and Neptune in Leo). They defined the new media of radio, movies, and TV. They were also the first generation with personalized transportation: cars and bicycles.

Ronald Reagan, the great communicator, was part of this generation. He started in radio and TV, and then moved to politics where he communicated his view of reality to great effect.

Many from this group created alternative realities, alternative ways of looking at our world. Among the artists, we notice: Modigliani, Chagall, Cocteau, Norman Rockwell, M.C. Escher, Walt Disney, Dr Seuss, Salvador Dali, Al Capp, Jackson Pollock, Tolkien. The realities they created were compelling.

During their lives both communication (movies, radio, TV) and transportation (autos, planes) were transformed. People's local environment was broadened to include the whole world – in a day you could find out about happenings in, or even travel to, another part of the world.

## Pluto in Cancer (1668–1692; 1914–1939)
## Qualities

- Family and food are intense focuses
- Family is everything, except when they cut off all their family – 'family values' generation
- Powerful characters
- Security paramount – gated communities when older
- Staying with the familiar is paramount

These are the people who grew up during the Depression. Family and food are the centers of their reality. Security is not just something to have – it is a must. Many of the people of this generation live in gated communities! Most of these people were sensitive and caring, or at least, highly emotional. Some had eating (Elvis Presley) or alcohol problems. This was a much more 'down home' generation than those following or preceding it. Patriotism for the 'home' country is strong.

Reality is based on 'family values' with family being 'everything'. Curiously, many of the members of this generation avoid family or are at odds with close family (Pluto is all-or-nothing with Cancer being family – this is the 'nothing' side of Pluto). Perhaps this occurs because power struggles tend to take place within the home, alienating people from their families. This group has voices that are 'huskier' than the Pluto in Gemini generation, who tend to have higher voices.

Many 'beatniks' were born with Pluto in Cancer – they avoided home and family for a life on the road where there is no security and no immediate family. Beat poetry was a way to pour out the intense emotions of the generation.

Pluto can 'wipe out' the qualities of the sign. Some tried to wipe out their emotionality or their upbringing: 'My difficult childhood had no effect on me.'

Emotionally, this is an intense generation. They can be tough and hard-shelled, showing little emotion, or they can be highly emotional. They can be totally dependent on others, or avoid dependency at all costs.

Although many of this generation will say 'family is everything', when you actually look at their actions they are not on speaking terms with many of their family! This is because they took to heart many of the hurts caused by the members of their family. So, in reality, family is nothing, thus showing the 'all or nothing' side of Pluto.

This generation had strong, unique personalities. The prior generation, with Pluto in Gemini, created whole worlds that we remember. This generation have powerful personalities; we remember the people themselves.

## Pluto in Leo (1692–1710; 1939–1956)
## Qualities

- Life lived intensely, fully
- Follow leaders blindly, or not at all
- Must be 'having fun'
- Must be creative in some form
- Can have large ego and be self-centered – 'me' generation
- Gamblers (or avoid risks)
- All or nothing about romance and extra-marital affairs

Pluto in Leo people are warm, fiery types. They must have fun, be entertained, or be entertaining. Famous people are mostly performers. There is a youth emphasis. They can be incredibly self-centered (the 'me' generation). Life force, heart, spirit, and 'self' form the basis of their reality. All have a strong life force.

They are all or nothing about leaders, either not following leaders or following them blindly (anarchist versus totalitarian). If the heart or core of something is right, it's real. They have extreme difficulty getting involved in things when their heart isn't involved; this played out strongly in the 1960s. Many of them follow their own heart in matters, even when it's an extreme gamble.

Speaking of gambling, this generation loves to gamble, to take risks. With Pluto the planet of all or nothing, others from this generation are completely risk-adverse.

Many are outside of the standard morality; they don't feel the rules apply to them (Leo is the sign of extra-marital relationships, which are both romantic and a gamble – a breaking away from the Cancerian home). Since Pluto is all or nothing, there are others who are completely into morality; these people eschew immoral behavior with great force. Some are immoral in earlier life and swing to the other extreme and become moral in later life. However, they are nowhere near as moralistic as the generation following with Pluto in Virgo.

Many are compelled to be creative: 'I am everything' (huge ego) or 'I am a big zero' (huge negative ego). If the core, the heart, of something is working, they're satisfied – they aren't bothered by details, as the Pluto in Virgo generation is. 'If it isn't fun, it isn't worth doing' is their motto. Their power comes through creativity.

One of the difficulties of the Pluto in Leo generation is when there is a large ego; then their reality, their morals, their life, and their country are the only ones that exist. This self-centered, narcissistic way of dealing with life causes great harm to themselves and those around them.

## Pluto in Virgo (1710–1724; 1956–1972)
### Qualities
- Compulsive about details, facts, and figures
- Obsessed with technology
- Workaholics or slackers
- Clubby
- Humble and into service
- Hard to connect with

This generation can be compulsive about details. That Plutonian all-or-nothing tendency can be focused on work, resulting in workaholics and slackers. They achieve power through technology or organizational skills. Some have Uriah Heep syndrome (power through humility).

This generation is much more quiet and serious than the Pluto in Leo generation that preceded them. They are also much more 'proper'.

When you are with them, you have a sense that you are either totally 'part of the club' or not part of the club. The cast of *Friends* and most of *Sex and the City* (with a Neptune in Scorpio influence), and even George and Elaine from *Seinfeld* are members of this generation; these ensemble casts are the 'clubs'.

This generation can be incredibly humble, picky, and work-oriented. Often, they are soft-spoken. Personal (and other) faults/problems are all or nothing. Being moralistic or amoral is an important polarity since Virgo rules morals and manners. They can be intensely low key, shy, or quietly reclusive.

Many can be highly critical (Virgo) and feel they gain power (Pluto) by finding faults (Virgo) in others – or they can be blind to faults! This generation has difficulty with mysticism and spiritual people since Virgo opposes Pisces. When they are into mysticism, it is through a 'system' or exercise (yoga, for example).

The most recent generation has Neptune in Scorpio with its cynicism; together with their ability to see faults, this can make them the 'yeah, right' generation. Just think of Elaine or George on *Seinfeld* or anybody on *Friends*. Virgo can be a sign of skepticism or doubt.

This generation gains power through their extreme knowledge of details – they are incredibly technical. The brains who populated the computer revolution came from this group.

The 'yes but no' push and pull of Virgo, and the Virgoan doubt often make Pluto in Virgo people hard to connect with.

They may like you – that shows when they meet you – but when pushed to make a commitment to get together later, they vacillate internally and put off making anything firm. This makes it hard to know where you stand with them, but it isn't personal; they have trouble finding their own solid ground within themselves.

For some, breaking down barriers and walls between people is their life's work. 'No man is an island,' said one of the members of this club. Virgo pigeonholing can be intensely applied, or smashed in that all-or-nothing Pluto way.

Because Virgo rules service, this is a generation of people who can see themselves as being of service to a larger whole. The highest members of this club see themselves as organizing people to a higher purpose. More generally, this is the generation that focused on the service economy.

See Uranus in Leo, Virgo, and Libra for people born in this sign from 1956 to 1972.

## Pluto in Libra (1724–1737; 1972–1984)
## Qualities
- Harmonious
- Relaxed
- Social justice important
- Transformed music and art – emphasis on outlaws and gangsters in younger years

This is a smooth, smiling, and harmonious generation. Power is conceived as being fair, socially aware, and gracious. They tend to try to remain relaxed and poised despite the most adverse circumstances. Everything must be fair. Relationships are what life is about. Relationships must be equal (if I call you, then, to be fair, you must call me).

Social justice is an important matter. So, too, is social networking. Libra considers everyone equal, and this generation can become incensed when a person or group is not considered equal. This generation is incredibly socially aware.

This is also the hip-hop generation who transformed music. On one side, this is the 'gangster' rap (Pluto rules gangsters and Libra rules artistic expression). On the other side, this is intense music where the underside of society is brought into popular culture. Rap is a Plutonian form of music.

Marriage is all or nothing – this generation wants to get married early to form an intense bond. When asked about marriage, they will often want to get married to 'get it over with'. When this generation gets into the newspapers, it is often over relationship or marriage problems.

This generation can be either lazy or hyperactive, the two phases of Libra that can become extreme when Pluto is added. Libra rules opinions so they spend much of their lives sharing opinions and ideas – the Internet was made for their social networking.

The first two years of the recent Pluto in Libra, 1972–1974, had Uranus in Libra as well. The years from 1974 to 1981 were when Uranus was in Scorpio. Finally, the years from 1981 to 1984 had Uranus in Sagittarius. Neptune was in Sagittarius the whole time Pluto was in Libra. Hence, there were three flavors of Pluto in Libra. See Uranus in Libra, Scorpio, and Sagittarius for people born in the 1972 to 1984 period.

## Pluto in Scorpio (1737–1749; 1984–1995)
### Qualities
- Intense
- Want to transform reality
- Deep, sometimes disturbed
- Psychological
- Sex is all or nothing

These are intense people. Monsieur Guillotin invented a more 'humane' and expeditious way to kill people. De Goya painted intensely emotional art. King George III with his need for power and domination created the environment for the American Revolution. Goethe plumbed the depth of the human psyche with his writing. The Marquis de Sade was the original sadist.

The current generation (1984–1995) grew up on virtual realities – they want to be able to transform reality. They too have a dark intensity, like the prior generation from the 1700s.

Already, many are playing roles in the movies as 'deep', sometimes disturbed, children who are beyond their years in knowledge, who won't put up with anything but bedrock reality. Most will have a deep, gut-level view into psychology, both their own and that of other people.

We can already predict that this generation will be all or nothing about sex. Some will be obsessed with it; others will be obsessed with avoiding it.

## Pluto in Sagittarius (1749–1762; 1995–2008)
## Qualities

- Visionaries
- Want a better world (utopian)
- Soaring art

These were visionaries (Blake, Nostradamus), or they based reality on being 'superior' (Marie Antoinette). Many showed a yearning for a better world. Religion played a strong part in their lives. The artists had soaring poetry (Dante) and music (Mozart). Of course, being Sagittarian, they can be sarcastic, proselytizing, and fanatical (Robespierre).

This generation tends to come into its own when Pluto is in Aquarius. Their aspirations are fulfilled as they gain the power to accomplish the reforms and improvements they demand. The oldest of this generation were 27 when the American Revolution started, and many were instrumental in the French Revolution.

## Pluto in Capricorn (1762–1778)
### Qualities

- Changed foundations; founders
- All or nothing about structure
- Understood limitations imposed by reality (Malthus' *Principle of Population*)
- Inner structures of nature (Fourier, Gauss, Ampère, Hegel)

Those born with Pluto in Capricorn had a deep understanding of nature, and, as with Malthus, a Saturnine view of humankind's prospects. The inner structures of electricity (Ampère), of periodic functions such as wave forms (Fourier), of the roots of mathematics (Gauss), and of how people form new paradigms (Hegel) all came from this generation.

Napoleon founded new institutions in France – imperialist, true, but new institutions, while Andrew Jackson did similar work in the United States to bring power to the people. Metternich, who followed Napoleon, tried to keep Europe united to put down insurrections arising from the people.

This generation fought the Napoleonic wars in Europe and therefore was the generation in which power came from the masses of the people conscripted into war rather than professional soldiers – power wasn't hierarchical (Capricorn) but diffuse. The wars of this generation were fought with Pluto in Pisces.

This was an austere generation, perhaps a bit stiff. The men in high society wore starched, dark clothing and the women had their 'place' – read Jane Austen for more details.

## Pluto in Aquarius (1778–1798)
### Qualities

- Freedom (Uranus rules Aquarius), freedom from oppression and slavery (Pluto)
- Power (Pluto) is with the people, the everyday person, and

primitive societies (Aquarius)
- Power is in ideals (Uranus)
- Friendship (Aquarius) is power
- Danger (Pluto) in technology (Aquarius)
- Investigations (Pluto) into electricity (Uranus rules Aquarius)

People born with Pluto in Aquarius tended to be unique individuals who prized their freedom and who fought for the freedom of others. The writers emphasized the dramatic in everyday people and events. Many had causes and ideals that were the focus of their lives.

Some of the greatest scientists and inventors of electricity (ruled by Uranus) such as Morse, inventor of the telegraph, and Faraday, who did many of the seminal experiments on electromagnetism, were born into this generation; also Ohm, who worked on electrical resistance.

Grimm's *Fairy Tales* and James Fenimore Cooper's *The Last of the Mohicans* were both about 'primitive' cultures, which Aquarius finds fascinating. Mary Schelley wrote *Frankenstein*, about the dangers of technology.

People who break others free, liberators such as Simon Bolivar and, to a lesser extent, Sam Houston and John Calhoun, are born with Pluto in Aquarius.

## Pluto in Pisces (1798–1822)
### Qualities
- Poets, storytellers, social conscience (Clara Barton, Dickens, Emerson, Whitman), compassion
- Victorian period of repressed people
- Awareness of fringe people, power through losing – great failures and stories of failure (Lincoln, Dumas, Dickens)
- Power through unity of outcasts (Marx, Engels)
- Power through the oceans (*Moby Dick*)

- Totally compassionate or not at all
- People with a lot of 'breadth' and understanding

Pisces rules compassion, the collective unconscious, mysticism, the ocean, and society's fringe element. But, perhaps most importantly, Pisces rules dreams. Since Pluto is reality, when Pluto is in Pisces at people's birth, they are obsessed with finding what is real within dreams, and how reality is really a dream, an illusion. For others, their dreams become more real than normal reality; these are the poets and storytellers born at this time.

Alcott, Dumas, Emerson, Thoreau, Hawthorne, Browning, Longfellow, Tennyson, Dickens, Poe, Whitman, Trollope, Melville – the list of poets and storytellers goes on and on. But less obvious are the people who promoted the odd and the fringe, such as P.T. Barnum – some of the people and objects he put on display were not real, but purely illusion.

Others who had compassion for the outcasts, the poor, included not only Dickens, but also Marx and Engels who invented communism. Pooling resources as in communism is idealistic and 'common', as Pisces is associated with the 12th house, a 'common' house. Also, Marx talked about unity (Pluto) among the workers, the outcasts of society (Pisces).

Perhaps the archetypical Pluto in Pisces author is Herman Melville, who wrote *Moby Dick*. This book is about an obsessed ocean-going (Pisces) captain who deals with violence (Pluto) from a whale who destroys him and his ship. Anyone who deals with Plutonian eruptions knows the quiet before the storm described in *Moby Dick* as the whale is below the ocean waiting to attack the boat.

Many of the older Victorians were born with Pluto here; since repression and denial are the negative sides of Pisces, this generation added this tone to the Victorian period. Queen Victoria herself had Pluto here and many planets in the twelfth house, the house of Pisces.

## Chapter 6

# Conjunct Generations

People born with an outer planet conjunct in their charts have an extra push, an extra energy to their lives. By conjunct, we mean that the planets are within eight degrees of each other in the natal chart. There are ten possible outer planet conjuncts. Some people have triple conjuncts; other people have two distinct outer planet conjuncts.

There are ten possible outer planet conjuncts: Jupiter-Saturn, Jupiter-Uranus, Jupiter-Neptune, Jupiter-Pluto, Saturn-Uranus, Saturn-Neptune, Saturn-Pluto, Uranus-Neptune, Uranus-Pluto, and Neptune-Pluto. The further along in this list, the more powerful the conjunct in the chart.

Any conjunct can act like one planet acting on the other, or like a merger of the energies. Each planet can be seen as acting on the other one.

Let's take an example: Jupiter-Uranus. Jupiter acting on Uranus means that the Uranian need for freedom, for joy, for spontaneity, for wisdom and insight, and for being rebellious is expanded, and even planned out, by the Jupiter. Uranian needs can be rationalized by the Jupiter. Jupiter is the planet of humor, so Jupiter will try to lighten up the Uranian energy, to make it into a joke.

On the flipside, Uranus acting on Jupiter makes the need for growth that Jupiter embodies more immediate and spontaneous. People with this conjunct would grow in spontaneous spurts, not in solid, predictable ways as other people would experience. They would open to new experience through a burst of energy, and suddenly.

The merger of Jupiter and Uranus would mean that

advancing by continuous growth and advancing by an electrical jump would become merged, so all the growth energy would be concentrated in one spot in the chart.

There are two ways to research what people with these conjuncts are like: looking at lists of famous people with the conjuncts and adding to the lists people you know personally, and looking at the sayings and actions of people from these lists. When looking at the quotes, look for ones that incorporate words from both the planets.

Of course, we could look at other aspects besides conjuncts, such as opposition, square, sextile, or trine. That would be a whole book in itself and we don't have space for it here. The same methods would apply for research of that book.

Let's look at each conjunct in depth and representative people who have it, in order to understand it.

## Jupiter conjunct Saturn

This conjunct happens every 20 years. For 200 years it stays in the same element; for the last 200 years it's been in earth. Then in 1980 it went into Libra, an air sign. In 2000 it went back to Taurus, an earth sign. For the next 100-plus years from now on, it will be in air signs.

This means that all the recent people born with Jupiter-Saturn conjunct are in earth signs except for those born around 1980. People born with this conjunct in signs that weren't air signs include Mary Baker Eddy, born in 1821, who founded Christian Science (she also had Uranus conjunct Neptune in Capricorn); Galileo, born in 1564, with the conjunct in Cancer; and Sir Isaac Newton, born 1642, with it in Pisces.

When you take the list of people with this conjunct and think about Jupiter acting on Saturn, you see that many were open to or aware of (Jupiter) pain and sorrow (Saturn). Many wanted to improve (Jupiter) on difficult situations (Saturn). Some made light (Jupiter) of problems (Saturn); others had an upbeat attitude

(Jupiter) about difficulties (Saturn). When there was a closed system (Saturn), many of this group opened it up (Jupiter). Others gave us new structural (Saturn) understanding (Jupiter).

Saturn acting on Jupiter resulted in some maintaining a solid, stable (Saturn) cheerfulness (Jupiter), no matter what (Saturn). Difficulties (Saturn) forced many to find the inherent possibilities and purpose (Jupiter). Limitations (Saturn) resulted in others not being cowed, but rather finding a rationale, a reason, or a way out (Jupiter). Many are what we would today call 'activists'.

When you merge these energies you see that the usual upbeat humor of Jupiter is tempered by the serious, controlled manner of Saturn. These people have a controlled humor and a lighter seriousness. Some are famous (Jupiter) for a craggy, tough, and steely exterior (Saturn).

In 1960 and 1961 the exact conjunction was in an earth sign (in this case, Capricorn), but the conjunct stayed within the eight-degree orb while Jupiter went into Aquarius. Famous people born with this conjunct with Saturn in Capricorn and Jupiter in Aquarius include George Clooney, Princess Diana, Melissa Etheridge, Michael J. Fox, Woody Harrelson, Mariel Hemingway, Eddie Murphy, and Barack Obama. Having Saturn in Capricorn (which accentuates it), and Jupiter in the hopeful, friendly, and humanitarian sign of Aquarius should make this group show the duality more forcefully. And it does.

George Cloony has the twinkly humor of Jupiter in Aquarius bubbling under the craggy looks of Saturn in Capricorn. Princess Diana opened up the closed world of British royalty and gave hope to the common man and woman (Jupiter in Aquarius) in spite of her difficulties. Melissa Etheridge opened up the closed world of rock and roll to lesbianism. Michael J. Fox played characters who were serious Republicans (Saturn in Capricorn) in the midst of a hippie family (Jupiter in Aquarius), or brought humor to the establishment. In later life, Michael has had to deal with physical limitations (Saturn, again) that he has surmounted with humor and hope (Jupiter in Aquarius). Woody Harrelson plays men with relentless humor in the face of limited circumstances – in real life, he's an activist (Jupiter in Aquarius versus Saturn in Capricorn). Eddie Murphy finds humor in difficult situations and rigid structures. Finally, Barack Obama ran on a platform of hope (Jupiter in Aquarius) that the American people can break out of a stranglehold of rigid structure (Saturn in Capricorn). So, in this small sampling of people born with the conjunct in 1961 we see most of the patterns we expected to see.

In 1940 and 1941 the conjunct was in Taurus. Taurus rules the throat and has been associated with singers. John Lennon, a singer who was born with this conjunct, wrote the song 'Working Class Hero', which is the other side of Taurus. This sign represents the raw means of production – working class men and women. Taurus is ruled by Venus; it's a sign of appreciation of the beauty and material pleasures of life. Unlike the prior group with Jupiter in one sign and Saturn in another, this group has Jupiter and Saturn in the same sign – the problem is the same as the solution.

Jupiter-Saturn produces activists. Besides John Lennon, there were Jesse Jackson, Richard Pryor, Joan Baez, Rennie Davis, and Frank Zappa who were part of this 1940s group. All were concerned with finding humor (Jupiter) in the establishment (Saturn). With Venus ruling this earth sign, there were some noted beauties in the group: Julie Christie, Carla Bruni (model and rock and roll consort), Elke Sommer, and Raquel Welch. Born during the 1980s conjunct in Libra, also ruled by Venus, was Serena Williams the tennis player.

The problem of the 1921 conjunct was Virgo: limitations imposed by putting people in boxes. Those with this conjunct expanded beyond mental limits placed by society. Betty Friedan brought women to their rightful position in society, while Jesse Helms, who also had the conjunct, fought against her (he was more disposed to the Saturn side). John Glenn broke the limits of earth and so did Gene Roddenberry of *Star Trek* fame. Gene saw the future as a place of egalitarianism between the races. Alex Haley went beyond prejudice by bringing people back to their roots.

From the 1901 conjunct in Capricorn: Louis Armstrong (1901), Gary Cooper (1901), Marlene Dietrich (1901), Charles Lindbergh (1902), Margaret Mead (1901), and Walt Disney (1901). Many of this group forged new organizations or ways of seeing organization. Walt Disney, for example, was revolutionary in art, conservative in politics, yet a lover of nature (*Bambi*). They grew (Jupiter) the establishment (Saturn and Capricorn).

Other famous people with the conjunct: Mary Baker Eddy (1821 in Aries), Thomas Jefferson (1743 with Saturn at 29 degrees Leo and Jupiter at five degrees Virgo), Nostradamus (1503 in Cancer conjunct Mars), and Sir Isaac Newton (1642 in mid Pisces). All broke out of limited ways of being (Saturn) and expanded our possibilities (Jupiter) or gave us new structural understanding.

## Jupiter conjunct Uranus

If you have this, aren't you cool! These people shine with the joy (Uranus) of nobility (Jupiter). Oftentimes, you get the feeling that they think they know better what is going on, and, damn it, they often do. This group wants to break out (Uranus) of the conventional (Jupiter) and the known (Jupiter). Many have a sparkly, bright (and slightly superior) twinkle in their eye. Others take a joy in knowing people who are famous or, at least, knowing everything about them. Often these people need lots of space (Jupiter) and freedom (Uranus) within the sign of the conjunct. Some have a 'wholesome' quality, although their reality may be quite a bit different. Uranus rules excitement and Jupiter expands whatever it touches – many in this group want constant excitement.

Starting with the most recent, Jennifer Aniston (Feb 11, 1969) has this conjunct in Libra. And, not surpisingly, most of her movies are about relationships (Libra) – and how Jennifer's character needs space and freedom to be a bit, well, wacky. Others from this period include Steffi Graf (Jun 14, 1969), Anne Heche (May 25, 1969), and Christian Slater (Aug 18, 1969). Christian definitely has that knowing twinkle and plays characters who break out of standard ways of relating.

Going back to 1954 and 1955, when the conjunct was in Cancer, we have Kirstie Alley (Jan 12, 1955), Sandra Bernhard (Jun 6, 1955), James Cameron (Aug 16, 1954), Kevin Costner (Jan 18, 1955), Chris Evert (Dec 21, 1954), Kelsey Grammer (Feb 20, 1955), Annie Lennox (Dec 25, 1954), Denzel Washington (Dec 28, 1954), Bruce Willis (Mar 19, 1955), Debra Winger (May 16, 1955), and Patrick Swayze (Aug 18, 1954). Kelsey Grammer plays a know-it-all snob (Jupiter) who is a bit odd (Uranus) underneath that noble exterior. Kirstie Alley has that wholesome girl-next-door feel, but with a bit of that alarming Uranus in Cancer need to break out of convention. Kevin Costner has that 'gee' quality of the boy next door and yet he tries to break out of that mold. The two Uranian rebels of the group are Sandra Bernhard, who derives humor from her rebellious nature, and Annie Lennox, who has made musical breakthroughs throughout her career. Denzel Washington, Bruce Willis, and Debra Winger all have the knowing twinkle we mentioned. Denzel and Bruce are often in dramatic action movies in which the usual humdrum world is broken by electric action. The familiar warmth of Jupiter in Cancer is made electrical by Uranus – think of the warmth of Kelsey Grammer, Kirstie Alley, Patrick Swayze, or Debra Winger.

Going back one conjunct lands us at 1941 with the conjunct in Taurus. Some people have a triple conjunct of Jupiter, Saturn, and Uranus. Some of the group with this conjunct are Ann Margret (Apr 28, 1941), Julie Christie (Apr 14, 1941), Bob Dylan (May 24, 1941), Ritchie Valens (May 13, 1941), Nora Ephron (May 19, 1941), and Paul Winfield (May 22, 1941). Bob Dylan has the conjunct in late Taurus conjunct his Sun in early Gemini. This is love of folk music and rebellion coming from the earthy people who sing folk songs – his hero was Woody Guthrie who combined folk music with pokes at the establishment. And Bob has that twinkle of mischievous Uranus under that knowledgeable look of Jupiter. Nora Ephron, the playwright, wrote,'Whenever I get married, I start buying *Gourmet* magazine' – there is the Taurean influence (*Gourmet*) combined with the humor of Jupiter and the joy of Uranus. Being cool for the Taurus group has a component of pleasure and appreciation.

The 1927 conjunct was in either Aries or Pisces and Aries. Alan King (Pisces, Dec 26, 1927), Althea Gibson (Aries, Aug 25, 1927), Janet Leigh (Jul 6, 1927), Roger Moore (Jupiter in Pisces and Saturn in Aries, Oct 14, 1927), and George C. Scott (Jupiter in Pisces and Saturn in Aries, Oct 18, 1927) had this placement. These people all had the coolness factor – and they definitely let you know it with all that Aries. Perhaps Alan King was a bit more self-deprecating with his conjunct in Pisces, but as for the rest, they exuded confidence and freedom to do what they wanted (Aries).

The wildest people with this conjunct are likely those born with it in Aquarius in 1914. How about Gypsy Rose Lee (Feb 9, 1914), Sir Alec Guinness (Apr 2, 1914), Jackie Coogan (Oct 26, 1914), or Dylan Thomas (Oct 27, 1914) for living wildly? Because Uranus rules Aquarius, the free, joyful, and odd qualities of Uranus are emphasized. This generation was cool because they were wild and unpredictable, and having a grand old time.

## Jupiter conjunct Neptune

This group has to make a big splash, with the 'big' being Jupiter and the 'splash' being Neptune. They want to have a large influence on others. Some want a grand image or to be very glamorous. Some dream of being rich or famous – or like to have the illusion of being that way. Others inspire almost a religious awe. Finally, others hide behind a large mask or illusion. Some became famous as poets. Many have watery eyes with that compassionate look of Neptune. But some are less emotional and more driven; they have a dream of being great and they put everything by the wayside that doesn't meet that ideal.

Neptune takes 14 years to a sign. When Jupiter, which takes 12 years to circle the zodiac, comes around to conjunct Neptune, it raises it to a higher level within that sign.

The most recent batch with this conjunct were born in 1984. Avril Lavigne (Neptune 29 Sagittarius and Jupiter 4 Capricorn, Sep 27, 1984) is a dramatic singer with this conjunct. She was born with Pluto in the first degree of Scorpio, which is what makes her so dark and intense. Getting back to the Jupiter-Neptune conjunct, she likes an accelerating (Jupiter) solid beat (Capricorn) that takes her to new levels (Neptune in Sagittarius). She likes to make a large splash and has that emotional outpouring that comes with the conjunct.

Going backward, the next group were born in 1971. Shannen Doherty (Sagittarius, Apr 12, 1971) was famous for her outbursts and wild times. But she too has those alluring, watery eyes and, with the conjunct in Sagittarius, she hates being boxed in. Mark Wahlberg is more driven as an actor with Jupiter in the last minutes of Scorpio and Neptune at the start of Sagittarius (Jun 5, 1971). Missy Elliott has a similar drive and the conjunct at the same place – she broke into the male-dominated world of rap. Finally, Lance Armstrong has the conjunct at the start of Sagittarius. He has fought to be the greatest cyclist and always dreams higher – he made his mark in the Tour de France, a far journey (Sagittarius) from his native Texas.

The 1958 conjunct in Scorpio has Ellen DeGeneres (Jan 26, 1958, both Scorpio), Tim Burton (Aug 25, 1958 with Jupiter at the end of Libra and Neptune in Scorpio), Scott Hamilton (Aug 28, 1958 with Jupiter in Libra and Neptune in Scorpio), Holly Hunter

(Mar 20, 1958 with both planets in Scorpio), Madonna (Aug 16, 1958 with Jupiter in Libra and Neptune in Scorpio), Sharon Stone (Scorpio, Mar 10, 1958), Andie MacDowell (Jupiter Libra and Neptune Scorpio, Apr 21, 1958), and Michael Jackson (Aug 29, 1958 with Jupiter at the end of Libra and Neptune in Scorpio). All members of this group have Neptune in Scorpio and all exude a magnetic energy, some more dark and sexual than others. They are all a combination of that dreamy look of Neptune with the dark magnetism of Scorpio. With Jupiter conjunct the Neptune, a touch of drama and grandiosity is added. Madonna, Sharon Stone, and Michael Jackson – there is a magnetic trio! Those with Jupiter in Libra may have a surface of beauty and smiling harmony, but that only amplifies the underlying swirling currents of Neptune in Scorpio.

Both John Lithgow (Oct 19, 1945 in Libra) and Henry Winkler (Oct 30, 1945) are pleasant and smiling (Libra), but they must be the social leaders (Jupiter) and trend-setters (Neptune) – and they play such roles as actors.

James Brown (May 3, 1933, conjunct Mars in Virgo), Carol Burnett (Apr 26, 1933, also conjunct Mars in Virgo), and Joan Collins (May 23, 1933, also conjunct Mars in Virgo) are part of the next group. James was famous for his choreography (Virgo) as well as his almost religious intensity. Carol Burnett is noted for her physical humor – she quickly rose to the top of the list of comedians of her time. Joan Collins played roles in which her, uh, campy criticalness (Virgo) and trappings (Neptune) of wealth (Jupiter) made others envious (see, I didn't use the 'B' word). Finally, Elizabeth Montgomery (Apr 15, 1933, conjunct Mars in Virgo) played a witch (very Virgo) who was upbeat and compassionate.

Great poets and writers included Emily Dickinson (Dec 10, 1830 in Capricorn), Omar Khayyam (Jul 25, 1050), and James Joyce (Feb 2, 1882 in Taurus). All had a great outpouring of sentiment springing from the conjunct.

## Jupiter conjunct Pluto

Here are people famous (Jupiter) for their focused intensity (Pluto). When they want to exert their power (Pluto) they invariably come out winners (Jupiter). Many see life as a struggle (Pluto) in which they desperately want to excel (Jupiter). Based on the sign, you can see what they are fighting for. You don't want to mess with these people.

Not only are they intense, they keep cranking it up. If what they are battling cranks it up, they will crank it up some more to almost superhuman levels. Many are famous (Jupiter) for their emotional force (Pluto) or their sexual magnetism (also Pluto). When they have a goal (Jupiter), they head for it with life-or-death intensity (Pluto).

As with Jupiter-Neptune, when Pluto is on the Scorpio side of the chart there is only one Jupiter-Pluto conjunct per sign. There may be two when Pluto is closer to Taurus and the transit of a sign stretches over 30 years.

The most recent group were born in 1981: Britney Spears (Pluto in Libra conjunct Jupiter in Scorpio, Dec 2, 1981) and Serena Williams (Sep 26, 1981 with the conjunct in Libra). Britney has an intensity in her marriage and relationships (Pluto in Libra) that is expanded by her need for intimacy and intensity (conjunct Jupiter in Scorpio). She first came to fame as a sexual schoolgirl and for her outrageous partying (Libra) and marriage (also Libra). Serena Williams plays a Libran game, tennis, with intensity and focus.

Will Smith exemplifies the 1968 conjunct in Virgo (with an added conjunct with Uranus at the end of Virgo). He plays roles where he is fighting battles against overwhelmingly (Jupiter) powerful (Pluto) and often alien (Pluto) forces, or where he is focused to excel (Jupiter again) over a vast range of competitors. With the conjunct in Virgo, he excels at getting the details of the acting perfect and works extremely hard.

Bill Gates (Oct 28, 1955) has the conjunct in Leo. He has

amassed great wealth and power by making Microsoft the center of the software industry and by, at times, bullying and overwhelming competitors. Also, he has remained focused on his business goals to the exclusion of everything else. Bjorn Borg (Jun 6, 1956) ruled men's tennis for years and was a focused competitor. Whoopi Goldberg (Nov 13, 1955) has little trouble telling people the truth or expressing herself fully (Leo) – much of her comedic talents lie in her intensity. Bill Maher (Jan 20, 1956) loves to push discussion to the limits, and political satire suits someone with Jupiter conjunct Pluto. Rounding out the people born under this conjunct is Joe Montana (Jun 11, 1956) who seemed to always find a way to overcome opponents and win the football game as a quarterback.

Going back a little further we have the 1943 generation. The most memorable person from this generation is Mick Jagger (Jul 26, 1943) who has his Sun conjunct Jupiter and Pluto in Leo – he embodies this conjunct. He cranks out his music with intensity in every performance, and still is doing it into his sixties. With the conjunct in Leo, he must be the center of attention. As the lead singer of The Rolling Stones, he is the center. All the conjuncts this year were in Leo.

A daredevil of the slopes is Jean-Claude Killy (Aug 30, 1943) who was just barely in control. At first, he was out of control, but then became a world-class skier. Arthur Ashe (Jul 10, 1943) in tennis and Bill Bradley (Jul 28, 1943) in basketball round out the sports heroes with this conjunct – with it in Leo, they all showed stagemanship and focused intensity. Finally, Robert De Niro (Aug 17, 1943) shows the raw power of an actor with this conjunct – he doesn't play light parts.

In 1931 the conjunct was in Cancer. James Dean (Feb 8, 1931) played intensely emotional parts (Cancer). Richard Alpert (Apr 6, 1931) became a spiritual leader and was known for taking LSD – the emotional component of eating is the realm of Cancer. Sean Connery (Aug 25, 1930) was a sexual icon as the daring James

Bond character. Gene Hackman (Jan 30, 1931) played many tough guy roles in which he had some intense goal. One person who showed little Cancerian emotion was the character Spock in *Star Trek*, played by Leonard Nimoy (Mar 26, 1931); his friend, who was intensely emotional, was Captain Kirk, played by William Shatner (Mar 22, 1931). Pluto is an all-or-nothing planet, so here one actor wiped out emotionality (Cancer) while another reveled in its intensity. Willie Mays was born on May 6, 1931.

Going back further, Johannes Kepler spent years unlocking the mysteries of the universe; he was born December 27, 1571 with the conjunct in Pisces. Pablo Picasso (Oct 25, 1881) had the conjunct in Taurus; he focused his life on art (Taurus is ruled by Venus). Pablo also had Saturn-Neptune conjunct in a chain with the Jupiter-Pluto conjunct. Martha Graham, the dancer, was born May 11, 1894 with Jupiter conjunct both Neptune and Pluto in Gemini; she pioneered new ways of moving (Gemini). Edgar Allan Poe (Jan 19, 1809) had Venus and Moon conjunct Jupiter and Pluto in Pisces; he pioneered whole new mediums (Pisces) such as horror tales and detective stories (both are under Pluto). Cecil B. DeMille created huge productions (Taurus) with Jupiter conjunct Pluto there – he was born August 12, 1881. Finally Mohandas Gandhi (Oct 2, 1869) fought for peace with the conjunct in Taurus; he fought with single-minded commitment to overcome the British in India using non-violent methods. Non-violence opposes others by non-action – this is a good Taurean method.

## Saturn conjunct Uranus

This starts the section of Saturn conjuncts with the transcendental planets. Saturn is the planet of accomplishment, taking things one step at a time, old age, the past, conservatism, seriousness, and structure but also fear, limitation, and defensiveness. It rules the inertia of the establishment, the part of society that doesn't want anything to change.

Saturn doesn't do that well in conjunct with the transcendentals that want to move forward and break out of limitations. At best, it becomes a channel for change. The most difficult conjunct you can have is conservative Saturn conjunct revolutionary Uranus. This is like having a conservative banker sitting next to a wild-eyed radical.

The people with this conjunct must find a way to make their internal bizarreness (Uranus) fit within the establishment structure (Saturn). Those who were successful forced the establishment to become a little looser, to change in order to accommodate the new energy they embodied. Others submerged that twinkle in their eyes within a stern exterior. Others never really came to an accommodation.

In the battle between Saturn and Uranus, the Saturn 'wins' when the freedom and joy of Uranus is squelched, and Uranus 'wins' when the structure breaks and oddness and bizarre behavior is allowed. This is like a shoot of Uranus breaking through the rock-hard solidity of the Saturn pavement. When this happens, you find a person with a unique (Uranus) ability (Saturn) who somehow accomplishes things in a non-linear fashion.

The most recent conjunct was around 1988, but as of the writing of this book, few of these people (who are only 21 years old) have had a chance to fight the good fight against the establishment. Both Rupert Grint (Aug 24, 1988) and Daniel Radcliffe (July 23, 1989), from the *Harry Potter* movies, are born with this conjunct. Rupert has it in Sagittarius while Daniel has it in Capricorn (actually a triple conjunct of Uranus-Saturn-Neptune). Already, Daniel is trying to break out of his role of Harry Potter by taking on antithetical roles. In the *Harry Potter* films both play roles in which they rebel against authority but within the establishment of the stone walls of Hogwarts.

The conjunct prior to that was in 1942 – there are 45 years between conjunctions. Since that conjunct was right on the

Gemini cusp, some have the conjunct in Taurus and others in Gemini.

Let's do the Taurus conjuncts first. Erica Jong (Mar 26, 1942, conjunct in Taurus) wrote the book *Fear of Flying*, about wanting to have freedom, joy, and independence (Uranus in Taurus) while the body (Saturn in Taurus) wants sensuality, comfort, and safety. Fear is Saturn and flying is Uranus. Carole King (Feb 9, 1942) wrote the songs for *Tapestry*, including the anthems for the liberated (Uranus) woman, the woman free (Uranus) of place and structure (Saturn), who can nurture and protect others (Taurus).

Martha Stewart (Aug 3, 1941) has this conjunct in Taurus but also has Sun conjunct Pluto in Leo. Martha excels at repurposing and changing (Uranus) old materials from around the home (Saturn in Taurus). She was convicted for illegal trading and was formerly a stock trader – both show her uneasy rapprochement with the establishment and her need for excitement and constant change when part of the structure.

John Irving (Mar 2, 1942) wrote *The World According to Garp*, a novel that twists the normal, placid world (Saturn in Taurus) by viewing things in a very odd way (Uranus); his conjunct in Taurus is also conjunct Mars, adding a bit of forcefulness to his smashing-out of structures.

Graham Nash (Feb 2, 1942) brings together the world of electric music and photography. His song 'Chicago (We Can Change the World)' shows his need to break out of the establishment and change things – he called his writing the 'lyrics of outrage'. He is also an innovator in digital (Uranus) photography and fine art (Taurus).

More traditional are Tammy Wynette (May 5, 1942) and Wayne Newton (Apr 3, 1942). They bring a certain electricity to their music, but stay within the structure, although it is the glitzy structure of Las Vegas for Wayne. Again, Taurus rules the throat and is often associated with singers.

Paul Simon (Oct 13, 1941) also has the conjunct in Taurus. He broke out of the mold with his performances with Garfunkel and his introduction of world music to audiences on the album *Graceland*. His bluesy, folksy sound shows the Taurean influence.

Muhammad Ali (Jan 17, 1942) refused to go into the US army. He said, 'No Viet Cong ever called me a nigger' and 'I know where I'm going and I know the truth, and I don't have to be what you want me to be. I'm free to be what I want.' That last statement is the heart of the conjunct in Taurus – the 'knowing' is Uranus and 'what you want me to be' is the Saturn in Taurus.

Bob Dylan (May 24, 1941) has a string of Saturn, Moon, Uranus, and Jupiter in Taurus, and the Jupiter is conjunct Sun in Gemini. Dylan feels the need to change and break free of the establishment through his emotions, ruled by the Moon. He puts all that change into words through his Sun in Gemini. Folk and country songs are about earthy, common people fighting the establishment and so he would resonate with them through his Saturn-Uranus in Taurus.

Finally, there is Aretha Franklin (May 25, 1942). First off, she is an electric singer with Uranus in Taurus. But she also symbolized the independent spirit of womanhood in such songs as 'Respect' and 'Sisters are Doing it for Themselves' with the duo Eurythmics.

The conjunct in Gemini is different; the focus here is on free speech and free thought, on breaking down barriers to the mind or to movement. Bobby Fischer (Mar 9, 1943) is famous for breaking the hold Russian players had at the top of the chess world. He was also strange and reclusive. Harrison Ford (Jul 13, 1942) has a twinkle in his eye as he breaks out of difficult situations with his wit and reflexes. Jerry Garcia (Aug 1, 1942) constantly questioned authority and broke with anything that blocked people from going where they wanted – that is this conjunct in Gemini. He said, 'It's pretty clear that what looked like it might have been some kind of counterculture is, in reality, just the plain old chaos of undifferentiated weirdness.'

Janis Joplin (Jan 19, 1943) was highly intelligent and so broke from her Texas upbringing. However, she remained a free thinker when she was at the top of her form in San Francisco, as her letters home attest.

Martin Scorsese (Nov 17, 1942) is constantly breaking out of his own mold – each of his films is different. From *Taxi Driver* (a good Gemini topic) to *Cape Fear* to *The Aviator* to *Kundun*, Scorsese is constantly changing the topic.

People from earlier eras include Queen Elizabeth I (Sep 17, 1533 in Cancer) who refused to become domestic and led her homeland against all manner of attacks. M.C. Escher (Jun 17, 1898 in Sagittarius) broke out of what is considered 'imaginable' to draw things that are totally 'off the wall'. Antoni Gaudi (Jun 25, 1852 in Taurus with Saturn in a triple conjunct with Uranus and Pluto) made concrete and stone into sculptures that were simultaneously organic (Taurus) and able to break free of our limited concept (Saturn) of practicality (also Taurus). Amelia Earhart (Jul 24, 1897 in Scorpio) was a woman adventurer and became a hero for breaking out of her sexual role (Scorpio) and letting her intensity and passion free. William Faulkner (Sep 25, 1897, also in Scorpio) shone a light on the deep, repressed secrets of the American South. Finally, Frank Capra (May 18, 1897 in Scorpio) showed how wisdom, joy, friendship, and freedom (Uranus) could break out of the sleazy, venal establishment (Saturn in Scorpio).

## Saturn conjunct Neptune

Neptune represents dreams and Saturn is the ability to accomplish, to manifest something. So Neptune conjunct Saturn gives the ability to make dreams happen in a practical way. Since Neptune is drugs as well, and Saturn is limitations, some of the people with this conjunct are famous for controlling their drug use, or trying to control others' drug use; in some cases the Neptune overflows the Saturn bounds, so to speak, and the person has difficulty controlling their own use.

Others embody a dream, a vision. Some fight a war between transcendence and practicality within themselves. The people who work best with this conjunct have their head in the clouds (Neptune) and their feet on the ground (Saturn).

When the Neptune overwhelms the Saturn there is a possibility for a person to dream of ways to accomplish rather than actually accomplishing something; this can even result in illusory accomplishments – upon closer inspection, they turn out to have no solid value. However, some people with this conjunct can accomplish through 'failing', by failing upward. Each failure is at a higher level until one day they don't fail. The difference between the first type and the second is that the second is learning, growing more solid and gaining more understanding with each of their failures.

Many of the people with this conjunct have compassion (Neptune) for those who are limited or poor (Saturn). Sometimes they combine this compassion with an ability to show the illusionary nature of the establishment that stops people from having resources.

Media or religious (Neptune) institutions (Saturn) – or, at least, new ways of expression – have been created by people with this conjunct. After all, a spiritual (Neptune) authority (Saturn) is one image for this conjunct. But most important, these people 'keep the dream' – they can maintain a dream for a long time and, eventually, show others its practical reality.

The most recent conjunct was in 1988–1989 in Capricorn. Since this is a Saturn aspect, we haven't seen much since this conjunct tends to have its effect as people get older, and the people who were born that year are barely 21.

Going back 36 years to the prior conjunction, we see the conjunction in Libra in 1952 and 1953. Roseanne Barr (Nov 3, 1952) is a comedian for the lower classes. She poked holes in the established (Saturn) images (Neptune) of women and society

(Libra) with her comedy act and TV show. Tim Allen (Jun 13, 1953) is another comedian who made fun of his own illusory seriousness and authority. Everything conspired to erode (Neptune) his masculine authority (Saturn), especially in his close relationships with others (Libra), resulting in hilarious moments. Jeff Goldblum (Oct 22, 1952) plays roles in which he, too, has a tenuous authority through his niceness (Libra again).

Christopher Reeve (Sep 25, 1952) had a gentle authority as Superman; after his accident he became an advocate for the disabled. Dennis Miller (Nov 3, 1953) is a libertarian who believes (Neptune) everyone should have the right to be left alone (Saturn), which makes him more sympathetic to the conservative side of the political spectrum (Saturn again).

In 1917 the conjunct was in Leo. As we mentioned, some here have boundary issues with drugs, and others form institutions. Betty Ford (Apr 8, 1918) has both bases covered by starting the Betty Ford Foundation after she had an extreme alcohol problem and needed help to overcome it.

Richard Boone (Jun 18, 1917), who played Paladin on TV, and Kirk Douglas (Dec 9, 1916), who played assorted action/adventure and dramatic roles, both had a deep image as serious actors (Saturn in Leo). Both had Saturn in the last degree of Cancer conjunct Neptune in Leo. William Holden (Apr 17, 1918) has a bass voice (like Richard Boone) and serious actor image. Dean Martin (Jun 17, 1917) maintained an image as a person who loved alcohol but had impeccable timing as a comedic straight man to Jerry Lewis. Lena Horne (Jun 30, 1917), a singer active in civil rights, and Susan Hayward (Jun 20, 1917) are women with this conjunct in Leo.

Finally, John F. Kennedy (May 29, 1917) with his emphasis on bravery (Leo) and sympathy for people's difficulties (Neptune-Saturn) was instrumental in civil rights as well. During the Cuban Missile Crisis, Kennedy bluffed and gambled (Leo), based on a deep intuitive understanding (Saturn-Neptune).

Prior conjuncts were 1882 in Taurus, 1846 in Aquarius, and 1809 in Sagittarius. Hazrat Inayat Khan (Jul 5, 1882) had a regal bearing as a religious authority (Taurus) and founded the Sufi Order, a mystical organization. Henry Kaiser (May 9, 1882) was a captain of industry (Taurus) who revolutionized ship manufacture, aluminum, and health care – he started a charitable foundation. Pablo Picasso (Oct 25, 1881) transformed art (Taurus, ruled by Venus) with a vision of abstract shapes, such as in cubism, and other distortions (a vision of 'solids' would be another description of the conjunct). Franklin Delano Roosevelt (Jan 30, 1882) was born wealthy (Taurus) but had sympathy for those suffering difficulties in the Great Depression.

Carry Nation (Nov 25, 1846) fought against alcoholism by attacking saloons with a hatchet after marrying an alcoholic – the battle to control drugs associated with this conjunct was intense and personal for her. Thomas Edison (Feb 11, 1847) represented the quintessential inventor (Aquarius) due to his ability to bring other inventors together in a group (also Aquarius) to form new physical (Saturn) mediums (Neptune) such as the phonograph, light bulb, and movie camera.

Edgar Allan Poe (Jan 19, 1809) was part of the 'dark romanticism' genre (where Saturn is dark and Neptune is romantic); he intensely disliked the 'pretenders and sophists' (Neptunians) among the transcendentalists and wrote satires about them.

Abraham Lincoln (Feb 12, 1809) and Charles Darwin (Feb 12, 1809) were born on the same day with the conjunct in Sagittarius. Lincoln freed the slaves and held high ideals about the union, while Darwin discovered evolution (Sagittarius), the theory of how species evolved over time. Evolution was promptly attacked by the conservative (Saturn) religious (Neptune in Sagittarius) contingent.

## Saturn conjunct Pluto

These planets both represent reality: Saturn is a practical reality, while Pluto is the underlying psychological reality. Saturn tries to solidify, to conserve, to limit, while Pluto tends to wipe out, to destroy, to reveal, to alienate, and to intensify. This conjunct is where the conservative establishment, and the conservative part of yourself, is forced to face reality. Every time you think you have it together through Saturn, it is blasted apart by Pluto's unnerving revelations of what is really happening.

Pluto acting on Saturn can make people have superhuman patience and endurance or it can place an impervious wall around some subjects (or countries). Many of the people who have this conjunct are heavy and intense people.

Pluto is all or nothing, life or death, or reality versus total wiping-out of reality. Some people with this conjunct can be obsessed (Pluto) with the past (Saturn), while others can wipe out the past and pretend it doesn't exist. This Plutonian wipe-out never has good results since destruction of one's environment through projection quickly results.

People with this conjunct are usually intensely grounded and focused on what is real. Difficulties are seen as just that; they rarely deter this person. Some with this conjunct try to 'make' reality. When practical difficulties make it obvious that something isn't going to happen, some people with this conjunct try to use their intensity and Plutonian force to 'make' it happen. However, when these people are opposed by a form of rigidity (Saturn) that they know is out of tune with the Plutonian reality, they can calmly let nature take its course and break through the opposition without effort when the natural course of things unfolds.

Since Pluto can be a peaceful calm based on inner reality and Saturn is accomplishment, some people can accomplish goals by calmly overcoming adversity. This can be almost Taoistic.

In Leo, for example, there is a need for intense and focused affection. Rarely do people with this conjunct have anything other than deep, long-lasting relationships.

With Saturn representing time and Pluto representing energies beyond the normally human, this conjunct represents extremely long or short periods of time. Sometimes people with this conjunct think in terms of lifetimes or billionths of a second.

The most recent conjunct was in 1982. Adam Lambert (Jan 29, 1982) of *American Idol* fame has the conjunct in Libra with it additionally conjunct Mars in Libra. Pluto in Libra represents intense artistic expression (hip-hop, for example) and to this is added a focused heaviness and force from the Mars. So Adam has an intense, aggressive, focused artistic intensity.

Another singer with this conjunct is Britney Spears (Dec 2, 1981). She has heavy and intense marriages and personal relationships (Libra). At one point she became unable to relate (Libra) to what was happening. She also has the same need for artistic expression as Adam.

An actress with the conjunct is Kirsten Dunst (Apr 30, 1982). She has very intense eyes and a focused demeanor. She has played in vampire movies, science fiction, as Spiderman's love interest, and as Marie Antoinette. She was treated for depression (Saturn) in 2008.

Going back 35 years, there is the Saturn-Pluto conjunct in 1947 in Leo. The women with this conjunct are hyper-realistic. For starters, Hillary Rodham Clinton (Oct 26, 1947) and Susan Sarandon (Oct 4, 1946) have this conjunct. Both are clear, intense, and solid. Hillary broke through the limitation on women running for president, and almost became the Democratic nominee.

There is an association with horror with the conjunct: Stephen King (Sep 21, 1947) tells dark, sinister, and dramatic tales; and Kathy Bates (Jun 28, 1948) has starred in a few horror movies.

Dark, sinister, and dramatic music, anyone? Both Alice Cooper (Feb 4, 1948) and David Bowie (Jan 8, 1947) have the conjunct.

Carlos Santana (Jul 20, 1947) broke into the mainstream of

rock and roll with Latin music. Ian Scott Anderson of Jethro Tull has Venus, Saturn, Pluto, and Sun conjunct in Leo – his music has heavy metal qualities. Also, he was the first to use a classical instrument, the flute, in rock and roll. His lyrics blast (Pluto) the established society and religion (Saturn). So both musicians broke barriers in rock and roll.

Tommy Lee Jones (Sep 15, 1946) has played heavy, intense, characters (often law officers) who, underneath, have understanding. Billy Crystal (Mar 14, 1948) stars in movies which often involve decades in the lives of the character he plays. Farah Fawcett (Feb 2, 1947) started her career in the action TV show *Charlie's Angels* but quickly took on heavy dramatic roles.

Other actresses with the conjunct include Sally Field (Nov 6, 1946), Barbara Hershey (Feb 5, 1948), and Patty Duke (Dec 14, 1946). All are serious dramatic actresses.

Directors with this conjunct are Steven Spielberg (Dec 18, 1946) and Oliver Stone (Sep 15, 1946). Steven brought new subjects to the cinema such as aliens and the Holocaust. Oliver Stone has made a career smashing establishment myths in a dramatic way.

Arnold Schwarzenegger (Jul 30, 1947) has broken through barriers as a body builder, an actor, and as a politician. Like Tommy Lee Jones, he played intense action-laden parts.

Al Gore (Mar 31, 1948) has the conjunct with Mars in Leo. Although he has come across as stiff and unemotional, he gets more animated when describing the catastrophes (Pluto) awaiting our planet due to global warming if we go beyond the natural limits (Saturn) of the earth.

The prior conjunct in early Cancer was in 1914 through 1915. However, some of the people with the conjunct had Pluto in Cancer with Saturn back in Gemini. Billie Holiday (Apr 7, 1915) transformed pop vocals and sang 'Strange Fruit', a song that brought lynching into public awareness. She had Saturn in Gemini and Pluto in Cancer, so the powerful and intense emotions represented by Pluto in Cancer were focused and communicated with Saturn in Gemini.

Jackie Coogan (Oct 26, 1914) was a child filmstar who was the first to sue his parents for spending all his earnings. He is also famous as Uncle Fester in the *Addams Family* TV series (humorous horror, you might say).

Hedy Lamarr (Nov 9, 1914) and Dorothy Lamour (Dec 10, 1914) were both glamorous actresses of the 1940s. Hedy Lamarr acted in a notorious nude scene that brought her to Hollywood's attention; this could be said to push the envelope on nudity in films. As an inventor, she also developed both radio-guided torpedoes and frequency hopping. Hedy Lamarr played 'sarong' roles in Tarzan and the 'Road' films, after being a singer and doing more serious roles.

Thomas Merton (Jan 31, 1915), a famous Catholic monk, wrote some 70 books on mysticism. He brought together Zen Buddhism and Roman Catholicism, breaking down the barrier between those two religions. He had Saturn in late Gemini (he was a writer) and Pluto in early Cancer. He was also intensely focused on social justice.

Earlier periods included 1883 in late Taurus, 1851 in late Aries, and 1819 to 1820 in Pisces. John Meynard Keynes (Jun 5, 1883, conjunct in Gemini) introduced Keynesian economics, bringing in an awareness of the longer economic cycles and the appropriate behavior in upswings and downswings. Hazrat Inayat Khan (Jul 5, 1882, with the conjunct in Taurus, also conjunct Pluto) was a Sufi spiritual teacher in the early part of the twentieth century. One of his sayings was 'Shatter your ideals on the rock of Truth', which partially shows how this triple conjunct influenced his life. Hazrat wanted to break down all barriers between religions (Neptune) and focus on the one eternal God, the only Being.

Bela Lugosi (Oct 20, 1882, Neptune, Saturn, Pluto) was the first horror star with this conjunct. Herman Melville (Aug 1,

1819, Pluto late Pisces, Saturn in Aries) wrote *Moby Dick*, a novel in which a whale from beneath the ocean (Pluto in Pisces) destroys a ship and an obsessed, dictatorial captain (Pluto conjunct Saturn in Aries). The silence before the whale smashes the ship is known to anyone who has had a Shiva/Plutonian experience.

Auguste Piccard (Jan 28, 1884, Pluto in Taurus, Saturn in Gemini) broke through barriers in the air and under the ocean in the first balloon to enter the stratosphere and the first bathyscope to go deep under the oceans.

Susan B. Anthony (Feb 15, 1820, Pluto, Saturn, and Venus conjunct in Pisces) was a women's rights advocate who broke through the barriers to feminine advancement. Finally, George Eliot (Nov 22, 1819, conjunct in Pisces) broke the barrier to women writers. She used a masculine pseudonym to get her writings accepted.

## Uranus conjunct Neptune

It's striking how many powerful women were born with this conjunct, including Susan B. Anthony, Clara Barton, Emily Brontë, Mary Baker Eddy, George Eliot, Florence Nightingale, and Queen Victoria. Admittedly, all of them were born with the conjunct in Capricorn or late Sagittarius from 1818 to 1825.

The most recent conjunct was in the early and mid 1990s in late Capricorn or early Aquarius. The two stars from this period, both quite young, are Abigail Breslin (Apr 14, 1996 – Neptune in Capricorn conjunct Uranus in Aquarius) and Miley Cyrus (Nov 23, 1992, Venus, Uranus, Neptune conjunct in Capricorn). Both are more grounded than the older generations of stars. We'll see whether powerful people emerge from this group.

As we said, the prior group was born around the 1820s. Not only were there powerful women but powerful men as well – both men and women started organizations or movements, many of which are going to this day. Powerful men included Prince

Albert, Sir Richard Burton, Ulysses Grant, Stonewall Jackson, Karl Marx, Herman Melville, Louis Pasteur, Johann Strauss, and Walt Whitman.

Each preceding conjunct is about 171 years earlier and 18 degrees back in the zodiac – this is not a common conjunct. Any aspect of the transcendental planets, especially a conjunct, is powerful. We would expect people born at that time to embody the qualities.

What are those qualities? Uranus is inspiration, which comes in a flash, while Neptune is intuition that comes in a nebulous manner, more as a feeling. These people would have flashes of intuition, like lightning in clouds.

For many born with this conjunct, their Uranian genius is in Neptunian compassion. They wish to find a way to help others by inspiring people. They can also inspire people with a dream or awaken them to an ideal.

The striving and wisdom of Uranus, added to the spiritual love and compassion of Neptune, can make people constantly strive to achieve an ideal; this can give longevity of purpose.

On the downside, there can be a tendency to be thrown off course by continual flashes, each flash inspiring a nebulous response. This can be addicting. However, the upside is the viral nature of the ideals; when these people hit their stride they can inspire larger and larger groups, with new recruits being 'turned on' by the Uranus to a Neptunian dream.

Neptune dissolves and merges, and Uranus takes joy in that dissolving and merging. So, many of the people with this conjunct want to dissolve the old structures and replace them with utopias in which everyone is equal because the old rigid hierarchies have dissolved.

Change is important to Uranians, and people with this conjunct fight for change based on a Neptunian vision or dream.

Susan B. Anthony (Feb 15, 1820 – Uranus late Sagittarius, Neptune early Capricorn) gave 100 speeches per year on women's rights for over four decades. She was originally also an abolitionist. She became the head of large groups of women fighting for the right to vote and for women's labor rights. She was the first real woman depicted on a US coin. Her gift was for public speaking and inspiring women to fight for their rights. Her dream was equal rights for women at the ballot box and equal pay for equal work – she witnessed men getting paid four times as much as women for the same job and women kept out of crafts and professions. So her dream was a world in which women were no longer beneath men but their equals.

Karl Marx (May 5, 1818, Uranus and Neptune in Sagittarius) also believed in equality; he believed class struggle would eventually lead to a classless state in which no class based on property would lord it over other people. What we today call communism was developed by Karl Marx. So Susan B. Anthony wanted men to no longer be in a class above women, and Karl Marx wanted the rich to no longer be in a class above the workers – there is starting to be a theme here.

Florence Nightingale (May 12, 1820 – Uranus in Sagittarius and Neptune in Capricorn) gave up the life of a rich, upper-class British woman to become a nurse who helped the sick. Her greatest work was done in the Crimean War where she fought for sanitary conditions and better nutrition for the army. Less known was her ability as a mathematician and statistician – she pioneered methods of charting that would allow politicians to visualize statistics. She had a calling from God and was also a feminist. Social service was her life's focus, as was the focus of Susan B. Anthony.

Mary Baker Eddy (Jul 16, 1821 – Uranus, Neptune, and Mars conjunct in Capricorn) founded Christian Science, a group devoted to healing people in a Christian manner. Eddy is another example of a woman with this conjunct who attracted people to a movement that continues up to the present.

Louis Pasteur (Dec 27, 1822 – Mercury, Sun, Neptune, Venus,

Uranus conjunct in Capricorn) made breakthroughs in the causes and cures of disease; his experiments supported the germ theory. Pasteurization, which he invented, helped rid milk of micro-organisms that cause disease. He also made discoveries in crystallography (light in hierarchical earthy structures – how Uranus in Capricorn!). The spread of disease is a Neptunian phenomenon, and he created a Uranian theory about that spread.

Among Americans, Stonewall Jackson (Jan 20, 1824 with the conjunct in Capricorn) was a brilliant strategist and tactician, who had an intuitive sense of how to fight battles. The image of a stone wall fits the Neptune in Capricorn. Ulysses Grant, also a brilliant general, was also known for his alcoholism (drugs are Neptune).

Clara Barton (Dec 25, 1821, Sun, Uranus, Neptune conjunct in Capricorn) was a nurse and the founder of the American Red Cross. She was also in charge of the search for missing men from the Union Army after being in charge of hospitals for the wounded during the American Civil War.

Finally, Queen Victoria (May 24, 1819, conjunct in Sagittarius) was the symbol of England for 63 years. Unlike the other women who founded institutions, she *was* an institution herself.

## Uranus conjunct Pluto

This conjunct alternately happens 112 years and 140 years apart. It stays in the same element for over 500 years; one conjunct may go forward into a new element, with the next conjunct falling back into the old element before future conjuncts remain in the new element.

The most recent conjunct peaked in 1966, although there were people with the conjunct from 1963 to 1969; all of the people with the conjunct have it in Virgo. We have a broad spectrum of people from this period to draw from.

Based on our knowledge of Uranus and Pluto, we would expect that these people would take a certain joy in being intense, would have an all-or-nothing need for freedom, could become obsessed with change for change's sake, could find joy in being powerful, or could find joy in pushing things to the limit.

Uranus could lighten up Pluto, resulting in more joy and spontaneity when in the world of intensity, power, and magnetism that is Pluto. Or Pluto could darken Uranus, resulting in the Uranian traits of freedom or joy becoming a compulsion.

Since the recent examples are all in Virgo, we have to abstract out the Virgo. Virgo can be clear-voiced or it can be more soft-spoken, almost shy, with a hoarse voice. Virgo is associated either with voluptuousness or with thin and petite body types.

Of people born in the 1960s with this conjunct, the voluptuous ones include Mira Sorvino, Brooke Shields, Anna Nicole Smith, Pamela Anderson, and Yasmine Bleeth. The petite include Calista Flockhart, Joan Cusack, and Celine Dion.

Virgo is associated with facts and figures, with work and service, with cleanliness and neatness, with doing it yourself. So, both accountants and handymen come under Virgo.

Of course, all of these people also have Neptune in Scorpio, which gives them a sexy, dark, cynical, and magnetic image.

From the election of 2008, both Michelle Obama and Sarah Palin have the conjunct. Sarah Palin (Feb 11, 1964) shows the joy in life and death, in power, which is associated with the conjunct. Michelle Obama (Jan 17, 1964) shows more of the subdued Virgo side – she was a health care administrator who wielded power but used it to serve people. Her joy (Uranus) is more in keeping it real (Pluto).

Will Smith (Sep 25, 1968 – Jupiter, Pluto, Uranus in Virgo conjunct Sun in Libra) has had a career that includes a few movies about aliens (Pluto) or being superhuman (Pluto) or dying (Pluto) or gaining wealth (Pluto). But he does the movies with a joy (Uranus) that makes the intensity a lot more palatable.

David Spade (Jul 22, 1966) plays roles in which he makes snide, critical comments (Pluto in Virgo), but has a twinkle when he does it (Uranus). Sarah Jessica Parker (Mar 25, 1965 – Mars, Uranus, Pluto conjunct) played the lead role in *Sex in the City*, which fits the conjunct with Mars but, of course, also the Neptune in Scorpio for the sex aspect. The urban aspect might be more the bustle of Virgo.

Among leading men with quiet sparkling intensity, we couldn't forget either Brad Pitt (Dec 18, 1963) or Keanu Reeves (Sep 2, 1964). Keanu has the Sun and Mercury conjunct the Uranus and Pluto, so he directly embodies the energies. He often portrays powerful, free beings in films like the *Matrix* series or *Little Buddha*. Brad Pitt has magnetism based on his good looks, but he also plays intense parts.

Adam Sandler (Sep 9, 1966) has self-deprecating humor; he often plays someone who is apparently unredeemable, but who finds the way to redemption by the end of the movie.

Many with this conjunct have a steely edge, but with some humor beneath it all, since they seem to be able to stand outside themselves (Pluto) and watch with humorous detachment (Uranus). Nicolas Cage (Jan 7, 1964), Halle Berry (Aug 14, 1968), and Robert Downey Jr (Apr 4, 1966) come to mind.

From prior periods we have Robert Louis Stevenson (Nov 13, 1850, Saturn, Uranus, Pluto conjunct in Aries) who reveled in tales of adventure (Aries) but also in dark characters (Pluto) who had a goodness underneath (Uranus). Vincent Van Gogh (Mar 30, 1853 in Taurus) saw life through a warped filter (Pluto), but he saw life with a brightness and focus (Uranus) that made his Impressionist paintings miraculous.

## Neptune conjunct Pluto

This is the longest conjunction pattern in astrology. The latest conjunction was at eight degrees Gemini in 1891 and 1892 (although people with the conjunct ran from 1885 to 1897). Prior conjuncts were 493 years earlier and five degrees back in the zodiac each time.

Gemini rules communication and transportation. These people created the very archetypes for media and travel; by 'media' I mean all forms of communication: radio, TV, newspapers, stage, art, dance, mystery, films, etc. Neptune is the images, the faith, and sympathy. When Pluto conjuncts it, those images and that faith undergo a transformation. For example, some people with this conjunct started to claim that 'God is dead' – if that isn't a loss of faith, what is?

Well, let's get the unpleasant part out of the way first. Adolf Hitler (Apr 20, 1889) and Goebbels, Goering, Hess, Ribbentrop, and Baron von Richtofen all had the conjunct. They redefined communication through radio and books by which they spread their hate, they created an archetype of a dictator, and they perfected modern methods of propaganda. And, although the Third Reich didn't last 493 years to the next conjunct, unfortunately their archetype may. You might say Hitler pioneered ego (Pluto) through mass media (Neptune in Gemini).

Edward G. Robinson (Dec 12, 1893) defined the gangster archetype in the movies. Norman Rockwell (Feb 3, 1894) created realistic paintings that depicted American life. Babe Ruth (Feb 6, 1895) was the consummate home-run hitter in baseball.

H.P. Lovecraft (Apr 20, 1890) created some amazing horror tales, and could be said to have improved the genre. He wrote, 'The process of delving into the dark abyss (Pluto) is the keenest form of fascination (Neptune).'

M.C. Escher (Jun 17, 1898) made sketches in which people walked along the ceilings and walls, water flowed downhill in a circular path (and each part appeared downhill), and fish flowed out of the paper – art as optical expression. He spoke of the 'nonsensicalness [Neptune] of what some take to be irrefutable certainties [Pluto]' and also said, 'I don't use drugs [Neptune]. My dreams [Neptune] are frightening enough [Pluto].'

Martha Graham (May 11, 1894) pioneered modern dance. Conrad Hilton (Dec 12, 1887, Neptune in Taurus conjunct Pluto in

Gemini) founded a chain of hotels to provide stable places (Neptune in Taurus) for travelers (Pluto in Gemini).

Henry Miller (Apr 4, 1891) created the archetypical erotic novel. Arthur Murray (Apr 4, 1895) started a chain of dance studios. The idea of business chains, such as those started by Arthur Murray and Conrad Hilton, was founded by this group with the conjunct in Gemini.

Al Jolson (Jun 7, 1886) starred in the first 'talkie', *The Jazz Singer*. Laurel and Hardy were the first comedy team in films.

The list goes on and on – there were so many people. Charles Atlas (Oct 30, 1893) was the first body builder to advertise nationally. Jack Benny (Feb 14, 1894) was one of the first comedians on both radio and TV, as was George Burns (Jan 20, 1896).

Rudolph Valentino (May 6, 1895) was the first theater heart-throb. Mae West (Aug 17, 1892) defined the type of woman who wasn't afraid to use her sexuality for humor. Charlie Chaplin (Apr 16, 1889) was a dramatic and comedic innovator. Amelia Earhart (Jul 24, 1897) was one of the first women heroes for physical daring.

Finally, J.R.R. Tolkien with his series *The Lord of the Rings* defined the modern fantasy novel.

Chapter 7

# Generations and Cycles of the USA and Europe

William Strauss and Neil Howe have done research on generational cycles of people in the United States; Arnold Toynbee did prior work, among others. The work here is based on Strauss and Howe, but deviates from their approach. For one thing, astrology and mysticism are brought into the mix. For another, Strauss and Howe see the length of generations as changing from approximately 28 years per generation to approximately 21 years. Here, we talk about two different generational patterns: a European pattern of approximately 28 years and a United States pattern of 21 years per generation. As the USA was born, the pattern switched over from 28 to 21 years. However, back in Europe, the 28-year pattern continued to the present day.

The switchover came around 1700, when the Saturn-Neptune conjunct was in Aries (1703) and Uranus was in late Gemini as Neptune entered Aries (1698). Interestingly, the next time this happens will be in 2026, when, for a brief period, the two generational patterns have the same starting point (but more on this later).

The generations we are talking about here concern the relationships of people to the major waves of change and growth in their larger cultures. People are born with outer planets in certain signs and aspects. These define their generational qualities, but whatever major events they went through such as wars and spiritual awakenings, and the time at which they went through them, also give context to their lives.

Generations happen in a pattern of four, with a spiritual awakening during the second generation and a major upheaval (usually a war) during the end of the last generation of the cycle (European) or right as the cycle starts (American). The generational cycle lasts for 108 years in Europe (4 x 28 = 112, but the last generation is 24 years so this brings the cycle down to 108) while it is only 84 years in the USA (4 x 21).

The European cycle is initiated by a Saturn conjunct with Neptune in a fire sign; this happens every 108 years. The USA cycle is initiated by Neptune on the Aries or Libra cusp with Uranus in early Gemini (Pluto is on a fixed cusp at these times); these are times of major convulsions for the USA. These were, in order: the Salem witch trials and the start of slavery (1692), the Declaration of Independence (1776), the Civil War (1861), and the attack on Pearl Harbor starting World War II (1941). The Neptune in Aries convulsions tend to be internal battles, within the USA, while the Libra convulsions tend to be wars with other countries. Therefore, the problems in 2025 will probably be concerned with structural issues within the USA, since Neptune will be on the Aries cusp.

Interestingly, there will be a convulsion in Europe, based on the European cycles, ending in 2026, since the Saturn-Neptune conjunction will be in early Aries. Typically, these convulsions have a build-up of ten to 20 years (during the 24 years from the last Saturn return to the prior conjunct point). Since we are already in the build-up period, we can see that wars dealing with the rapid depletion of the world's supply of fossil fuels, and the corresponding lack of energy, will probably be the cause of the problems – not to mention global warming which results from the burning of fossil fuels.

Each cycle of four generations has a fiery generation, an earthy generation, an airy generation, and a watery generation – this is just like the cycle of signs in the zodiac. For example, in the zodiac we see that Aries, fire, is followed by Taurus, earth, which is followed by Gemini, air, which is followed by Cancer, water.

The fire generation is spiritual; it breaks out of the materialism it sees in the prior generations. This group includes great orators and actors. However, their driving force and guiding spirit comes from within. They are born in the aftermath of a crisis that shattered the complacency of the world and leads them into finding what is underneath the outward reality.

The earth generation are survivors. Typically they are left to fend for themselves as youth, since they grew up amidst people searching inwardly who didn't care about children – they were trying to become independent of the world spiritually. This generation's religion is more fundamentalist, and based on surviving during life and even after death. 'Everyone else is a loser, but you will survive,' they think. They want to survive death and be winners, just as they want to survive and be winners in life. Since their chances are slim, they are not afraid to take chances to break out of the mass of mediocrity. This is a crafty and cynical generation – they have to be, to survive.

Next come the air generation. This generation works in groups – everyone is treated equally. All are expected to work together to achieve some apparently impossible goal. The miracle is how often they pull it off. Extroversion is prized; they are socially driven. The downfall comes if this generation loses its integrity and tries to achieve a goal that is unworthy. This is the generation that has to deal with the crisis. They give to the larger whole, and expect the larger whole to give to them. When the crisis comes, this is the generation – in young adulthood to early middle age – that must deal with it.

The water generation is sensitive and artistic. But they can also be concerned with trivia and procedure when the 'house' is burning down. Sometimes this generation goes for meticulously crafted compromise instead of simply doing the right thing. However, the art that defines whole cultures is created by this generation, since they incorporate within themselves the intensity and crisis surrounding them as they grew up. Their parents try to shelter them, but they can feel the difficulties nonetheless.

## The European Generations

As we said, these generations happen every 108 years based on the Saturn-Neptune conjunct in a fire sign. The conjuncts happen a trine back each time – if one conjunct is in Leo, the next will be in Aries. The first three generations of the cycle take almost one complete cycle of Saturn back to the point of the conjunct; in this time Uranus goes four signs and Neptune two signs. The last generation is shorter since Saturn only has to go two-thirds of the zodiac to get to the new conjunct. The turmoil that defines the whole next cycle typically happens during the birth of this last generation.

The next Saturn-Neptune conjunct in a fire sign will be in the beginning of Aries in 2026 at 1 Aries. Previous conjuncts were:

| | |
|------|----------------|
| 1164 | 27 Sagittarius |
| 1271 | 24 Leo |
| 1380 | 21 Aries |
| 1486 | 17 Sagittarius |
| 1594 | 14 Leo |
| 1703 | 12 Aries |
| 1809 | 7 Sagittarius |
| 1917 | 5 Leo |

As you can see, the conjuncts cycle backwards within the fire signs. There were periods where there were no Saturn-Neptune conjuncts in fire signs. The years from 661 to 1164 were such a period. If we go back to the conjunct in Taurus in 1057, this was around the time of the Norman invasion of England in 1066 and probably could 'stand in' for a fire conjunct. (This could do with more research.)

The temper of the age, the practical challenge, is often

indicated by the fire sign where the conjunction takes place. For example, Sagittarius rules both religion and exploration: the years from 1486 to 1594 were the years of discovery – including, most notably, the voyages of Columbus – but also a time of religious turmoil during the Protestant Reformation. The years from 1594 to 1703 started with the end of Elizabeth's reign and Shakespeare (acting is Leo) but then went through a period of questioning of the power of the king (Leo) versus parliament. Throughout this period the kings of England thought of themselves as ruling by divine right, while parliament felt that they ruled by the consent of the people.

The 1703 period was about empire, and whose empire would rule (Aries). At the beginning it seemed like the British Empire would prevail, but after the American and French revolutions and the rise of the Napoleonic Empire, this was in doubt. By the 1809 period, Napoleon had conquered all of Europe except Britain. He quickly went downhill, however, and rule passed to more democratic institutions. European empires expanded until they had conquered the entire world (Sagittarius) but then imploded in World War I and the communist revolution in 1917.

The current period has been one of dictators (Leo) and struggles between parliaments and heads of state, between corporations, which control much of the media, and government – true democracy has been challenged. Leo prefers power centralized in people, like the prior 1594–1703 period. Although we may not think of it, radio and TV are centered around acting, with Europe focused on this acting (Leo).

The European generations are:

| | | |
|------|------|-------------|
| Fire | 1164 | Sagittarius |
| Earth | 1192 | |
| Air | 1220 | |
| Water | 1248 | |
| Fire | 1271 | Leo |

| Earth | 1299 | |
| Air | 1327 | |
| Water | 1365 | |
| Fire | 1380 | Aries |
| Earth | 1408 | |
| Air | 1436 | |
| Water | 1464 | |
| Fire | 1486 | Sagittarius |
| Earth | 1514 | |
| Air | 1542 | |
| Water | 1570 | |
| Fire | 1594 | Leo |
| Earth | 1622 | |
| Air | 1650 | |
| Water | 1678 | |
| Fire | 1703 | Aries |
| Earth | 1731 | |
| Air | 1759 | |
| Water | 1787 | |
| Fire | 1809 | Sagittarius |
| Earth | 1837 | |
| Air | 1865 | |
| Water | 1893 | |
| Fire | 1917 | Leo |
| Earth | 1945 | |
| Air | 1973 | |
| Water | 2001 | |
| Fire | 2026 | Aries |

Fire is our equivalent of the 'Prophet' generation (described by Strauss and Howe), earth is the 'Nomad' generation, air is the 'Hero' generation, and water is the 'Artist' generation. Fire comes from inside and is inner-directed (Prophet), earth wants to make a mark and is concerned with survival (Nomad), air is outer-directed and social (Hero), while water reacts to all the outer stimuli to create an inner synthesis (Artist).

The 1164 conjunct in Sagittarius was during the reign of Henry II of England (1154–1189) and coincided with the tension between Thomas à Becket and Henry, which resulted in Thomas's murder in 1170. This was the time of the twelfth-century renaissance, when England was put on a solid footing. Henry ruled much of France as well as England. Throughout this generational cycle (1164–1270), the emphasis was on religion and foreign adventures, such as the Crusades – both religion and foreign countries are Sagittarian. Richard the Lionheart, John, and Henry III were the monarchs during this time.

From 1164 to 1192, during the fire period, many famous musicians, poets, and philosophers were born, including Wolfram von Eschenbach, German poet; Vogelweide, German minnesinger; and Saadi, a Persian poet. In 1214, during the earth period from 1192 to 1220, Roger Bacon, a famous scientist, was born. Henry III was born in 1207 (earth) – he was known for his 'simplicity' and aesthetics. Edward I was born in 1239 (air) – he believed in rule with the aid of parliament. The poet Dante Alighieri was born in 1265 during a water period, as was the mystic Meister Eckhart, born in 1260; also during this water period Giotto was born, in 1266.

The crisis in 1264 between king and nobles resulted in the first true English parliamentary meetings in 1265 and the formalization of a mechanism for the Magna Carta. This was the crisis prior to the 1271 conjunct starting the next cycle of generations. Pluto entered Capricorn in 1270, which also signaled a change in government. The Magna Carta was produced during late Pluto in Sagittarius.

The next conjunct, one that initiated a series of generations, was in 1271, in Leo. Hafiz was born in 1320, during an earth period. Chaucer, 1340, air; Van Eyck, Dutch painter, 1370, water; Ghiberti, sculptor, 1378, water. During this Leo period, the emphasis was on centralizing rule in England and France. These older periods will require more research to discover who was born in each period and their qualities, and the qualities of their lives in succeeding periods. Although the Black Death occurred in the air part of this period (1349), its effects lasted into the next cycle.

The conjunction in 1380 was in Aries. Thirty years before, in 1349, the Black Death killed one-third of the population of Europe and it reoccurred, in lesser forms, for decades. The population didn't start to increase again until the mid-1400s – nearly the entire period from 1380 to 1486 was under this pall. Strauss and Howe describe the last two segments of this period, the air and water period, in *The Fourth Turning*. All subsequent periods are also described in that book (although, after 1703, they are the American periods which we will describe in the next section).

Richard II, who was born in 1367 (water), was emotional, violent, and tyrannical; he was overthrown and murdered by Henry IV. Richard was king from 1377 to 1399, the last of the Plantagenets. The man who overthrew him, Henry IV, was the first of the Lancastrian and York dynasty. The sources of crisis for those years were the Black Death and the reign of Richard II, since the Black Prince, who was the natural successor, had died before him. In 1380 Charles VI, 'the Mad', assumed the French throne; in 1392 he went mad and was replaced by his brother, the Duke of Orleans. There was a lot of black in those years.

In 1380, Thomas à Kempis, a German mystic, was born (fire). Joan of Arc was born in 1412 (earth); she died in 1431 at the age of 19. Joan was responsible for a French awakening to the country's destiny, independent of England. This awakening was responsible for the French pushing England out and reclaiming their country. At this time there occurred the Great Schism, when there were two popes, one French and the other Roman. In 1408 the process of the end of this schism was begun; by the end of the earth period the Schism was ended.

Gutenburg, who invented printing, was born in 1396 (late fire) during the Neptune-Pluto conjunction that peaked in Gemini in 1399 (the first one in Gemini). The awakening that resulted from printing (1450, air generation) gave birth to the Renaissance.

This air period ended with the War of the Roses, an English civil war, between the houses of York and Lancaster; the final battle was in 1471, shortly after the water period started. Printing came to England in 1476. This was the start of the humanist period in England as Greek, Roman, and other texts, uncensored by the church, made their way into the hands of the general public. As usual, this period was a precursor to the Sagittarian period to follow. The period ended with the short reign of the 'princes in the Tower' (of London).

As is typical with periods initiated by a conjunct in Aries, there was battling for position: for nearly the entire period, the power was in the hands of both the Yorkists and the Lancastrians. But there was also a change in viewpoint of the world marked by the invention of printing. Christopher Columbus was born in 1451 (air). The children born during the water phase were imbued with this humanist (Sagittarian) spirit; famous people included Erasmus, Machiavelli, Vasco da Gama, Dürer, Thomas More, Martin Luther (1483, almost fire), Michelangelo, and Copernicus. Nearly all were involved in creating new ways of seeing the world (Aries) or in expanding the known physical or spiritual world (Sagittarius).

In 1485, to initiate the Sagittarian fire cycle, Henry VII started the Tudor reign (1485–1603) in England. In Spain, at this time, the reign of Ferdinand and Isabella (started in 1479) succeeded in pushing out the Moors (Islam) and the Jews (the other two western religions besides Christianity – Sagittarius rules religion), but also in furthering a wave of exploration (Sagittarius) by Christopher Columbus in 1492.

The Reformation (1517) defined the 1486 cycle: this was an

awakening during an earth period as the fiery Prophet generation came of age. The entire cycle was Sagittarian, hence concerning religion and foreign affairs. Pluto entered Capricorn in 1516 while Neptune was in Aquarius from 1506 to 1520. When Pluto enters Capricorn there is a need to become independent: new powers are born which split off from a major power of the time – in this case, the Roman Catholic Church. Neptune in Aquarius signaled a revolutionary change (Aquarius) in religion (Neptune).

In England, Henry VIII reigned from 1509 to 1547 – this was the entire earth or awakening period during which England broke free from Roman Catholicism and became Protestant. Henry brought England into the Renaissance with his love of art and philosophy. He was a true Sagittarian ruler. This period ended with the Spanish Armada crisis in 1588 during the water generational period from 1570 to 1594, as the English defeated the massive Spanish Armada.

The next cycle started in 1594 with the conjunction in Leo. Queen Elizabeth was at the end of her reign that lasted from 1558 to 1603. Pluto had entered Aries in 1577, starting a new era of power politics. England was in the midst of a glorious period that produced Queen Elizabeth I and Shakespeare, a great playwright, as befits a Leo period. The series of generations ended with the Glorious Revolution in 1689 during the water period. Note that the crisis for European generations typically happens five to 15 years from the end of the water cycle (we will see that it is different for American generations). See Strauss and Howe for more information on this cycle.

In 1703 the American cycle diverged from the European cycle. However, the European cycle continued onward and European affairs are based on this Saturn-Neptune, 106-year cycle to the present day. As in the prior Aries conjunct in 1380, this was a battle between France and England for European supremacy. In 1380 the battle remained within France; by the end of the 1703 cycle, it enveloped all of Europe with the French Revolution and Napoleon's takeover of Europe.

In England, Anne, the last of the Stuarts, reigned from 1702 to 1714. After her came the Hanoverian dynasty with the Georges (George I, II, and III) reigning throughout this cycle (the dynasty ended in 1901). The Hanoverians brought on the American Revolution due to their intransigence, and they lived through the French Revolution, with their prime ministers and parliament mostly handling affairs.

The French Revolution / Napoleon crisis started two years into the water generation in 1789, which saw the start of the French Revolution, and lasted until six years into the next cycle in 1815 with the defeat of Napoleon at Waterloo. However, the start of the end for Napoleon was in 1808 during the Iberian campaign.

During the 1809 to 1917 period, the emphasis was again outside of Europe, as it had been in the 1486 period when the Europeans explored the entire globe. However, in this period the Europeans conquered the whole world, carving it up among various European countries. Two alliances of countries went to war during the implosion in World War I, after the world had run out of places to conquer in the early 1890s during the Neptune-Pluto conjunction. World War I was fought during the end of the water period, from 1914 to 1917.

The awakening in 1848, during the earth period, was to Marxism, democracy, and nationalism. Marxism triumphed in 1917 when Russia became communist as World War I ended. The 1840s was the period of the Romantics – poetry and art had a diffuse, idealistic Neptunian aura. The Pre-Raphaelite Brotherhood of artists flourished at this time. Dickens and other writers woke people up to the poverty and misery of the lower classes under industrialization – this cycle was the height of industrialization.

The period from 1893 to 1917, the water period, saw the birth of many English writers, politicians, and actors who defined the mid-twentieth century: Harold Macmillan, Aldous Huxley, J.B. Priestley, Anthony Eden, Charles Laughton, Noel Coward, Evelyn Waugh, W.H. Auden, and Ian Fleming. These were the people who were aged 22 to 46 when the policy of appeasement was used with Hitler in 1939. Strauss and Howe note that people in the water generation are 'wishy-washy', which would explain that generation's support of this policy.

During the 1960s, the European fire (Prophet) generation were 15 to 43 years old – this is why the English were the driving force for rock and roll during these years. The American fire generation was four to 20 years old in 1960; they were 14 to 30 in 1969 when the phrase 'Don't trust anyone over 30' was popular. Nearly all of the fire generation in America had Pluto in Leo as well (1939-1956); those over 30 in 1969 had Pluto in Cancer. Many weren't old enough to be accomplished musicians during the 1960s – fortunately, this was the time when the American artist (water) generation was the earlier generation. American rock and rollers of the time were drawn from them.

## The American Generations

The American generational pattern is based on three mutually reinforcing cycles:

1) Uranus in the first ten degrees of Gemini, which happens every 84 years
2) Neptune on the cusp of Aries or Libra, which happens every 84 years
3) Pluto near one of the following fixed cusps: Taurus, Leo, or Aquarius

## Uranus in Gemini

1690–1697, Neptune enters Aries, 1697, Pluto in Leo 1692–1712
1774–1782, Neptune enters Libra, 1778, Pluto in Aquarius 1777–1798

1858–1866, Neptune enters Aries, 1861, Pluto in Taurus 1851–1883

1941–1948, Neptune enters Libra, 1942, Pluto in Leo 1937–1958

2025–2032, Neptune enters Aries, 2025, Pluto in Aquarius, 2023–2043

Each American generational cycle is started by Uranus entering Gemini, and Neptune entering either Aries or Libra. Each generation is a quarter of the 84-year cycle, which is 21 years. Uranus goes a square (90 degrees) each generation, and thus is near the start of a mutable sign when each generation starts. Neptune goes one and a half signs or a semi-square (45 degrees) each generation.

It is interesting to note that the last time the American and European generations synched up was in 1690 (1703); the next time is 2025. The generations start within a year of each other in 2025 and 2026.

Unlike the European generations, in which the crisis starts during the water generation's time, in the American pattern the crisis starts immediately when Uranus reaches the place in Gemini, and Neptune crosses the Aries or Libra cusp. For example, the Civil War started within minutes of Neptune entering Aries.

When Neptune enters Aries the crisis is internal to the USA; when it enters Libra the crisis is with external (international) enemies. The two prior Neptune-in-Aries periods were the Salem witch trials and the Civil War. The prior Neptune-in-Libra periods were the Revolutionary War and World War II.

Uranus is at the start of Gemini (air sign), Virgo (earth), Sagittarius (fire), and Pisces (water) for each of the four generations. Therefore the fire or Prophet generation has more emphasis on communicating in the American generations, which, after all, is what a prophet does. The earth generation has the doubt and survivalist qualities of Virgo, but also the organizational skills and craftiness. The air generation is mixed with the lofty enthusiasm of Sagittarius, but also the elitism. The water generation has all the artistic ability and empathy of Pisces, but suffers from the lack of will and need to conform.

The Salem witch trials were in 1692. This period from 1690 to 1697 (Uranus in Gemini) was exactly the period of the French and Indian wars between Massachusetts and French Canada, as well. These twin problems defined the crisis of the 1692 period. 1692 was exactly 84 years prior to 1776 and the Declaration of Independence.

The American generations are:

| | |
|------|------|
| Fire | 1692 |
| Earth | 1713 |
| Air | 1734 |
| Water | 1755 |
| Fire | 1776 |
| Earth | 1797 |
| Air | 1818 |
| Water | 1839 |
| Fire | 1861 |
| Earth | 1882 |
| Air | 1903 |
| Water | 1924 |
| Fire | 1942 |
| Earth | 1963 |
| Air | 1984 |
| Water | 2005 |
| Fire | 2026 |

Although the American generations intrinsically have this pattern, during the two cycles from 1692 to 1861, the generational pattern was a mixture of European with American, with the usual adjustment for what was happening astrologically. The unique pattern of the American Revolution and the prolonged splitting-off of the USA from England, intermixed with the events in Europe, led to two skewed cycles that were intermixed as well. In many cases the 21-year period was 'pushed back' to coincide with the European cycle, so fire became water, earth became fire, etc. In the 1692 cycle, however, people were born right after the crisis and so had a predisposition to fire even though they were born in a water cycle in Europe.

The American crises are typically short-lived: the Salem witch trials only lasted a year; the Civil War and World War II each were four years. However, the American Revolution lasted from 1776 to 1783, a total of seven years. The American Constitution that grounded the USA wasn't completed until 1788, so, in fairness, the crisis could be said to have lasted for 12 years.

### 1692 Fire (Water in Europe 1678–1703)
Benjamin Franklin (Jan 17, 1706)

### 1713 Fire (Fire in Europe 1703–1731)
Father Junipero Serra (Nov 24, 1713), Samuel Adams (Sep 27, 1722), George Washington (Feb 22, 1732)

### 1734 Earth (Earth in Europe 1731–1759)
Robert Morris (Jan 31, 1734), Daniel Boone (Nov 2, 1734), Paul Revere (Jan 1, 1735), John Adams (Oct 30, 1735), Patrick Henry (May 29, 1736), James Watt (1736), John Hancock (Jan 23, 1737), Thomas Paine (1737), Ethan Allen (Jan 21, 1738), Benedict Arnold (Jan 14, 1741), Thomas Jefferson (Apr 13, 1743), John Jay (Dec 12, 1745), John Hancock (1746), John Paul Jones (1747), James Madison (1751), Betsy Ross (1752)

### 1755 Air (Air in Europe 1759–1787)
Nathan Hale (1755), Aaron Burr (1756), James Monroe (1758), Noah Webster (Oct 16, 1758), John Jacob Astor (Jul 17, 1763), Eli Whitney (Dec 8, 1765), Andrew Jackson (1767), John Quincy

Adams (Jul 11, 1767), Dolly Madison (1768), DeWitt Clinton (1769), Sir Walter Scott (Aug 15, 1771), Meriwether Lewis (Aug 18, 1774)

## 1776 Water

Henry Clay (1777), Washington Irving (Apr 3, 1783), Samuel F.B. Morse (1791), Zebulon Pike (1779), Daniel Webster (Jan 18, 1782), John Calhoun (Mar 18, 1782), Zachary Taylor (Nov 24, 1784), John James Audubon (Apr 26, 1785), Davy Crockett (Aug 17, 1786), James Fenimore Cooper (Sep 15, 1789), John Tyler (Mar 29, 1790), James Buchanan (Apr 23, 1791), Sam Houston (1793)

## 1797 Fire

Nat Turner (Oct 2, 1800), Ralph Waldo Emerson (May 25, 1803), Nathaniel Hawthorne (Jul 4, 1804), William Lloyd Garrison (Dec, 1805), Robert E. Lee (Jan 19, 1807), Edgar Allan Poe (Jan 19, 1809), Jefferson Davis (1808), Abraham Lincoln (Feb 12, 1809), Harriet Beecher Stowe (Jun 14, 1811), Nathaniel Currier (1813), Henry David Thoreau (Jul 12, 1817)

Further, the American cycle was losing ground on the European cycle. The European fire generation wasn't due until 1809 and the crisis there of the French Revolution and Napoleon started in the 1790s and lasted until 1815. The result was that the post-crisis generation, the fire generation in the USA, was pushed into what is usually the earth generation, 1797 to 1818. The people who became the Transcendentalists – Emerson, Thoreau, etc. – were born in this period, as were Abraham Lincoln and Jefferson Davis, the two main politicians of the Civil War, not to mention the abolitionists such as William Lloyd Garrison and Harriet Beecher Stowe.

This made the earth generation from 1818 to 1839 double as both the earth and air generation: the earth generation since these were the people born and growing up during the transcendental awakening; the air generation since these were the people who had to step up to being the heroes of the Civil War. The fire generation had Pluto in Pisces, and Neptune in Scorpio (1792–1807), which tended to make them attuned to the power of mysticism and the intuition and, with Neptune the ruler of Pisces, in Scorpio, wanting to transform spirituality and find a mystical reality.

## 1818 Earth/Air

Frederick Douglas (1818), Walt Whitman (1819), Susan B. Anthony (Feb 15, 1820), Ulysses S. Grant (Apr 27, 1822), Stonewall Jackson (Jan 21, 1824), Levi Strauss (Feb 26, 1829), Emily Dickinson (1830), James Whistler (1834), Mark Twain (Nov 30, 1835), Winslow Homer (1836), Grover Cleveland (Mar 18, 1837), John Pierpont Morgan (Apr 17, 1837)

The earth/air generation of 1818 to 1839 had Pluto in Aries (1821–1851) and Neptune in Sagittarius that was conjunct Uranus in Capricorn (in 1821, on the cusp of Capricorn). Those born after 1834 had Neptune in Aquarius. With the Aries power driving them, this was a dynamic generation with intense personalities well aware of the forces of history and humankind. Pluto in Aries made them survivors, while Neptune conjunct Uranus in Capricorn helped them fuse the United States into truly united states – the Union, a single entity. Emerson wrote on self-reliance, a key Aries trait, while living through this period.

## 1839 Water

Thomas Nast (1840), Edison (Feb 11, 1847), Alexander Graham Bell (Mar 3, 1847), Joseph Pulitzer (Apr 10, 1847), Tiffany (1848), Wyatt Earp (Mar 19, 1848), Howard Pyle (1853), Andrew Mellon (Mar 24, 1855), Woodrow Wilson (1856), Clarence Darrow (Apr 18, 1857), Theodore Roosevelt (1858), Grandma Moses (1860)

From 1839 to 1861 was the water generation, who had to live through the Civil War as children or young soldiers. These were the inventors, idealists, and artists who thrived in the Gilded Age

(Pluto in Taurus) through the beginning of the twentieth century.

## 1861 Fire

Edith Wharton (1862), William Randolph Hearst (Apr 29, 1863), Alfred Stieglitz (1864), Frank Lloyd Wright (1867), Wilbur Wright (Apr 16, 1867), Harry Houdini (Mar 24, 1874), Robert Frost (Mar 26, 1874), Maxfield Parrish (1870), Albert Einstein (Mar 14, 1879), Douglas MacArthur (Jan 26, 1880), Max Weber (1881)

Starting in 1861, the generations were firmly onto the 84-year cycle with four 21-year generations that has lasted up to the present day. The fire generation that started in 1861 were the innovators of the twentieth century. Included in this generation were William Randolph Hearst who created the first information empire, Frank Lloyd Wright who transformed architecture by making it conform to the nature surrounding it, Wilbur Wright who invented the airplane, and Albert Einstein who transformed physics. They came of age during the Neptune-Pluto conjunct.

## 1882 Earth

Edward Hopper (1882), Rockwell Kent (1882), N.C. Wyeth (1882), Franklin Delano Roosevelt (Jan 30, 1882), Rube Goldberg (1883), Damon Runyan (1884), Chester Nimitz (Feb 24, 1885), Edna Ferber (1885), Ezra Pound (1885), Sinclair Lewis (1885), Ty Cobb (1886), Georgia O'Keefe (1887), Jim Thorpe (1888), Knute Rockne (Mar 4, 1888), George Kaufman (1888), Hubble (1889), Charlie Chaplin (Apr 16, 1889), Man Ray (1890), Eisenhower (1890), Grant Wood (1891), Compton (1892), Edna St Vincent Millay (1892), Cole Porter (1893), Norman Rockwell (1894), James Thurber (1894), Jack Benny (Feb 14, 1894), Babe Ruth (Feb 6, 1895), Buckminster Fuller (1895), J. Edgar Hoover (Jan 1, 1895), Dorothea Lange (1895), Thornton Wilder (Apr 17, 1897), Al Capone (Jan 17, 1899), Margaret Mitchell (1900), Walt Disney (1901), Ansel Adams (1902), Charles Lindbergh (Feb 4, 1902)

The earth generation of 1882 to 1903 were the core of the

twentieth century in the USA. This generation was born during the Neptune-Pluto conjunct that enhanced them. So, in terms of the cycles of US history, they were the earth generation, born into difficult times when they had to fend for themselves and survive; they would tend to have a need to accomplish things in spite of the odds. But the conjunct made them archetypical twentieth (through twenty-fourth!) century men and women. These were the generals and the US president during World War II. As is typical of earth, they were as hard on themselves as they were on others; these were not people who would cut you any slack.

## 1903 Air

Willem de Koonig (1904), Jon Gnagy (1907), Theodore Roszak (1907), Lee Krasner (1908), Lyndon Baynes Johnson (1908), Al Capp (1909), Charles Addams (1912), Ronald Reagan (1911), Jackson Pollock (1912), Richard Nixon (1913), Jimmy Hoffa (Feb 14, 1913), Frank Sinatra (Dec 12, 1915), Andrew Wyeth (1917), J.F. Kennedy (1917), Ray Harryhausen (1920)

These were the GIs, the people who fought World War II. They gave to the greater whole and, in return, they got from the greater whole through the GI bill and social security.

They had Pluto in Gemini until 1912 to 1914, after which it was in Cancer. Neptune was in Cancer until 1914 through 1916 and then was in Leo. Uranus was in Capricorn, Aquarius, and Pisces during this time. Before 1914, these were the communicators (Pluto in Gemini) with an emotional message (Neptune in Cancer); the people born after this were more intensely emotional (Pluto in Cancer) but appreciated a good time and were more expressive (Neptune in Leo). With Uranus completing the zodiac, all had a broad vision of the world.

## 1924 Water

Jimmy Carter (1924), Aman (1928), Andy Warhol (1928), Martin Luther King Jr (Jan 15, 1929), Jules Feiffer (1929), Claes

Oldenberg (1929), Gahan Wilson (1930), Yoko Ono (1933), Christo (1935), Peter Max (1937), Maya Angelou (Apr 4, 1928), Stanley Kubrick (Jul 26, 1928), Jacqueline Kennedy Onassis (Jul 28, 1929), George Steinbrenner (Jul 4, 1930), Dan Rather (Oct 31, 1931), Edward Kennedy (Feb 22, 1932), Dick Gregory (Oct 12, 1932), Gloria Steinem (Mar 25, 1934), Bill Moyers (Jun 5, 1934), Mary Tyler Moore (Dec 29, 1936), Madeleine Albright (May 15, 1937), Dustin Hoffman (Aug 8, 1937), Pat Buchanan (Nov 2, 1938), Francis Coppola (Apr 7, 1939), Smokey Robinson (Feb 19, 1940)

This group lived through World War II as children. Their parents tried to shield them from the horrors of war and the Great Depression, not always successfully. All had Pluto in Cancer with Neptune in Leo or Virgo. Uranus went through Aries and Taurus giving them a drive to be individuals, in your face individuals if necessary. However, with Neptune in Virgo for the majority of this generation, they idealize themselves as servants and try to keep a 'clean' image.

## 1942 Fire

Chevy Chase (Oct 8, 1943), Joni Mitchell (Nov 7, 1943), Diana Ross (Mar 26, 1944), Michael Douglas (Sep 25, 1944), Donald Trump (Jun 14, 1946), George W. Bush (Jul 6, 1946), David Letterman (Apr 12, 1947), Hillary Rodham Clinton (Oct 26, 1947), Andrew Lloyd Webber (Mar 22, 1948), Richard Simmons (Jul 12, 1948)

These were the children of the 1960s awakening, the 'flower children', protesters, and revolutionaries. But they were also the 'me' generation in the 1980s. All had Pluto in Leo, and Neptune in Libra. Most have Uranus in Gemini, but some have Uranus in Cancer.

## 1963 Earth

Brad Pitt (Dec 18, 1963), Sarah Jessica Parker (Mar 25, 1965),

Adam Sandler (Sep 9, 1966), Julia Roberts (Oct 28, 1967), Celine Dion (Mar 30, 1968), Tony Hawk (May 12, 1968), Barry Sanders (Jul 16, 1968), Halle Berry (Aug 14, 1968), Will Smith (Sep 25, 1968), Marilyn Manson (Jan 5, 1969), Matthew Perry (Aug 19, 1969), River Phoenix (Aug 23, 1970), Tonya Harding (Nov 12, 1970), Shawn Wayans (Jan 19, 1971), Winona Ryder (Oct 29, 1971), Penelope Cruz (Apr 28, 1974), Leonardo DiCaprio (Nov 11, 1974), Charlize Theron (Aug 7, 1975), Reese Witherspoon (Mar 22, 1976), Sarah Michelle Geller (Apr 14, 1977), Katherine Heigl (Nov 24, 1978), Clay Aiken (Nov 30, 1978), Nick Carter (Jan 28, 1980), Ben Savage (Sep 13, 1980), Elijah Wood (Jan 28, 1981)

This generation was born during the height of the 1960s and, in general, wanted no part of it. They survived the 1960s and 1970s and all the 'New Age', and continue surviving. This generation became the heart of the evangelical movement's followers ('We will survive through Christ'). Unlike the fire generation, they went to college not to find themselves, but to get a good career. These were the foot soldiers in the dotcom crash, but also for the computer and Internet rushes.

The younger members have Uranus-Pluto in Virgo and Neptune in Scorpio (1963–1969); later members have Pluto in Libra (1982), Neptune in Sagittarius (1970), and Uranus in Libra, Scorpio, or Sagittarius. The Pluto-in-Libra and Neptune-in-Sagittarius generation is much more wide-eyed and optimistic, of course, than the Pluto-in-Virgo with Neptune-in-Scorpio portion of this generation who reflect more of the difficulties of growing up as children in the 1960s.

### 1984 Air

This generation was inaugurated by Pluto entering Scorpio, and Neptune entering Capricorn. This is one tough generation! They will need to be to deal with the mid-2020 struggles. They are already honing their networking skills with the Internet, cell phones, computers, digital video, etc.

## 2004 Water

This generation is just being born as this book is being written. Although this generation technically starts in 2005, Uranus entering Pisces in 2004 will make the people born that year resonate more with the water generation.

## Chapter 8

# Generational People

This is a list of famous people's birth dates. The first section is for people born with Jupiter or Saturn in particular signs. The Jupiter people list goes with the Jupiter Generations section, and the Saturn list with the Saturn Generations section.

The second section is for Uranus, Neptune, and Pluto. To find people's Uranus, Neptune, and Pluto signs, go backwards in the listing to the first Uranus, the first Neptune, and the first Pluto you encounter. That is their placements for these three planets. For example: John Ritter (Sep 17, 1948) was born with Uranus in Cancer, Neptune in Libra, and Pluto in Leo since those are the first instance of each planet immediately preceding his name. Since Pluto can take up to 32 years per sign, you may have to go back pages to find it.

## Jupiter and Saturn People
### Jupiter People

### Jupiter in Aries

Douglas Adams, Mario Andretti, Burt Bacharach, Bonnie Blair, Tom Brokaw, Sir Richard Burton, John Cleese, Johnny Depp, Hermann Goering, Betty Grable, Marilu Henner, Paul Hogan, Helen Hunt, John Hurt, Anjelica Huston, Michael Keaton, Gina Lollabrigida, Rob Lowe, Billy Martin, Demi Moore, Jack Nicklaus, Chuck Norris, Conan O'Brien, Al Pacino, Gregory Peck, Rosie Perez, Brad Pitt, Smokey Robinson, Steven Seagal, Jane Seymour, George Bernard Shaw, Jackie Stewart, Lily Tomlin, Al Unser, Jesse Ventura, Johnny Weissmuller, Mae West, Oscar Wilde, Robin Williams, Kate Winslet, Reese Witherspoon, Tiger Woods

## Jupiter in Taurus

Ann-Margret, Charles Atlas, Dan Aykroyd, Joan Baez, Roseanne Barr, John Barrymore, Orson Bean, Pat Benatar, Jack Benny, Bob Bergland, Richard Boone, James Brolin, Joyce Brothers, Sandra Bullock, Buffalo Bill Cody, Bob Crane, Cecil B. DeMille, Placido Domingo, Faye Dunaway, Bob Dylan, Eddie Fisher, Calista Flockhart, Henry Fonda, Terry Gilliam, David Hasselhoff, Teri Hatcher, Audrey Hepburn, Jesse Jackson, Tom Jones, James Joyce, John F. Kennedy, Chaka Khan, Martin Luther King, Lenny Kravitz, Martin Landau, Bruce Lee, John Lennon, Dean Martin, Joan Miro, Liam Neeson, Ryan O'Neal, Jack Paar, Pablo Picasso, Richard Pryor, Christopher Reeve, Keanu Reeves, Norman Rockwell, Franklin D. Roosevelt, Elke Sommer, Ringo Starr, Patrick Stewart, Mao Tse-tung, Andy Warhol, Raquel Welch, Frank Zappa

## Jupiter in Gemini

Muhammad Ali, Gracie Allen, Tim Allen, Ed Asner, Jane Austen, Pearl Bailey, Ellen Barkin, Kim Basinger, Alexander Graham Bell, Clara Bow, Dick Button, Kate Capshaw, Jackie Chan, Lon Chaney, Dick Clark, Cindy Crawford, David Crosby, Sandra Dee, Charles Dickens, Phyllis Diller, Arthur Conan Doyle, Robert Duvall, Clint Eastwood, Thomas Edison, Michael Eisner, Aretha Franklin, Greta Garbo, Kahlil Gibran, Kathie Lee Gifford, Samuel Goldwyn, Martha Graham, Susan Hayward, Patty Hearst, Paul Horn, Lena Home, Aldous Huxley, Amy Irving, John Irving, Erica Jong, Grace Kelly, Hazrat Inayat Khan, Nikita Khrushchev, Carole King, Alfred Kinsey, Cyndi Lauper, Ursula LeGuin, Charles Lindbergh, Courtney Love, Myrna Loy, Imelda Marcos, Linda McCartney, Steve McQueen, Jessica Mitford, Maria Montessori, Graham Nash, Carry Nation, Bob Newhart, Jacqueline Onassis, Dorothy Parker, Dennis Quaid, Helen Reddy, Anne Rice, Theodore Roosevelt, Leon Russel, Arthur Schlesinger, Jerry Seinfeld, Brooke Shields, Alicia Silverstone, Martha

Stewart, Barbra Streisand, Mike Wallace, Barbara Walters, Oprah
Winfrey, Tammy Wynette, Glenn Yarborough, Jesse Colin Young

## Jupiter in Cancer

Kirstie Alley, Richard Alpert, Fiona Apple, Ernie Banks, James
Barrie, Melvin Belli, James Belushi, Polly Bergen, Sandra
Bernhard, Leonard Bernstein, Art Carney, Leslie Caron, Kurt
Cobain, Nat King Cole, Sean Connery, Kevin Costner, John
Cusack, James Dean, Laura Dern, Chris Evert, Harrison Ford,
Anne Francis, Annette Funicello, Jerry Garcia, Kelsey Grammer,
Gene Hackman, George Harrison, Rita Hayworth, Jimi Hendrix,
Katharine Hepburn, Janis Joplin, Frida Kahlo, Annie Lennox,
Liberace, Barry Manilow, Leonard Nimoy, Marcel Proust, Lynn
Redgrave, Adam Sandler, Martin Scorsese, William Shatner,
Patrick Swayze, Kathleen Turner, Mark Twain, Bruce Willis,
Debra Winger

## Jupiter in Leo

Eddie Albert, Don Ameche, Pamela Anderson Lee, Patricia
Arquette, Arthur Ashe, Anne Bancroft, Ray Bradbury, Bill
Bradley, Brandy, George Burns, Enrico Caruso, Johnny Cash,
Chevy Chase, John Cipollina, Harry Connick Jr, Howard Cosell,
Elvis Costello, Roger Daltry, Angela Davis, Bette Davis, Geena
Davis, Robert De Niro, John Denver, Angie Dickinson, Celine
Dion, Mike Douglas, Douglas Fairbanks Sr, Federico Fellini, F.
Scott Fitzgerald, Ian Fleming, Joe Frazier, Bill Gates, Mitzi
Gaynor, Whoopi Goldberg, Robert Goulet, Arsenio Hall, Rex
Harrison, Leona Helmsley, Hedda Hopper, Julio Iglesias, Mick
Jagger, Lyndon Johnson, Edward Kennedy, John Kerry, Nicole
Kidman, Billie Jean King, Peggy Lee, Alan Leo, George Lucas, Bill
Maher, Penny Marshall, Burgess Meredith, Ethel Merman, Joni
Mitchell, Joe Montana, Jim Morrison, Randy Newman, Peter
O'Toole, Annie Oakley, Frank Oz, Jimmy Page, Emily Post, Dan
Rather, Debbie Reynolds, Geraldo Rivera, Eleanor Roosevelt,

Diana Ross, Maria Shriver, Mira Sorvino, James Stewart, Elizabeth Taylor, Jack Webb

## Jupiter in Virgo

Loni Anderson, F. Lee Bailey, Boris Becker, Wallace Beery, Halle Berry, Janet Blair, Yasmine Bleeth, Joan Blondell, Victor Borge, James Brown, Carol Burnett, Ellen Burstyn, Michael Caine, Frank Capra, Carol Channing, Eric Clapton, Montgomery Clift, Joan Collins, Rita Coolidge, David Copperfield, Macaulay Culkin, Bo Derek, Danny DeVito, Michael Douglas, Hugh Downs, Amelia Earhart, Ralph Waldo Emerson, Nanette Fabray, Jerry Falwell, Mimi Farina, Mia Farrow, Dianne Feinstein, Carrie Fisher, Errol Flynn, John Fogarty, Dennis Franz, Steffi Graf, Dick Gregory, Tom Hanks, Anne Heche, Judy Holliday, Harry Houdini, Burl Ives, Quincy Jones, Al Jolson, Timothy Leary, Spike Lee, Meadowlark Lemon, Shari Lewis, Phil Mahre, Jayne Mansfield, Bob Marley, Joseph McCarthy, Rod McKuen, Mohammed, Carmen Miranda, Samuel F.B. Morse, Martina Navratilova, Yoko Ono, Sylvia Plath, Ezra Pound, Christina Ricci, Rob Reiner, Paul Reiser, Molly Ringwald, Joan Rivers, Julia Roberts, Gene Roddenberry, Jane Russell, Will Smith, Rod Stewart, Stephen Stills, Gene Wilder, Venus Williams

## Jupiter in Libra

Hank Aaron, Steve Allen, Jennifer Aniston, Georgio Armani, Prince, Kevin Bacon, Alec Baldwin, Brigitte Bardot, Annette Bening, Candice Bergen, Robert Blake, Bill Blass, Pat Boone, Peter Boyle, Ashleigh Brilliant, Charles Bronson, Helen Gurley Brown, Tim Burton, George W. Bush, Rory Calhoun, Naomi Campbell, Pierre Cardin, Joan Caulfield, Paul Cézanne, Marc Chagall, Richard Chamberlain, Cyd Charisse, Cher, Winston Churchill, Van Cliburn, Bill Clinton, Tim Conway, Robin Cousins, Jacques Cousteau, Robert Cummings, Doris Day, Donovan, Barbara Eden, M.C. Escher, Douglas Fairbanks Jr, Jose

Feliciano, Judy Garland, George Gershwin, Melanie Griffith, Goldie Hawn, William R. Hearst, Michael Jackson, Tommy Lee Jones, Naomi Judd, Carl Jung, Diane Keaton, Jack Kerouac, Charles Kuralt, John Lithgow, Jennifer Lopez, Bette Midler, Dan Millman, Liza Minnelli, Van Morrison, Bill Moyers, Ralph Nader, Leslie Nielsen, Nick Nolte, Drew Pearson, Michelle Pfeiffer, Gilda Radner, Ronald Reagan, Carl Reiner, Jimmy Rogers, Linda Ronstadt, George Segal, Christian Slater, Gloria Steinem, Oliver Stone, Mother Teresa, George Washington, Betty White, Flip Wilson, Henry Winkler

## Jupiter in Scorpio
Kareem Abdul-Jabbar, André Agassi, Jason Alexander, Herb Alpert, Julie Andrews, James Arness, Rosanna Arquette, Fred Astaire, Lucille Ball, Anne Baxter, Linda Blair, Humphrey Bogart, David Bowie, Charlotte Brontë, Brett Butler, James Cagney, Al Capone, Diahann Carroll, Elridge Cleaver, Glenn Close, Noel Coward, Aleister Crowley, Jamie Lee Curtis, Dalai Lama, Matt Damon, Ruby Dee, Ellen DeGeneres, Joan Didion, Patty Duke, Kirsten Dunst, Farrah Fawcett, Sally Field, Redd Foxx, Ava Gardner, Uri Geller, Danny Glover, Arlo Guthrie, Tonya Harding, Mata Hari, Jean Harlow, Emmylou Harris, Ernest Hemingway, Charlton Heston, Alfred Hitchcock, Holly Hunter, Elton John, Magic Johnson, Stephen King, Henry Kissinger, David Koresh, Queen Latifah, Charles Laughton, Jerry Lee Lewis, Jack London, Norman Mailer, Charles Manson, Rocky Marciano, Melina Mercouri, Dudley Moore, Vladimir Nabokov, Napoleon, Camilla Parker Bowles, Elvis Presley, Vincent Price, Ronald Reagan, Auguste Rodin, Ginger Rogers, Carl Sagan, Carlos Santana, Susan Sarandon, Arnold Schwarzenegger, Nicole Brown Simpson, O.J. Simpson, Britney Spears, Steven Spielberg, Danielle Steel, Sally Struthers, Donald Sutherland, Jimmy Swaggart, Peter Tchaikovsky, Uma Thurman, Jules Verne, Kurt Vonnegut, George Washington Carver, Tennessee Williams, James Wood

## Jupiter in Sagittarius

Charles Addams, Ben Affleck, Alan Alda, Woody Allen, Gregg Allman, Ursula Andress, Lauren Bacall, Kathy Bates, William Blake, Marlon Brando, George Bush, John Cage, Glen Campbell, Jimmy Carter, Maurice Chevalier, Alice Cooper, Nicolaus Copernicus, Billy Crystal, Ted Danson, Bobby Darin, Cameron Diaz, Phil Donahue, Richard Dreyfuss, T.S. Elliot, Queen Elizabeth I, Peggy Fleming, Al Gore, Tipper Gore, Phil Hartman, Sonja Henie, Barbara Hershey, Hermann Hesse, Benny Hill, Abbie Hoffman, Buddy Holly, Oliver Wendell Holmes, Dennis Hopper, Jill Ireland, Jeremy Irons, Barbara Jordan, Gene Kelly, Margot Kidder, Val Kilmer, Don Knotts, Kris Kristofferson, John Laroquette, Art Linkletter, John Madden, John McEnroe, Olivia Newton-John, Stevie Nicks, Roy Orbison, Sean Penn, Bernadette Peters, David Hyde Pierce, Robert Redford, Burt Reynolds, Knute Rockne, Hillary Rodham Clinton, Winona Ryder, Bobby Seale, Sam Shepard, Brad Steiger, Cat Stevens/Yusuf Islam, James Taylor, Danny Thomas, Henri Toulouse-Lautrec, Spencer Tracy, Steven Tyler, Tracey Ullman, Vincent Van Gogh, Gloria Vanderbilt, Dennis Weaver

## Jupiter in Capricorn

Louis Armstrong, Jim Backus, Warren Beatty, John Belushi, Yogi Berra, Bono, Abigail Breslin, Elizabeth Barrett Browning, Lenny Bruce, Art Buchwald, William F. Buckley, Richard Burton, George Carlin, David Carradine, Johnny Carson, Carlos Castaneda, Charlie Chaplin, Gary Cooper, Bill Cosby, Tony Curtis, Sammy Davis Jr, Gerard Depardieu, Walt Disney, Isadora Duncan, Shelley Duvall, Enrico Fermi, Roberta Flack, Gerald Ford, George Foreman, Connie Francis, Morgan Freeman, Clark Gable, Richard Gere, Amy Grant, Daryl Hannah, Woody Herman, Adolph Hitler, James Hoffa, Dustin Hoffman, Rock Hudson, Saddam Hussein, Samuel L. Jackson, Bruce Jenner, Waylon Jennings, Andy Kaufman, Danny Kaye, John F. Kennedy

Jr, Robert Kennedy, Rudyard Kipling, Vivien Leigh, Jack Lemmon, Charles Lindbergh, Heather Locklear, Julia Louis-Dreyfus, Shelley Long, Karl Marx, Peter Max, Margaret Mead, Mary Tyler Moore, Jack Nicholson, Richard Nixon, Gwyneth Paltrow, Tom Paxton, Suzanne Pleshette, Sylvia Porter, Bonnie Raitt, Venessa Redgrave, Carl Sandburg, Peter Sellers, Rod Serling, Red Skelton, Tom Smothers, Bruce Springsteen, Donna Summer, Loretta Swit, Margaret Thatcher, Ivana Trump, Dick Van Dyke, Gore Vidal, Sigourney Weaver, H.G. Wells, Oscar Wilde, Jane Wyman, Loretta Young, Roger Zelazny

## Jupiter in Aquarius

Ansel Adams, Horatio Alger, Susan B. Anthony, Elizabeth Arden, Tallulah Bankhead, Tyra Banks, Lionel Barrymore, Shelley Berman, Chuck Berry, Jon Bon Jovi, Tycho Brahe, Jeff Bridges, Matthew Broderick, Mel Brooks, Jerry Brown, Pat Buchanan, Karen Carpenter, Jim Carrey, Lewis Carroll, David Cassidy, Fidel Castro, Agatha Christie, George M. Cohan, John Coltraine, Jeff Conaway, Jackie Coogan, Sheryl Crow, Marie Curie, Miles Davis, Princess Diana, Albert Einstein, Dwight D. Eisenhower, Melissa Etheridge, Morgan Fairchild, W.C. Fields, Jane Fonda, Michael J. Fox, Stan Freberg, Peter Gabriel, Robin and Maurice Gibb, Allen Ginsberg, Woody Harrelson, Hugh Hefner, Thor Heyerdahl, Anthony Hopkins, William Hurt, Billy Joel, Immanuel Kant, Evel Knievel, Hedy Lamar, Dorothy Lamour, k.d. lang, Jessica Lang, Stan Laurel, Gypsy Rose Lee, Jerry Lewis, H.P. Lovecraft, Groucho Marx, Anne McCaffrey, Herman Melville, Michelangelo, Marilyn Monroe, Eddie Murphy, Bill Murray, Ogden Nash, Rosie O'Donnell, Barack Obama, Jane Pauley, Randy Quaid, Richard Rodgers, Dennis Rodman, Kenny Rogers, Martin Short, Sissy Spacek, Tori Spelling, Mark Spitz, Meryl Streep, Ed Sullivan, Ted Turner, Liv Ullmann, Jon Voight, Lindsay Wagner, Alan Watts, Walt Whitman

## Jupiter in Pisces

Paula Abdul, Louisa May Alcott, Charles Barkley, Drew Barrymore, Harry Belafonte, Ingrid Bergman, Sarah Bernhardt, Irma Bombeck, Fanny Brice, Eddie Cantor, Fritjof Capra, Mary Cassatt, Tracy Caulkins, Cesar Chavez, Claudette Colbert, Judy Collins, Francis Ford Coppola, Joan Crawford, Bing Crosby, Tom Cruise, Joan Cusack, Charles Darwin, Leonardo da Vinci, Leonardo DiCaprio, Max Ernst, Phil Everly, Jodie Foster, Sigmund Freud, David Frost, Zsa Zsa Gabor, Marvin Gaye, Arthur Godfrey, Cary Grant, Lorne Greene, Cathy Guisewite, Oliver Hardy, Billie Holiday, Bob Hope, Jean Houston, Peter Hurd, Olivia Hussey, Peter Jennings, Michael Jordan, Johannes Kepler, Alan King, Coretta Scott King, Jay Leno, Abraham Lincoln, Ray Manzarek, Henry Miller, Sal Mineo, Roger Moore, Sir Isaac Newton, Friedrich Nietzsche, Anais Nin, George Orwell, Edgar Allan Poe, Sidney Poitier, Cole Porter, Tom Poston, Diana Rigg, Will Rogers, Jerry Rubin, Kurt Russell, Ally Sheedy, Frank Sinatra, Grace Slick, Dick Smothers, Wesley Snipe, Dr Benjamin Spock, Joseph Stalin, Leopold Stokowski, J.R.R. Tolkien, Tina Turner, Booker T. Washington, Muddy Waters, Orson Welles, Stevie Wonder, Natalie Wood, Frank Lloyd Wright, Wilbur Wright, Peter Yarborough

# Saturn People

## Saturn in Aries

Eddie Albert, Don Ameche, Pamela Anderson Lee, Mario Andretti, Jennifer Aniston, Jim Bakker, Clara Barton, Boris Becker, Halle Berry, Victor Borge, Abigail Breslin, Tom Brokaw, Jerry Brown, Pat Buchanan, Sir Richard Burton, George Carlin, John Cleese, Johnnie Cochran, Judy Collins, Harry Connick Jr, Francis Ford Coppola, Bill Cosby, Bette Davis, Celine Dion, Mary Baker Eddy, Albert Einstein, Phil Everly, Douglas Fairbanks Jr, Ian Fleming, Errol Flynn, Peter Fonda, Morgan Freeman, Marvin Gaye, Barry Goldwater, Cuba Gooding Jr, Dustin Hoffman, Paul

Hogan, Jean Huston, John Hurt, Saddam Hussein, Burl Ives, Peter Jennings, Waylon Jennings, Lyndon Johnson, Ashley Judd, Helen Keller, Nicole Kidman, Evel Knievel, Carole Lombard, Douglas MacArthur, Ray Manzarek, Herman Melville, Don Meredith, Sal Mineo, Carmen Miranda, Samuel Morse, Jack Nicklaus, Florence Nightingale, Chuck Norris, Rudolph Nureyev, Richard Petty, Lisa Marie Presley, Diana Rigg, Molly Ringwald, Julia Roberts, Smokey Robinson, Kenny Rogers, Will Rogers, Jerry Rubin, Rosalind Russel, William Saroyan, Grace Slick, Anna Nicole Smith, Will Smith, Dick Smothers, Mira Sorvino, Joseph Stalin, Robert Lewis Stevenson, Jackie Stewart, Fran Tarkenton, Lee Trevino, Ted Turner, Tina Turner, Liv Ullmann, Al Unser, George Washington, Simon Wiesenthal, Cale Yarborough, Peter Yarrow, Susannah York, Roger Zelazny

## Saturn in Taurus

John Adams, Charles Addams, André Agassi, Muhammad Ali, Ann-Margret, John Jacob Astor, Jim Backus, Joan Baez, Tammy Faye Bakker, Lucille Ball, John Barrymore, Beau Bridges, James Brolin, Anita Bryant, Naomi Campbell, Lon Chaney, Julie Christie, Jacques Cousteau, David Crosby, Robert Cummings, Matt Damon, Cecil B. DeMille, Sandra Dee, Neil Diamond, Shannen Doherty, Placido Domingo, Faye Dunaway, Bob Dylan, Michael Eisner, Cass Elliot, Shelley Fabres, Alexander Fleming, Aretha Franklin, Benjamin Franklin, Art Garfunkel, Antoni Gaudi, Kahlil Gibran, Terry Gilliam, Steffi Graf, Ulysses Grant, Jean Harlow, Valerie Harper, Sonja Henie, L. Ron Hubbard, Hubert Humphrey, Jesse Jackson, Joan of Arc, Tom Jones, Erica Jong, James Joyce, Henry Kaiser, Danny Kaye, Hazrat Inayat Khan, Carole King, Queen Latifah, Bruce Lee, John Lennon, Jennifer Lopez, Bela Lugosi, Matthew McConaughey, Yvette Mimieux, Graham Nash, Wayne Newton, Richard Nixon, Ryan O'Neal, Al Pacino, River Phoenix, Pablo Picasso, Vincent Price, Richard Pryor, Ronald Reagan, Helen Reddy, Ginger Rogers, Roy

Rogers, Franklin D. Roosevelt, Pete Rose, Claudia Schiffer, Percy Bysshe Shelley, Paul Simon, Christian Slater, Ringo Starr, Martha Stewart, Patrick Stewart, Leopold Stokowski, Igor Stravinsky, Barbra Streisand, Pierre Teilhard de Chardin, Mother Teresa, Danny Thomas, Uma Thurman, Lily Tomlin, Vincent Van Gogh, Dionne Warwick, Raquel Welch, Tennessee Williams, Virginia Woolf, Tammy Wynette, Jesse Colin Young, Loretta Young, Frank Zappa

### Saturn in Gemini

Ben Affleck, Arthur Ashe, Bill Bradley, John Cage, Albert Camus, Oleg Cassini, Coco Chanel, Chevy Chase, Julia Child, Nicolaus Copernicus, Michael Crichton, Roger Daltry, Alighieri Dante, Angela Davis, Robert De Niro, Catherine Deneuve, John Denver, Cameron Diaz, Linda Evans, Bobby Fischer, Larry Flynt, Gerald Ford, Harrison Ford, Joe Frazier, Sigmund Freud, Annette Funicello, Zsa Zsa Gabor, Jerry Garcia, Newt Gingrich, Lorne Greene, George Harrison, Bob Hayes, Jimi Hendrix, Woody Herman, Billie Holiday, Hedda Hopper, Julio Iglesias, Mick Jagger, Janis Joplin, John Kerry, Jean-Claude Killy, Billie Jean King, Dorothy Lamour, Gypsy Rose Lee, Monica Lewinsky, Art Linkletter, Joe Louis, George Lucas, Barry Manilow, Penny Marshall, Thomas Merton, John Mitchell, Joni Mitchell, Harry Morgan, Jim Morrison, Mussolini, Joe Namath, Randy Newman, Oliver North, Frank Oz, Vance Packard, Jimmy Page, Thomas Paine, Gwyneth Paltrow, Joe Pesci, Sylvia Porter, Lynn Redgrave, Eleanor Roosevelt, Diana Ross, Winona Ryder, Gale Sayers, Martin Scorsese, Robert Shapiro, Red Skelton, John Phillip Sousa, Harry Truman, Lech Walesa, Christopher Walken, Booker T. Washington, Muddy Waters, Alan Watts, Orson Welles, Richard Widmark, Oscar Wilde, Brian Wilson, Jane Wyman

### Saturn in Cancer

Loni Anderson, Fatty Arbuckle, Eddie Arcaro, Honore de Balzac,

Tyra Banks, Drew Barrymore, Jeff Beck, Wallace Beery, Candice Bergen, Ingrid Bergman, Jacqueline Bisset, Richard Boone, Rita Mae Brown, Anthony Burgess, Gary Busey, George W. Bush, Cher, Eric Clapton, Ty Cobb, Jackie Coogan, Rita Coolidge, Clarence Darrow, Marquis de Sade, Olivia de Haviland, Danny DeVito, Leonardo DiCaprio, Donovan, Kirk Douglas, Sandy Duncan, Mimi Farina, Mia Farrow, John Fogarty, Dennis Franz, Betty Grable, Goldie Hawn, Thor Heyerdahl, Al Jolson, Naomi Judd, Diane Keaton, John F. Kennedy, Hedy Lamarr, John Lithgow, Bob Marley, Dean Martin, Eugene McCarthy, Michelangelo, Bette Midler, Dan Millman, Hayley Mills, Liza Minnelli, Van Morrison, Napoleon, Nostradamus, Jack Paar, George Patton, Gregory Peck, Ezra Pound, Gilda Radner, Martha Raye, Rob Reiner, Linda Ronstadt, Jonas Salk, Monica Seles, Tom Selleck, Mary Shelley, Frank Sinatra, Sylvester Stallone, Rod Stewart, Stephen Stills, Dylan Thomas, Sophie Tucker, Jules Verne, Woodrow Wilson, Henry Winkler, Neil Young

## Saturn in Leo

Kareem Abdul-Jabbar, Spiro Agnew, Duane Allman, Fiona Apple, Pearl Bailey, James Barrie, Kathy Bates, Beethoven, Irving Berlin, Leonard Bernstein, Ruben Blades, David Bowie, Tom Bradley, William Jennings Bryant, Richard Byrd, Art Carney, Florence Chadwick, Charlie Chaplin, Maurice Chevalier, Connie Chung, Bill Clinton, Hillary Rodham Clinton, Glenn Close, Jean Cocteau, Nat King Cole, Alice Cooper, Billy Crystal, Pierre Curie, Phyllis Diller, Snoop Doggy Dog, Arthur Conan Doyle, Richard Dreyfuss, Patty Duke, T.S. Eliot, Farrah Fawcett, Sally Field, Peggy Fleming, Dick Fosbury, Uri Geller, Barry Gibb, Danny Glover, Al Gore, Tipper Gore, Billy Graham, Arlo Guthrie, Barbara Hershey, Conrad Hilton, Adolph Hitler, William Holden, Lena Horne, Jeremy Irons, Thomas Jefferson, Billy Joel, Elton John, Brian Jones, Tommy Lee Jones, Stephen King, John Larroquette, Stan Laurel, Liberace, H.P. Lovecraft, Freddie

Mercury, Jessica Mitford, Thelonious Monk, Stevie Nicks, Vaslav Nijinsky, Eugene O'Neill, Annie Oakley, Camilla Parker Bowles, Eva Peron, Bernadette Peters, Jim Plunkett, Dan Quayle, Oral Roberts, Jackie Robinson, Knute Rockne, Teddy Roosevelt, Carlos Santana, Susan Sarandon, Arnold Schwarzenegger, Georges Seurat, Alicia Silverstone, O.J. Simpson, Steven Spielberg, Cat Stevens/Yusuf Islam, Oliver Stone, James Taylor, Cheryl Tiegs, Leo Tolstoy, Steven Tyler, Abigail Van Buren, Versace, Diane von Furstenberg, Mike Wallace, Casper Weinberger, Ted Williams, James Woods, Tiger Woods, Brigham Young

## Saturn in Virgo

Jane Addams, Louisa May Alcott, Horatio Alger, Johann S. Bach, John Belushi, Daniel Berrigan, Ray Bradbury, Johannes Brahms, Brandy, Fanny Brice, Jeff Bridges, Dave Brubeck, Pearl Buck, Eddie Cantor, Karen Carpenter, Lewis Carroll, Carol Channing, Agatha Christie, Montgomery Clift, Natalie Cole, Howard Cosell, Macauley Culkin, Gerard Depardieu, René Descartes, Emily Dickinson, Dore, Mike Douglas, Hugh Downs, Alexandre Dumas, Shelley Duvall, Dwight D. Eisenhower, Ralph Waldo Emerson, Nanette Fabray, Morgan Fairchild, Federico Fellini, George Foreman, Betty Friedan, Peter Gabriel, Phyllis George, Richard Gere, John Glenn, Cathy Guisewite, Phil Hartman, William Randolph Hearst, Leona Helmsley, O. Henry, Judy Holiday, Katie Holmes, Victor Hugo, William Hurt, Olivia Hussey, Anjelica Huston, Betty Hutton, Samuel L. Jackson, Bruce Jenner, Don Johnson, Andy Kaufman, Deborah Kerr, Margot Kidder, Cheryl Ladd, Timothy Leary, Peggy Lee, Jay Leno, Shelley Long, Linda Lovelace, Barbara Mandrell, Jayne Mansfield, Groucho Marx, Henry Miller, Bill Murray, Olivia Newton-John, Jane Pauley, Mary Pickford, Cole Porter, Randy Quaid, Bonnie Raitt, Basil Rathbone, Christina Ricci, Sugar Ray Robinson, Gene Roddenberry, Jane Russell, Kurt Russell, Jane

Seymour, Cybill Shepherd, Martin Short, Sissy Spacek, Mark Spitz, Bruce Springsteen, Leopold Stokowski, Meryl Streep, Donna Summer, Twiggy, Peter Ustinov, Jesse Ventura, Lindsay Wagner, George Wallace, Sigourney Weaver, Jack Webb, Mae West, Esther Williams, Robin Williams, Venus Williams, Stevie Wonder, Steve Wozniak, Whitney Young

## Saturn in Libra

Douglas Adams, Steve Allen, Tim Allen, June Allyson, James Arness, Roseanne Arnold, Charles Atlas, Jane Austen, Dan Aykroyd, Anne Baxter, Pat Benatar, Jack Benny, Bill Blass, Charles Bronson, Helen Gurley Brown, Elizabeth Barrett Browning, George Bush, Rory Calhoun, Maria Callas, Pierre Cardin, Cyd Charisse, Marcia Clark, Camille Claudel, Jackie Cooper, Leonardo da Vinci, Doris Day, Ruby Dee, Bob Dole, Kirsten Dunst, Henry Ford, Redd Foxx, Ava Gardner, Judy Garland, Crystal Gayle, Bob Geldof, J. Paul Getty, Kathie Lee Gifford, Hermann Goering, Jeff Goldblum, John Goodman, Jay Gould, Martha Graham, John Gray, Oliver Hardy, David Hasselhoff, Jessie Helms, Marilu Henner, Charlton Heston, Aldous Huxley, Amy Irving, Michael Keaton, Jack Kerouac, Chaka Khan, Nikita Khrushchev, Alfred Kinsey, Henry Kissinger, Don Knotts, Charles Lamb, Cyndi Lauper, Norman Mailer, Henry Mancini, Rocky Marciano, Dick Martin, George McGovern, Melina Mercouri, Joan Miro, Mohammed, Liam Neeson, Leslie Nielsen, Alfred Noble, Dorothy Parker, Christopher Reeve, Carl Reiner, Cathy Rigby, Edward G. Robinson, Norman Rockwell, Isabella Rossellini, Phyllis Schlafly, Britney Spears, Charles Steinmetz, Gale Storm, J.R.R. Tolkien, Toulouse-Lautrec, Arthur Treacher, Mao Tse-tung, Kurt Vonnegut, Bill Walton, George Washington Carver, Dennis Weaver, James Whistler, Betty White, Shelley Winters, William Yeats, Yogananda, Franco Zeffirelli

## Saturn in Scorpio

Kirstie Alley, Lauren Bacall, Ellen Barkin, Kim Basinger, James Belushi, Shelley Berman, Yogi Berra, Chuck Berry, Bjorn Borg, Marlon Brando, Mel Brooks, Lenny Bruce, Art Buchwald, William F. Buckley, George Burns, Richard Burton, Barbara Bush, James Cameron, Truman Capote, Frank Capra, Kate Capshaw, Johnny Carson, James Earl Carter, Fidel Castro, Jackie Chan, Cheiro, John Coltrane, David Copperfield, Elvis Costello, Kevin Costner, Marie Curie, Tony Curtis, Miles Davis, Sammy Davis Jr, John Delorean, Amelia Earhart, Empress Elizabeth, Chris Evert, William Faulkner, Arthur Fiedler, F. Scott Fitzgerald, Stan Freberg, Bill Gates, Mel Gibson, Allen Ginsberg, Johann von Goethe, Whoopi Goldberg, Kelsey Grammer, Robert Graves, Merv Griffen, Gus Grissom, Matt Groening, H.R. Haldeman, Dorothy Hamill, Tom Hanks, Warren G. Harding, Patty Hearst, Hugh Hefner, Benny Hill, J. Edgar Hoover, Rock Hudson, Lee Iacocca, Robert Kennedy, Johannes Kepler, Francis Scott Key, B.B.King, Rudyard Kipling, Angela Lansbury, Laplace, Jack Lemmon, Annie Lennox, Jerry Lewis, Martin Luther, Anne McCaffrey, Dennis Miller, Marilyn Monroe, Joe Montana, Arthur Murray, Patricia Neal, Paul Newman, Sam Peckinpah, Juan Peron, Pol Pot, Freddie Prinze, Dennis Quaid, Steve Reeves, Babe Ruth, Telly Savalas, Albert Schweitzer, Jerry Seinfeld, Peter Sellers, Rod Serling, Maria Shriver, Howard Stern, Patrick Swayze, James Thurber, Arturo Toscanini, John Travolta, Mark Twain, Leslie Uggams, Rudolph Valentino, Dick Van Dyke, Stevie Ray Vaughan, Gore Vidal, Denzel Washington, H.G. Wells, Bruce Willis, Oprah Winfrey, Debra Winger, Jonathan Winters, Frank Lloyd Wright, Wilbur Wright, Malcolm X

## Saturn in Sagittarius

Maya Angelou, Prince, Ed Asner, Fred Astaire, Burt Bacharach, Kevin Bacon, Alec Baldwin, Orson Bean, Harry Belafonte,

Annette Benning, Larry Bird, Humphrey Bogart, Irma Bombeck, Frank Borman, Tycho Brahe, Joyce Brothers, Tim Burton, Dick Button, James Cagney, Al Capone, Kit Carson, Lillian Carter, Rosalynn Carter, Paul Cézanne, Neville Chamberlain, Cesar Chavez, Frederic Chopin, Rosemary Clooney, Robin Cousins, Noel Coward, Xavier Cugat, Jamie Lee Curtis, Charles Darwin, Geena Davis, Ellen DeGeneres, Bo Derek, Phillip K. Dick, Dr Tom Dooley, Robert Duvall, M.C. Escher, Carrie Fisher, Eddie Fisher, Leon Fleischer, Anne Frank, Gandhi, James Garner, George Gershwin, Andy Gibb, Althea Gibson, Pancho Gonzales, Melanie Griffith, Che Guevara, Arsenio Hall, Linda Hamilton, Scott Hamilton, Thomas Hardy, Helen Hayes, Ernest Hemingway, Heinrich Himmler, Holly Hunter, Michael Jackson, Grace Kelly, Alan King, Coretta Scott King, Martin Luther King, Eartha Kitt, Harvey Korman, Judith Krantz, Martin Landau, Charles Laughton, Spike Lee, Ursula LeGuin, Janet Leigh, Nicolai Lenin, Abraham Lincoln, Gina Lollabrigida, James Lovell, Andie MacDowell, James Madison, Madonna, Bill Maher, Imelda Marcos, Billy Martin, Henri Matisse, Roddy McDowell, Walter Mondale, Roger Moore, Vladimir Nabokov, Martina Navratilova, Bob Newhart, Gary Oldman, Jacqueline Onassis, Patti Page, Norman V. Peale, Michelle Pfeiffer, Edgar Allan Poe, Sidney Poitier, Tom Poston, Leontyne Prince, Ernie Pyle, Ronald Reagan, Paul Reiser, Auguste Rodin, George C. Scott, Beverly Sills, Neil Simon, Sharon Stone, Gloria Swanson, Tchaikovsky, Shirley Temple Black, Paul Volker, Barbara Walters, Andy Warhol, Emile Zola

## Saturn in Capricorn

Ansel Adams, Buzz Aldrin, Jason Alexander, Richard Alpert, Marie Antoinette, Louis Armstrong, Neil Armstrong, Tai Babilonia, Anne Bancroft, Antonio Banderas, Ernie Banks, Polly Bergen, Bono, Leslie Caron, Enrico Caruso, Dick Clark, George Cloony, Sean Connery, Calvin Coolidge, Gary Cooper, James

Dean, Princess Diana, Charles Dickens, Angie Dickinson, Marlene Dietrich, Walt Disney, David Duchovny, Clint Eastwood, Nelson Eddy, Melissa Etheridge, Fabio, Enrico Fermi, Michael J. Fox, Anne Francis, Clark Gable, Mitzi Gaynor, Frank Gifford, Mikhail Gorbachev, Robert Goulet, Amy Grant, Dick Gregory, Wayne Gretzky, Bob Guccione, Gene Hackman, Jessica Hahn, Daryl Hannah, Woody Harrelson, Mariel Hemingway, Audrey Hepburn, Oliver Wendell Holmes, Paul Horn, Washington Irving, Henry James, Magic Johnson, Jim Jones, Immanuel Kant, Bob Kaufman, Edward Kennedy, Val Kilmer, David Koresh, k.d. lang, Carl Lewis, Charles A. Lindbergh, Heather Locklear, Henry Cabot Lodge, Guy Lombardo, Julia Louis-Dreyfus, Jeanette MacDonald, Willie Mays, John McEnroe, Steve McQueen, Margaret Mead, Harvey Milk, John Milton, Toni Morrison, Rupert Murdoch, Eddie Murphey, Ogden Nash, Leonard Nimoy, Barack Obama, Ross Perot, David Hyde Pierce, Sylvia Plath, Emily Post, Marcel Proust, Rasputin, Dan Rather, Richard Rogers, Dennis Rodman, Bertrand Russell, William Shatner, Willy Shoemaker, John Steinbeck, George Steinbrenner, Adlai Stevenson, Ed Sullivan, Rip Torn, Spencer Tracy, Tracey Ullman, Ethel Waters, Robert Anton Wilson, Orville Wright, Glenn Yarborough, Boris Yeltsin

### Saturn in Aquarius

Hank Aaron, Paula Abdul, Konrad Adenauer, Danny Aiello, Georgio Armani, Tracy Austin, F. Lee Bailey, Tallulah Bankhead, Brigitte Bardot, Charles Barkley, Ralph Bellamy, Edgar Bergen, Sarah Bernhardt, Otto Von Bismark, Bonnie Blair, Robert Blake, William Blake, Jon Bon Jovi, Pat Boone, Ashleigh Brilliant, Matthew Broderick, Charlotte Brontë, Garth Brooks, James Brown, Carol Burnett, Edgar Rice Burroughs, Ellen Burstyn, Lord Byron, Nicolas Cage, Michael Caine, Joseph Campbell, Jim Carrey, Johnny Cash, Richard Chamberlain, Winston Churchill, Van Cliburn, Buffalo Bill Cody, Claudette Colbert, Joan Collins,

Tim Conway, Joan Crawford, Davy Crockett, Bing Crosby, Sheryl Crow, Aleister Crowley, Tom Cruise, Joan Cusack, Miley Cyrus, Salvador Dali, Johnny Depp, Christian Dior, Jeanne Dixon, Barbara Eden, Brian Epstein, Emilio Estevez, Patrick Ewing, Jerry Falwell, Chris Farley, Dianne Feinstein, Bridget Fonda, Jodie Foster, A.J. Foyt, Anatole France, Robert Frost, Yuri Gagarin, Greta Garbo, Arthur Godfrey, Cary Grant, Joan Hackett, Teri Hatcher, Bob Hope, Harry Houdini, Whitney Houston, Howard Hughes, Helen Hunt, Quincy Jones, Michael Jordan, Carl Jung, Larry King, Charles Kuralt, Shari Lewis, Jack London, Sophia Loren, Peter Lorre, Rob Lowe, Shirley MacLaine, Thomas Mann, Jayne Mansfield, Charles Manson, Roger Maris, Rod McKuen, Elizabeth Montgomery, Demi Moore, Bill Moyers, Mozart, Ralph Nader, Carry Nation, Friedrich Nietzsche, Anais Nin, Nick Nolte, Kim Novak, Conan O'Brien, Rosie O'Donnell, Tatum O'Neal, Peter O'Toole, Omar Khayyam, Yoko Ono, George Orwell, Rosie Perez, Brad Pitt, Elvis Presley, Charley Pride, Debbie Reynolds, Ann Richards, Joan Rivers, Jimmy Rogers, Carl Sagan, Omar Sharif, Ally Sheedy, B.F. Skinner, Wesley Snipes, Dr Spock, Gertrude Stein, Gloria Steinem, Quentin Tarantino, Elizabeth Taylor, Marisa Tomei, Bobby Unser, Johnny Weissmuller, Lawrence Welk, Gene Wilder, Flip Wilson

## Saturn in Pisces

Alan Alda, Gracie Allen, Woody Allen, Herb Alpert, Ursula Andress, Julie Andrews, Susan B. Anthony, Richard Bach, Lionel Barrymore, Warren Beatty, Samuel Beckett, Alexander Graham Bell, Melvin Belli, Clara Bow, Craig Breedlove, Sandra Bullock, Glen Campbell, David Carradine, Diahann Carroll, Pablo Casals, Edgar Cayce, Wilt Chamberlain, Eldridge Cleaver, Kurt Cobain, Cindy Crawford, John Cusack, the Dalai Lama, Bobby Darin, Laura Dern, Phil Donahue, Robert Downey Jr, Isadora Duncan, Wyatt Earp, Thomas Edison, Werner Erhard, Geraldine Ferraro, W.C. Fields, Roberta Flack, Henry Fonda, Jane Fonda, Connie

Francis, Paul Gaugin, Buddy Guy, Merle Haggard, Rex Harrison, Gary Hart, Katharine Hepburn, Seymour Hersh, Hermann Hesse, Judd Hirsch, Abbie Hoffman, Buddy Holly, Anthony Hopkins, Dennis Hopper, Paul Hornung, Jill Ireland, Janet Jackson, Wynonna Judd, Frida Kahlo, Ken Kesey, Sandy Koufax, Lenny Kravitz, Kris Kristofferson, Téa Leoni, Jerry Lee Lewis, Courtney Love, Myrna Loy, John Madden, Karl Marx, Peter Max, Zubin Mehta, Burgess Meredith, Ethel Merman, Dudley Moore, Mary Tyler Moore, Sir Isaac Newton, Jack Nicholson, Sir Laurence Olivier, Aristotle Onassis, Roy Orbison, Sarah Jessica Parker, Pavarotti, Tom Paxton, Suzanne Pleshette, Robert Redford, Vanessa Redgrave, Keanu Reeves, Burt Reynolds, Robespierre, Yves Saint-Laurent, Carl Sandburg, Adam Sandler, John Paul Sartre, Antonin Scalia, Bobby Seale, Kyra Sedgwick, Charlie Sheen, Brooke Shields, Upton Sinclair, Tom Smothers, Barbara Stanwyck, Brad Steiger, Donald Sutherland, Loretta Swit, Queen Victoria, Walt Whitman

## Uranus, Neptune, and Pluto People

Pluto Aries (cycles of zodiac start with this sign): 375 BC–343 BC; 132 BC–99 BC; 112–144; 356–387; 600–633; 844– 75; 1088–1119; 1332–1363; 1578–1607; 1822–1852; 2067–2097

**Pluto Aries**: May 4, 1577 – Aug 28, 1577; Mar 19, 1578 – Oct 27, 1578; Jan 30, 1579 – Jul 7, 1606; Aug 22, 1606 – May 10, 1607; Oct 26, 1607 – Mar 28, 1608

**Pluto Taurus**: Jul 7, 1606 – Aug 22, 1606; May 10, 1607 – Oct 26, 1607; Mar 28, 1608 – Jul 9, 1638; Oct 22, 1638 – May 24, 1639; Dec 15, 1639 – Apr 10, 1640

**Pluto Gemini**: Jul 9, 1638 – Oct 22, 1638; May 24, 1639 – Dec 15, 1639; Apr 10, 1640 – Jul 24, 1668; Dec 8, 1668 – Jun 8, 1669; Feb 10, 1670 – Apr 13, 1670

**Uranus Pisces**: Mar 19, 1668 – Aug 29, 1668; Jan 10, 1669 – Jun 24,

1675; Jul 15, 1675 – Mar 19, 1676

**Pluto Cancer:** Jul 24, 1668 – Dec 8, 1668; Jun 8, 1669 – Feb 10, 1670; Apr 13, 1670 – Sep 2, 1692; Dec 30, 1692 – Jul 12, 1693; Mar 15, 1694 – May 8, 1694

**Neptune Aquarius:** Mar 1, 1670 – Jul 8, 1670; Jan 1, 1671 – Mar 3, 1684; Sep 14, 1684 – Jan 1, 1685

Addison, English essayist (May 1, 1672)

**Uranus Aries:** Jun 24, 1675 – Jul 15, 1675; Mar 19, 1676 – May 21, 1683; Oct 28, 1683 – Mar 11, 1684

**Neptune Pisces:** Mar 3, 1684 – Sep 14, 1684; Jan 1, 1685 – Apr 30, 1697; Sep 8, 1697 – Mar 1, 1698

**Uranus Taurus:** May 21, 1683 – Oct 28, 1683; Mar 11, 1684 – Jul 10, 1690; Nov 4, 1690 – Apr 28, 1691

**Pluto Leo:** Sep 2, 1692 – Dec 30, 1692; Jul 12, 1693 – Mar 15, 1694; May 8, 1694 – Oct 17, 1710

**Uranus Gemini:** Jul 10, 1690 – Nov 4, 1690; Apr 28, 1691 – Jul 31, 1697

Voltaire (Nov 21, 1694), Tiepolo, Italian painter (Mar 5, 1696), Maurice Green (Aug 12, 1696), Prevost, French novelist (Apr 1, 1697), Richard Savage, English author (1697)

**Neptune Aries:** Apr 30, 1697 – Sep 8, 1697

**Neptune Pisces:** Sep 8, 1697 – Mar 1, 1698

Canaletto, painter (Oct 28, 1697)

**Uranus Cancer:** Jul 31, 1697 – Dec 16, 1697; May 18, 1698 – Jul 31, 1704

William Hogarth, English painter (Nov 10, 1697)

**Neptune Aries:** Mar 1, 1698 – Jul 3, 1710

**Uranus Leo:** Jul 31, 1704 – Mar 11, 1705; May 3, 1705 – Sep 27, 1710

Dick Turpin, English highwayman (Sep 21, 1705), Benjamin Franklin (Jan 17, 1706), Henry Fielding, English author (Apr 22, 1707), Samuel Johnson (Sep 18, 1709)

**Pluto Virgo:** Oct 17, 1710 – Jan 19, 1711; Aug 17, 1711 – Apr 19, 1712; Jun 1, 1712 – Nov 14, 1724

**Neptune Taurus:** Jul 3, 1710 – Sep 3, 1710, Apr 22, 1711 – Dec 8, 1711, Feb 12, 1712 – Jun 11, 1724

**Uranus Virgo:** Sep 27, 1710 – Feb 23, 1711, Jul 13, 1711 – Nov 22, 1716

David Hume, Scottish philosopher, historian (Apr 26, 1711), Lemonossov, Russian chemist (Nov 8, 1711), Kitty Clive, English actress (1711), Frederick the Great (Jan 24, 1712), Rousseau (Jun 28, 1712), Fournier, French printer, engraver (1712), John Shore, trumpeteer, invented tuning fork, Soufflot, French architect (Jul 22, 1713), Diderot, French philosopher (Oct 5, 1713), Alicia Cockburn, Scottish poet (Oct 8, 1713), Laurence Sterne, English novelist (Nov 24, 1713), Father Junipero Serra (Nov 24, 1713), Gluck, German composer (Jul 2, 1714), Helvetius, French philosopher (Jan 26, 1715), De Condillac, French philosopher (Sep 30, 1715), Lancelot 'Capability' Brown, English landscape designer (1716)

**Uranus Libra:** Nov 22, 1716 – Feb 18, 1717; Sep 4, 1717 – Oct 29, 1723

Thomas Gray, English poet – 'No man is an island' (Dec 26, 1716), Empress Maria Theresa of Austria (May 13, 1717), Horace Walpole, English statesman (Sep 24, 1717), D'Alembert, French mathematician and chemist (Nov 17, 1717), Maria Agnesi, Italian mathematician and philosopher (May 16, 1718), Samuel Foote, dramatist and actor (Jan 27, 1720), Bonnet, Swiss entomologist (Mar 13, 1720), Prince Charles Stuart, 'Young Pretender' (Dec 31, 1720 ), Madame Pompadour (Dec 29, 1721), Samuel Adams (Sep 27, 1722), Joshua Reynolds, English painter (Jul 16, 1723)

**Uranus Scorpio:** Oct 29, 1723 – Jun 18, 1724; Jul 27, 1724 – Jan 9, 1730; May 4, 1730 – Oct 28, 1730

Immanuel Kant, writer, philosopher (Apr 22, 1724)

**Pluto Libra:** Nov 14, 1724 – Feb 22, 1725; Sep 9, 1725 – Dec 5, 1736

**Neptune Gemini:** Jun 11, 1724 – Dec 3, 1724; Apr 12, 1725 – Aug 6, 1737

Casanova (Apr 5, 1725), Thomas Gainsborough (May 14, 1727), Captain James Cook (Oct 27, 1728), Edmund Burke (Jan 12, 1729), Gotthold Lessing (Jan 22, 1729), Catherine the Great (Apr 21, 1729), Moses Mendelssohn, German-Jewish philosopher (Sep 6, 1729), Von Steuben, German general in American Civil War (Sep 17, 1730), Ramon de la Cruz (Mar 28, 1731), Beaumarchais, French dramatist (Jan 24, 1732), Mesmer (May 23, 1734), George Romney, English painter (Dec 15, 1734), Lagrange, mathematician (Jan 25, 1736), Coulomb, physicist (Jun 14, 1736)

**Uranus Sagittarius**: Jan 9, 1730 – May 4, 1730; Oct 28, 1730 – Jan 25, 1737

George Washington (Feb 22, 1732), Haydn (Mar 31, 1732), Robert Morris (Jan 31, 1734), Daniel Boone (Nov 2, 1734), Paul Revere (Jan 1, 1735), John Adams (Oct 30, 1735), Patrick Henry (May 29, 1736), James Watt (1736)

**Pluto Scorpio**: Dec 5, 1736 – Apr 4, 1737; Oct 1, 1737 – Dec 10, 1748; Jun 8, 1749 – Oct 6, 1749

John Hancock (Jan 23, 1737)

**Uranus Capricorn**: Jan 25, 1737 – Jun 21, 1737; Nov 16, 1737 – Mar 12, 1744; Jun 30, 1744 – Dec 31, 1744

Thomas Paine (Jan 29, 1737)

**Neptune Cancer**: Aug 6, 1737 – Dec 2, 1737

**Neptune Gemini**: Dec 2, 1737 – Jun 6, 1738

Ethan Allen (Jan 21, 1738), King George III (Jun 4, 1738)

**Neptune Cancer**: Jun 6, 1738 – Aug 2, 1751

Herschel (Nov 15, 1738), James Boswell, Scottish author (Oct 29, 1740), Benedict Arnold (Jan 14, 1741), Emperor Joseph II (Mar 13, 1741), Houdon, French sculptor (Mar 20, 1741), Thomas Jefferson (Apr 13, 1743), Cagliostro (Jun 2, 1743), Elbridge Gerry (Jul 17, 1744), De Lamarck (Aug 1, 1744), Volta (Feb 18, 1745), Benjamin Rush, US physician (Dec 24, 1745), De Goya (Mar 30, 1746), Mirabeau, Jean-Paul Marat, the Marquis de Sade,

**Uranus Aquarius:** Mar 12, 1744 – Jun 30, 1744; Dec 31, 1744 – Feb 29, 1752; Oct 3, 1752 – Dec 13, 1752

John Jay (Dec 12, 1745), John Hancock (1746), John Paul Jones (1747)

**Pluto Sagittarius:** Dec 10, 1748 – Jun 8, 1749

Laplace (Mar 28, 1749)

**Pluto Scorpio:** Jun 8, 1749 – Oct 6, 1749

Goethe (Aug 28, 1749)

**Pluto Sagittarius:** Oct 6, 1749 – Jan 7, 1762

James Madison (Mar 16, 1751)

**Neptune Leo:** Aug 2, 1751 – Feb 16, 1752; May 31, 1752 – Oct 9, 1764

Betsy Ross (Jan 1, 1752)

**Uranus Pisces:** Feb 29, 1752 – Oct 3, 1752; Dec 13, 1752 – May 13, 1759

Talleyrand (Feb 2, 1754), Alexander Hamilton (Jan 11, 1755), Nathan Hale (1755), Marie Antoinette (Nov 2, 1755), Wolfgang Amadeus Mozart (Jan 27, 1756), Aaron Burr (1756), William Blake (Nov 28, 1757), James Monroe (Apr 28, 1758), Robespierre (May 6, 1758), Noah Webster (Oct 16, 1758), Robert Burns (Jan 25, 1759)

**Uranus Aries:** May 13, 1759 – Sep 1, 1759

**Uranus Pisces:** Sep 1, 1759 – Mar 1, 1760

**Uranus Aries:** Mar 1, 1760 – May 3, 1767

**Pluto Capricorn:** Jan 7, 1762 – Jul 8, 1762

**Pluto Sagittarius:** Jul 8, 1762 – Nov 9, 1762

**Pluto Capricorn:** Nov 9, 1762 – Apr 3, 1777

John Jacob Astor (Jul 17, 1763)

**Neptune Virgo:** Oct 9, 1764 – Jan 27, 1765

**Neptune Leo:** Jan 27, 1765 – Aug 9, 1765

**Neptune Virgo:** Aug 9, 1765 – Oct 18, 1778

Robert Fulton (Nov 14, 1765), Eli Whitney (Dec 8, 1765), Malthus (Feb 14, 1766), John Dalton (Sep 6, 1766), Andrew Jackson (Mar 15, 1767)

**Uranus Taurus**: May 3, 1767 – Nov 29, 1767
John Quincy Adams (Jul 11, 1767)
**Uranus Aries**: Nov 29, 1767 – Feb 15, 1768
**Uranus Taurus**: Feb 15, 1768 – Jun 19, 1774
Dolly Madison (1768), Napoleon Bonaparte (Aug 15, 1769), DeWitt Clinton (1769), Wordsworth (Apr 7, 1770), William Clark (Aug 1, 1770), Hegel (Aug 27, 1770), Ludwig van Beethoven (Dec 16, 1770), Sir Walter Scott (Aug 15, 1771), Fourier (Apr 7, 1772), Samuel Taylor Coleridge (Oct 21, 1772), William Henry Harrison (Feb 9, 1773), Prince Metternich (May 15, 1773)
**Uranus Gemini**: Jun 19, 1774 – Dec 1, 1774
Meriwether Lewis (Aug 18, 1774), Ann Seton (Aug 28, 1774)
**Uranus Taurus**: Dec 1, 1774 – Apr 8, 1775
Ampere (Jan 20, 1775), Charles Lamb (Feb 10, 1775)
**Uranus Gemini**: Apr 8, 1775 – Jul 12, 1781
Jane Austen (Dec 16, 1775), Gauss (Apr 30, 1777)
**Pluto Aquarius**: Apr 3, 1777 – May 28, 1777
**Pluto Capricorn**: May 28, 1777 – Jan 26, 1778
H.C. Oersted (Aug 14, 1777), Henry Clay (1777)
**Pluto Aquarius**: Jan 26, 1778 – Aug 21, 1778
**Pluto Capricorn**: Aug 21, 1778 – Dec 1, 1778
**Pluto Aquarius**: Dec 1, 1778 – Apr 11, 1797
Clement Clarke Moore (Jul 15, 1779), Scott Key (Aug 1, 1779), Zebulon Pike (1779)
**Neptune Libra**: Oct 18, 1778 – Mar 25, 1779
**Neptune Virgo**: Mar 25, 1779 – Aug 20, 1779
**Neptune Libra**: Aug 20, 1779 – Nov 2, 1792
J.A.D. Ingres, painter (Aug 24, 1780), Bernhard Bolzano, Austrian mathematician (Oct 5, 1781), Daniel Webster, politician, orator (Jan 18, 1782), Paganini, composer, violinist (Oct 27, 1782)
**Uranus Cancer**: Jul 12, 1781 – Jan 12, 1782
**Uranus Gemini**: Jan 12, 1782 – Apr 28, 1782

John Calhoun (Mar 18, 1782)

**Uranus Cancer:** Apr 28, 1782 – Oct 14, 1787

Martin Van Buren (Dec 5, 1782), Washington Irving (Apr 3, 1783), Simon Bolivar (Jul 24, 1783), Peter von Cornelius, German painter (Sep 23, 1783), Zachary Taylor (Nov 24, 1784), John James Audubon (Apr 26, 1785), Oliver Perry, US naval hero (Aug 3, 1785), David Wilkie, Scottish painter (Nov 18, 1785), William Beaumont (Nov 21, 1785), Nicholas Biddle, US financier (Jan 8, 1786), Grimm, folklorist (Feb 24, 1786), Davy Crockett (Aug 17, 1786)

**Uranus Leo:** Oct 14, 1787 – Nov 28, 1787

Daguerre, photography pioneer (Nov 18, 1787)

**Uranus Cancer:** Nov 28, 1787 – Jul 14, 1788

Lord Byron (Jan 22, 1788), Schopenhauer (Feb 22, 1788)

**Uranus Leo:** Jul 14, 1788 – Sep 9, 1794

James Fenimore Cooper (Sep 15, 1789), John Tyler (Mar 29, 1790), James Buchanan (April 23, 1791), Samuel Morse (Apr 27, 1791), Charles Babbage (Dec 26, 1791), Percy Bysshe Shelley, poet (Aug 4, 1792)

**Neptune Scorpio:** Nov 2, 1792 – May 15, 1793

Lobachevsky, Russian mathematician (Dec 1, 1792), Waldmuller, painter (Jan 15, 1793)

**Neptune Libra:** May 15, 1793 – Sep 2, 1793

**Neptune Scorpio:** Sep 2, 1793 – Jan 28, 1806

Sam Houston (1793), Commodore Matthew Perry (Apr 10, 1794)

**Uranus Virgo:** Sep 9, 1794 – Mar 20, 1795

**Uranus Leo:** Mar 20, 1795 – Jun 21, 1795

**Uranus Virgo:** Jun 21, 1795 – Nov 1, 1800

John Keats (Oct 31, 1795), James K. Polk (Nov 2, 1795), Thomas Carlyle, Scottish historian (Dec 4, 1795), Franz Schubert (Jan 31, 1797), German Emperor William I (Mar 22, 1797)

**Pluto Pisces:** Apr 11, 1797 – Jul 21, 1797

**Pluto Aquarius**: Jul 21, 1797 – Feb 17, 1798

Mary Wollstonecraft Shelley (Aug 30, 1797)

**Pluto Pisces**: Feb 17, 1798 – Sep 28, 1798

Delacroix (April 26, 1798)

**Pluto Aquarius**: Sep 28, 1798 – Dec 26, 1798

**Pluto Pisces**: Dec 26, 1798 – Apr 16, 1822

Balzac (May 20, 1799), Pushkin (May 26, 1799), Millard Fillmore (Jan 7, 1800), John Brown (May 9, 1800), Nat Turner (Oct 2, 1800)

**Uranus Libra**: Nov 1, 1800 – Mar 18, 1801

Charles Goodyear (Dec 29, 1800)

**Uranus Virgo**: Mar 18, 1801 – Aug 18, 1801

William Seward (May 16, 1801)

**Uranus Libra**: Aug 18, 1801 – Jan 7, 1807

Bellini, opera composer (Nov 1, 1801), Victor Hugo (Feb 26, 1802), Waldopere (Jul 24, 1802), Alexandre Dumas (Jul 24, 1802), Ralph Waldo Emerson (May 25, 1803), Bulwer-Lytton (May 25, 1803), Joseph Paxton, English architect (Aug 3, 1803), Berlioz (Dec 11, 1803), Nathaniel Hawthorne (Jul 4, 1804), Franklin Pierce (Nov 23, 1804), Disraeli (Dec 21, 1804), Hans Christian Andersen (Apr 2, 1805), Mazzini, Italian revolutionary (Jun 22, 1805), Alexis de Tocqueville (Jul 29, 1805), Hamilton, mathematician (Aug 4, 1805), William Lloyd Garrison (Dec, 1805)

**Neptune Sagittarius**: Jan 28, 1806 – Apr 6, 1806

Elizabeth Barrett Browning (Mar 6, 1806)

**Neptune Scorpio**: Apr 6, 1806 – Nov 21, 1806

John Stuart Mill (May 20, 1806)

**Neptune Sagittarius**: Nov 21, 1806 – Jul 11, 1807

**Uranus Scorpio**: Jan 7, 1807 – Mar 4, 1807

Robert E. Lee (Jan 19, 1807 – Saturn conjunct Uranus), Henry Longfellow (Feb 27, 1807)

**Uranus Libra**: Mar 4, 1807 – Oct 13, 1807

Garibaldi (Jul 4, 1807)

**Neptune Scorpio:** Jul 11, 1807 – Sep 12, 1807

**Neptune Sagittarius:** Sep 12, 1807 – Feb 5, 1820

**Uranus Scorpio:** Oct 13, 1807 – Dec 20, 1813

Jefferson Davis (Jun 3, 1808), Andrew Johnson (Dec 29, 1808), Louis Braille (Jan 4, 1809), Edgar Allan Poe (Jan 19, 1809), Felix Mendelssohn (Feb 3, 1809), Abraham Lincoln (Feb 12, 1809), Charles Darwin (Feb 12, 1809 – born same day as Lincoln), Gogol (Mar 31, 1809), Tennyson (Aug 6, 1809), Kit Carson (Dec 24, 1809), Gladstone (Dec 29, 1809), Frederic Chopin (Feb 22, 1810), Schumann (Jun 8, 1810), P.T. Barnum (Jul 5, 1810), Bunsen (Mar 31, 1811), Harriet Beecher Stowe (Jun 14, 1811), Thackeray (Jul 18, 1811), Dupré, Franz Liszt (Oct 22, 1811), Charles Dickens (Feb 7, 1812), Robert Browning (May 7, 1812), Richard Wagner (May 22, 1813), Giuseppe Verdi (Oct 10, 1813), Nathaniel Currier (1813)

**Uranus Sagittarius:** Dec 20, 1813 – Jun 2, 1814

**Uranus Scorpio:** Jun 2, 1814 – Oct 9, 1814

**Uranus Sagittarius:** Oct 9, 1814 – Jan 6, 1821

Otto von Bismarck (Apr 1, 1815), Anthony Trollope (Apr 24, 1815), Charlotte Brontë (Apr 21, 1816), Henry David Thoreau (Jul 12, 1817), Frederick Douglas (1818), George Elliot, Karl Marx (May 5, 1818), Emily Brontë (Jul 30, 1818), Queen Victoria (May 24, 1819), Walt Whitman (May 31, 1819), Abner Doubleday (Jun 26, 1819), Herman Melville (Aug 1, 1819), Anne Brontë (Jan 17, 1820)

**Neptune Capricorn:** Feb 5, 1820 – Jun 2, 1820

William Tecumseh Sherman (Feb 8, 1820), Susan B. Anthony (Feb 15, 1820), Herbert Spencer (Apr 27, 1820), Florence Nightingale (May 12, 1820),

**Neptune Sagittarius:** Jun 2, 1820 – Dec 6, 1820

Mormons founded (1820), Friedrich Engels (Nov 28, 1820)

**Neptune Capricorn:** Dec 6, 1820 – Feb 13, 1834

**Uranus Capricorn:** Jan 6, 1821 – Jul 22, 1821

James Longstreet (Jan 8, 1821), Nathan Bedford Forrest (Jul

13, 1821), Mary Baker Eddy (Jul 16, 1821)

Sir Richard Burton (Mar 19, 1821 – Sun conjunct Pluto conjunct Jupiter and Mercury in Aries, Uranus conjunct Neptune), Mary Baker Eddy (Jul 16, 1821 – Uranus conjunct Neptune, Jupiter conjunct Saturn in Aries)

**Uranus Sagittarius**: Jul 22, 1821 – Oct 23, 1821

Helmholtz (Aug 31, 1821)

**Uranus Capricorn**: Oct 23, 1821 – Feb 18, 1828

Fyodor Dostoevsky (Nov 11, 1821 – Mercury conjunct Uranus conjunct Neptune, Jupiter conjunct Saturn in Aries), Gustave Flaubert (Dec 12, 1821), Clara Barton (Dec 25, 1821 – Sun conjunct Uranus conjunct Neptune, Jupiter conjunct Saturn in Aries), Schliemann, German archeologist (Jan 6, 1822), Rutherford B. Hayes (Oct 4, 1822), Louis Pasteur (Dec 27, 1822 – Mercury conjunct Uranus conjunct Neptune)

**Pluto Aries**: Apr 16, 1822 – Sep 19, 1822

Ulysses S. Grant (Apr 27, 1822 – Uranus-Neptune conjunct), Gregor Mendel, founder of genetics (Jul 22, 1822)

**Pluto Pisces**: Sep 19, 1822 – Mar 3, 1823

**Pluto Aries**: Mar 3, 1823 – May 20, 1851

Thomas 'Stonewall' Jackson (Jan 21, 1824), Johann Strauss (Oct 25, 1825), Gustave Moreau, French painter (Apr 6, 1826), William Holman Hunt, Pre-Raphaelite painter (Apr 2, 1827), Joseph Lister, English surgeon (Apr 5, 1827), Jules Verne (Feb 8, 1828), George Meredith, English novelist (Feb 12, 1828), Leo Tolstoy (Aug 28, 1828)

**Uranus Aquarius**: Feb 18, 1828 – Jul 31, 1828

Ibsen (Mar 20, 1828), Hippolyte Adolphe Taine, French thinker and historian (Apr 21, 1828), Jean Henri Dumont, Red Cross founder (May 8, 1828), Dante Gabriel Rossetti (May 12, 1828)

**Uranus Capricorn**: Jul 31, 1828 – Dec 10, 1828

**Uranus Aquarius**: Dec 10, 1828 – Apr 29, 1835

Levi Strauss (Feb 26, 1829), Louis Gottschalk, American painter/composer (May 8 1829), Cantor, mathematician (Aug

23, 1829), Chester A. Arthur (Oct 5, 1829), Anton Rubinstein, Russian painter/composer (Nov 28, 1829), Camille Pissarro, painter (Jul 10, 1830), Alfred Waterhouse, architect, among first to use structural ironwork (Jul 19, 1830), Francis Joseph I (Aug 18, 1830), Porfiro Diaz (Sep 15, 1830), Belva Lockwood, American lawyer, first woman before Supreme Court, nominated for US president (Oct 24, 1830), Emily Dickinson (Dec 10, 1830), Lord Leighton (Dec 31, 1830), Foreign Legion founded (Mar 9, 1831), Madame Blavatsky (Aug 12, 1831), James Clerk Maxwell, physicist who discovered laws of electricity (Nov 13, 1831), James Garfield (Nov 19, 1831), Gustave Dore (Jan 6, 1832), Horatio Alger (Jan 13, 1832), Edouard Manet (Jan 23, 1832), Lewis Carroll (Jan 27, 1832), Sir William Crookes, chemist (Jun 17, 1832), Louisa May Alcott (Nov 29, 1832), Chinese Gordon (Jan 28, 1833), Johannes Brahms (May 7, 1833), Benjamin Harrison (Aug 20, 1833), Edward Burne-Jones, Pre-Raphaelite English painter (Aug 28, 1833), Alfred Nobel (Oct 21, 1833), Edwin Booth (Nov 13, 1833), John Singleton Mosby (Dec 6, 1833)

**Neptune Aquarius**: Feb 13, 1834 – Jul 31, 1834

William Morris (Mar 24, 1834), Bartholdi, sculptor of Statue of Liberty (Apr 2, 1834), James Whistler (Jul 11, 1834), Edgar Degas (Jul 19, 1834)

**Neptune Aquarius**: Jul 31, 1834 – Dec 17, 1834

**Neptune Aquarius**: Dec 17, 1834 – Apr 26, 1847

**Uranus Pisces**: Apr 29, 1835 – Jul 13, 1835

**Uranus Pisces**: Jul 13, 1835 – Feb 11, 1836

Mark Twain (Nov 30, 1835), Samuel Butler (Dec 4, 1835), Sir Lawrence Alma-Tadema (Jan 8, 1836)

**Uranus Pisces**: Feb 11, 1836 – Apr 20, 1843

Ramakrishna (Feb 18, 1836), Winslow Homer (Feb 24, 1836), Bret Harte (Aug 25, 1836), William Gilbert (Nov 18, 1836), Grover Cleveland (Mar 18, 1837), John Pierpont Morgan (April 17, 1837), Wild Bill Hickok (May 27, 1837), Sitting Bull

(1837), Charles 'Tom Thumb' Stratton (Jan 4, 1838), John Muir (Apr 21, 1838), Georges Bizet (Oct 25, 1838), Paul Cézanne (Jan 19, 1839), Modest Mussorgsky (Mar 21, 1839), John D. Rockefeller (Jul 8, 1839), George Armstrong Custer (Dec 5, 1839), Emile Zola (April 2, 1840), Peter Ilyich Tchaikovsky (Apr 25, 1840), Auguste Rodin (Nov 12, 1840), Claude Monet (Nov 14, 1840), Thomas Nast (1840), Pierre Auguste Renoir (Feb 25, 1841), Oliver Wendell Holmes (Mar 8, 1841), William James (Jan 11, 1842), Arthur Sullivan (May 13, 1842), Ambrose Bierce (Jun 24, 1842), William McKinley (Jan 29, 1843), Henry James (Apr 15, 1843)

**Uranus Aries**: Apr 20, 1843 – Oct 1, 1843

**Uranus Pisces**: Oct 1, 1843 – Feb 10, 1844

**Uranus Aries**: Feb 10, 1844 – Jul 8, 1850

Anatole France (April 16, 1844), Mary Cassat (May 22, 1844), Henry John Heinz (Oct 11, 1844), Nietzsche (Oct 15, 1844), Sarah Bernhardt (Oct 22, 1844), William 'Buffalo Bill' Cody (Feb 26, 1846), George Westinghouse (Oct 6, 1846), Carry Nation (Nov 25, 1846), Thomas Alva Edison (Feb 11, 1847), Alexander Graham Bell (Mar 3, 1847), Joseph Pulitzer (Apr 10, 1847)

**Neptune Pisces**: Apr 26, 1847 – Jul 11, 1847

**Neptune Aquarius**: Jul 11, 1847 – Feb 17, 1848

Jesse James (Sep 5, 1847)

**Neptune Pisces**: Feb 17, 1848 – Oct 15, 1848

Louis Comfort Tiffany (Feb 18, 1848), Wyatt Earp (Mar 19, 1848), Paul Gauguin (Jun 7, 1848 – Uranus conjunct Pluto)

**Neptune Aquarius**: Oct 15, 1848 – Dec 6, 1848

**Neptune Pisces**: Dec 6, 1848 – Apr 13, 1861

Luther Burbank (Mar 7, 1849), Ivan Pavlov (Sep 26, 1849)

**Uranus Taurus**: Jul 8, 1850 – Sep 3, 1850

**Uranus Taurus**: Sep 3, 1850 – Apr 15, 1851

Robert Louis Stevenson (Nov 13, 1850 – Uranus conjunct Pluto)

**Uranus Taurus:** Apr 15, 1851 – Jun 2, 1858
**Pluto Taurus:** May 20, 1851 – Oct 14, 1851
**Pluto Aries:** Oct 14, 1851 – Apr 7, 1852
**Pluto Taurus:** Apr 7, 1852 – Dec 12, 1852
**Pluto Aries:** Dec 12, 1852 – Feb 14, 1853
André Michelin (Jan 16, 1853), José Marti (Jan 28, 1853)
**Pluto Taurus:** Feb 14, 1853 – Jul 21, 1882
Van Gogh (Mar 30, 1853 – Uranus conjunct Pluto), Bat Masterson (Nov 24, 1853), C.W. Leadbetter (Feb 16, 1854), Oscar Wilde (Oct 16, 1854), Arthur Rimbaud (Oct 20, 1854), John Philip Sousa (Nov 6, 1854), Percival Lowell (Mar 13, 1855), Dr Daniel Hale Williams (Jan 18, 1856), Booker T. Washington (Apr 5, 1856), L. Frank Baum, writer of stories about strange lands (May 5, 1856 – Sun conjunct Uranus, Venus conjunct Pluto), Sigmund Freud (May 6, 1856 – Sun conjunct Uranus), Robert E. Peary (May 6, 1856), Nicola Tesla (Jul 9, 1856), George Bernard Shaw, writer with quick, earthy wit (Jul 26, 1856 – Moon conjunct Uranus), Louis Brandeis (Nov 13, 1856), Woodrow Wilson (Dec 28, 1856), Lord Baden-Powell (Feb 22, 1857), Clarence Darrow (Apr 18, 1857), Sir Edward Elgar (Jun 2, 1857), William H. Taft (Sep 15, 1857), Joseph Conrad (Dec 3, 1857),
**Uranus Gemini:** Jun 2, 1858 – Jan 1, 1859
Teddy Roosevelt, conservationist, revolution through land management (Oct 27, 1858)
**Uranus Taurus:** Jan 1, 1859 – Mar 14, 1859
Kaiser William II (Jan 27, 1859), Sholem Aleichem (Feb 18, 1859)
**Uranus Gemini:** Mar 14, 1859 – Jun 27, 1865
Pierre Curie (May 15, 1859), Sir Arthur Conan Doyle (May 22, 1859), John Dewey (Oct 20, 1859), Billy the Kid (Nov 23, 1859), Georges Seurat (Dec 2, 1859 – Sun conjunct Uranus), Chekhov (Jan 29, 1860), Herman Hollerith (Feb 29, 1860), James Barrie (May 9, 1860), Mahler (Jul 7, 1860), Lizzie Borden (Jul 19,

1860), Annie Oakley (Aug 13, 1860), Grandma Moses (Sep 7, 1860), John J. Pershing (Sep 13, 1860), Juliette Low (Oct 31, 1860), Rudolph Steiner (Feb 25, 1861)

**Neptune Aries:** Apr 13, 1861 – Oct 1, 1861

**Neptune Pisces:** Oct 1, 1861 – Feb 14, 1862

James Naismith (Nov 6, 1861), Edith Wharton (Jan 24, 1862)

**Neptune Aries:** Feb 14, 1862 – Jun 8, 1874

Debussy (Aug 22, 1862), O. Henry (Sep 11, 1862), Vivekanada (Jan 12, 1863), William Randolph Hearst (April 29, 1863 – Sun conjunct Pluto, Venus conjunct Uranus), Henry Ford (Jul 30, 1863), Alfred Stieglitz (Jan 1, 1864), Richard Strauss (Jun 11, 1864), Toulouse-Lautrec (Nov 24, 1864), William Butler Yeats (Jun 13, 1865 – Sun conjunct Uranus, Venus conjunct Pluto)

**Uranus Cancer:** Jun 27, 1865 – Feb 17, 1866

Rudyard Kipling (Dec 30, 1865 – Uranus conjunct ascendant)

**Uranus Gemini:** Feb 17, 1866 – Mar 27, 1866

**Uranus Cancer:** Mar 27, 1866 – Sep 14, 1871

H.G. Wells (Sep 21, 1866 – Mars conjunct Uranus), Wilbur and Orville Wright (Wilbur: Apr 16, 1867), Frank Lloyd Wright (Jun 8, 1867), Marie Curie (Nov 7, 1867), Gandhi (Oct 2, 1869), Matisse (Dec 31, 1869), Lenin (April 22, 1870), Maxfield Parrish (Jul 25, 1870), Proust (Jul 10, 1871 – Sun conjunct Uranus)

**Uranus Leo:** Sep 14, 1871 – Dec 31, 1871

Stephen Crane (Nov 1, 1871)

**Uranus Cancer:** Dec 31, 1871 – Jun 29, 1872

**Uranus Leo:** Jun 29, 1872 – Aug 25, 1878

Beardsley (Aug 21, 1872), Emily Post (Oct 27, 1872), Gertrude Stein (Feb 3, 1874), Harry Houdini (Mar 24, 1874), Robert Frost (Mar 26, 1874)

**Neptune Taurus:** Jun 8, 1874 – Sep 30, 1874

Herbert Hoover (Aug 10, 1874 – Sun conjunct Uranus)

**Neptune Aries:** Sep 30, 1874 – Apr 7, 1875

Churchill (Nov 30, 1874), Schweitzer (Jan 14, 1875), D.W. Griffith

(Jan 22, 1875), Ravel (Mar 7, 1875)

**Neptune Taurus:** Apr 7, 1875 – Aug 16, 1887

Edgar Rice Burroughs (Sep 1, 1875), Rilke (Dec 4, 1875), Jack London (Jan 12, 1876), Mata Hari (Aug 7, 1876 – Mars conjunct Uranus), Willa Cather (Dec 7, 1873), Pablo Casals (Dec 29, 1876), Edgar Cayce (Mar 18, 1877), Isadora Duncan (May 26, 1877), Hermann Hesse (Jul 2, 1877), Carl Sandburg (Jan 6, 1878), Martin Buber (Feb 8, 1878)

**Uranus Virgo:** Aug 25, 1878 – Oct 14, 1884

Upton Sinclair (Sep 20, 1878), E.M. Forester (Jan 1, 1879), Albert Einstein (Mar 14, 1879), Ethel Barrymore (Aug 15, 1879), Will Rogers (Nov 4, 1879), Trotsky (Nov 7, 1879), Klee (Dec 18, 1879), Stalin (Dec 21, 1879), Mac Sennett (Jan 17, 1880), Douglas MacArthur (Jan 26, 1880), W.C. Fields (Jan 29, 1880), Alice Bailey (Jun 16, 1880), Helen Keller (Jun 27, 1880), Cecil B. DeMille (Aug 12, 1881), Picasso (Oct 25, 1881), Max Weber (1881), A.A. Milne (Jan 18, 1882), Virginia Wolfe (Jan 25, 1882), Franklin Delano Roosevelt (Jan 30, 1882), James Joyce (Feb 2, 1882), John Barrymore (Feb 15, 1882), Leopold Stokowski (Apr 18, 1882), Stravinski (Jun 17, 1882), Rockwell Kent (Jun 21, 1882)

**Pluto Gemini:** Jul 21, 1882 – Oct 9, 1882

Edward Hopper (Jul 22, 1882), Samuel Goldwyn (Aug 27, 1882)

**Pluto Taurus:** Oct 9, 1882 – Jun 2, 1883

N.C. Wyeth (Oct 22, 1882), Lon Chaney (Apr 1, 1883), Douglas Fairbanks (May 23, 1883)

**Pluto Gemini:** Jun 2, 1883 – Dec 4, 1883

Franz Kafka (Jul 3, 1883), Rube Goldberg (Jul 4, 1883)

**Pluto Taurus:** Dec 4, 1883 – Apr 19, 1884

**Pluto Gemini:** Apr 19, 1884 – Sep 10, 1912

Harry Truman (May 8, 1884), Damon Runyan (Oct 4, 1884), Eleanor Roosevelt (Oct 11, 1884)

**Uranus Libra:** Oct 14, 1884 – Apr 11, 1885

Sinclair Lewis (Feb 7, 1885), Chester Nimitz (February 24, 1885)

**Uranus Virgo**: Apr 11, 1885 – Jul 29, 1885

**Uranus Libra**: Jul 29, 1885 – Dec 10, 1890

D.H. Lawrence (Sep 11, 1885), Niels Bohr (Oct 7, 1885), Ezra Pound (Oct 30, 1885), George Patten (Nov 11, 1885), David Ben-Gurion (Oct 16, 1886), Ed Wynn (Nov 9, 1886), Ty Cobb (Dec 18, 1886), Artur Rubinstein (Jan 28, 1887), Fatty Arbuckle (Mar 24, 1887), Chagall (Jul 7, 1887), Edna Ferber (Aug 15, 1887)

**Neptune Gemini**: Aug 16, 1887 – Sep 20, 1887

**Neptune Taurus**: Sep 20, 1887 – May 26, 1888

Chiang Kai-shek (Oct 31, 1887), Georgia O'Keefe (Nov 15, 1887), Boris Karloff (Nov 23, 1887), John Foster Dulles (Feb 25, 1888), Knute Rockne (Mar 4, 1888), Irving Berlin (May 11, 1888)

**Neptune Gemini**: May 26, 1888 – Dec 27, 1888

Jim Thorpe (May 28, 1888), Joe Kennedy (Sep 6, 1888), Maurice Chevalier (Sep 12, 1888), Eugene O'Neill (Oct 16, 1888), Harpo Marx (Nov 23, 1888)

**Neptune Taurus**: Dec 27, 1888 – Mar 22, 1889

**Neptune Gemini**: Mar 22, 1889 – Jul 19, 1901

Arnold Toynbee (Apr 14, 1889), Charlie Chaplin (April 16, 1889), Adolph Hitler (Apr 20, 1889), Jean Cocteau (Jul 5, 1889), Erle Stanley Gardner (Jul 17, 1889), Walter Lippman (Sep 23, 1889), Nehru (Nov 14, 1889), George Kaufman (Nov 16, 1889), Hubble (Nov 29, 1889), Nijinsky (Mar 12, 1890), Ho Chi Minh (May 19, 1890), Hedda Hopper (Jun 2, 1890), Stan Laurel (Jun 16, 1890), Groucho Marx (Oct 2, 1890), Eisenhower (Oct 14, 1890), De Gaulle (Nov 22, 1890)

**Uranus Scorpio**: Dec 10, 1890 – Apr 5, 1891

Ronald Colman (Feb 9, 1891), David Sarnoff (Feb 27, 1891)

**Uranus Libra**: Apr 5, 1891 – Sep 26, 1891

Cole Porter (Jun 9, 1891)

**Uranus Scorpio:** Sep 26, 1891 – Dec 2, 1897

Fanny Brice (Oct 29, 1891), Henry Miller (Dec 26, 1891 – Uranus conjunct Moon and Mars), J.R.R. Tolkien (Jan 3, 1892), Hal Roach (Jan 14, 1892), Oliver Hardy (Jan 18, 1892), Grant Wood (Feb 13, 1892), Lowell Thomas (Apr 6, 1892), Baron Von Richthofen (May 2, 1892), Cole Porter (Jun 9, 1892), Basil Rathbone (Jun 13, 1892), Pearl S. Buck (Jun 26, 1892), Mae West (Aug 17, 1892), Leo G. Carroll (Oct 25, 1892), Francisco Franco (Dec 4, 1892), J. Paul Getty (Dec 15, 1892), Jimmy Durante (Feb 10, 1893), Andres Segovia (Feb 21, 1893), Mary Pickford (Apr 8, 1893), Harold Lloyd (Apr 20, 1893), Edna St Vincent Millay (1892), Joan Miro (Apr 20, 1893), Cole Porter (1893), Karl Menninger (Jul 23, 1893), Mae West (Aug 17, 1893), Dorothy Parker (Aug 22, 1893), Spring Byington (Oct 17, 1893), Gummo Marx (Oct 23, 1893), Charles Atlas (Oct 30, 1893 – Sun conjunct Uranus), Edward G. Robinson (Dec 12, 1893), Robert Ripley (Dec 25, 1893), Mao Tse-tung (Dec 26, 1893), Norman Rockwell (Feb 3, 1894), Jack Benny (Feb 14, 1894), Bessie Smith (Apr 15, 1894), Nikita Khrushchev (Apr 17, 1894), Martha Graham (May 11, 1894), Dashiell Hammett (May 27, 1894), Fred Allen (May 31, 1894), Edward VIII, King of England (Jun 23, 1894), Alfred Kinsey (Jun 23, 1894), Arthur Treacher (Jul 23, 1894), Walter Brennan (Jul 25, 1894), Aldous Huxley (Jul 26, 1894), e.e. cummings (Oct 14, 1894), Brooks Atkinson (Nov 28, 1894), James Thurber (Dec 8, 1894), Arthur Fiedler (Dec 17, 1894), J. Edgar Hoover (Jan 1, 1895), John Ford (Feb 1, 1895), Babe Ruth (Feb 6, 1895), Shemp Howard (Mar 17, 1895), Arthur Murray (Apr 4, 1895), Rudolph Valentino (May 6, 1895), Bishop Fulton Sheen (May 8, 1895), Velikovsky (Jun 10, 1895), Jack Dempsey (Jun 24, 1895), R. Buckminster Fuller (Jul 12, 1895), Oscar Hammerstein II (Jul 12, 1895), George 'Machine Gun' Kelly (Jul 18, 1895), Bert Lahr (Aug 13, 1895), Bud Abbott (Oct 2, 1895), Buster Keaton (Oct 4, 1895), Juan Peron (Oct 8, 1895),

Busby Berkeley (Nov 29, 1895), George Burns (Jan 20, 1896), William Wellman (Feb 29, 1896), Wallis Simpson (Jun 19, 1896), Jean Piaget (Aug 9, 1896), Raymond Massey (Aug 30, 1896), F. Scott Fitzgerald (Sep 24, 1896), Lillian Gish (Oct 14, 1896), Ruth Gordon (Oct 30, 1896), Ethel Waters (Oct 31, 1896), Ira Gershwin (Dec 6, 1896), Marion Davies (Jan 3, 1897), Marian Anderson (Feb 27, 1897), Walter Winchell (Apr 7, 1897), Frank Capra (May 18, 1897), Moe Howard (Jun 19, 1897), Walter Pidgeon (Sep 23, 1897), William Faulkner (Sep 25, 1897), Cyril Ritchard (Dec 1, 1897)

**Uranus Sagittarius**: Dec 2, 1897 – Jul 3, 1898

Zasu Pitts (Jan 3, 1898), Gracie Fields (Jan 9, 1898), Bertolt Brecht (Feb 10, 1898), Paul Robeson (Apr 9, 1898), Golda Meir (May 3, 1898), Bennett Cerf (May 25, 1898), Norman Vincent Peale (May 31, 1898), M.C. Escher (Jun 17, 1898)

**Uranus Scorpio**: Jul 3, 1898 – Sep 11, 1898

Alexander Calder (Jul 22, 1898), Amelia Earhart (Jul 24, 1898), Preston Sturges (Aug 29, 1898), Shirley Booth (Aug 30, 1898)

**Uranus Sagittarius**: Sep 11, 1898 – Dec 20, 1904

George Gershwin (Sep 26, 1898), René Magritte (Nov 21, 1898), C.S. Lewis (Nov 29, 1898), Emmett Kelly (Dec 9, 1898), Irene Dunne (Dec 20, 1898), Al Capone (Jan 17, 1899), Gloria Swanson (Mar 27, 1899), August Anheuser Busch Jr (Mar 28, 1899), Vladimir Nabokov (Apr 23, 1899), Duke Ellington (Apr 29, 1899), Fred Astaire (May 10, 1899), Chief Dan George (Jun 24, 1899), Charles Laughton (Jul 1, 1899), E.B. White (Jul 11, 1899), James Cagney (Jul 17, 1899), Ernest Hemingway (Jul 21, 1899), Alfred Hitchcock (Aug 13, 1899), Charles Boyer (Aug 28, 1899), Bruce Catton (Oct 9, 1899), Pat O'Brien (Nov 11, 1899), Eugene Ormandy (Nov 18, 1899), Hoagy Carmichael (Nov 22, 1899), Noel Coward (Dec 16, 1899), Humphrey Bogart (Dec 25, 1899), Xavier Cugat (Jan 1, 1900), Adlai E. Stevenson Jr (Feb 5, 1900), Luis Buñuel (Feb 22, 1900), Spencer Tracy (Apr 5, 1900), Antoine de Saint-Exupéry (Jun 29, 1900),

Zelda Fitzgerald (Jul 24, 1900), Elizabeth, the Queen Mother (Aug 4, 1900), Claude Pepper (Sep 8, 1900), Helen Hayes (Oct 10, 1900), Lotte Lenya (Oct 18, 1900), Margaret Mitchell (Nov 8, 1900), Aaron Copland (Nov 14, 1900), Clark Gable (Feb 1, 1901), Zeppo Marx (Feb 25, 1901), Linus Pauling (Feb 28, 1901), Gary Cooper (May 7, 1901)

**Neptune Cancer:** Jul 19, 1901 – Dec 25, 1901

Rudy Vallee (Jul 28, 1901), Louis Armstrong (Aug 4, 1901), Ben Blue (Sep 12, 1901), Ed Sullivan (Sep 28, 1901), Paul Ford (Nov 2, 1901), Lee Strasberg (Nov 17, 1901), Walt Disney (Dec 5, 1901 – Sun conjunct Uranus and opposed Pluto), Margaret Mead (Dec 16, 1901)

**Neptune Gemini:** Dec 25, 1901 – May 21, 1902

Marlene Dietrich (Dec 27, 1901), Langston Hughes (Feb 1, 1902), Charles Lindbergh (Feb 4, 1902), Lyle Talbot (Feb 8, 1902), Ansel Adams (Feb 20, 1902), John Steinbeck (Feb 27, 1902), Bobby Jones (Mar 17, 1902), David O. Selznick (May 10, 1902), Ayatollah Khomeini (May 17, 1902)

**Neptune Cancer:** May 21, 1902 – Sep 23, 1914

Guy Lombardo (Jun 19, 1902), John Dillinger (Jun 28, 1902), Richard Rodgers (Jun 28, 1902 – Sun conjunct Neptune on ascendant), George Murphy (Jul 4, 1902), Gracie Allen (Jul 26, 1902), Ogden Nash (Aug 19, 1902), Ansel Adams (1902), Larry Fine (Oct 5, 1902), Ray Kroc (Oct 5, 1902), Strom Thurmond (Dec 5, 1902), Margaret Hamilton (Dec 9, 1902), Ralph Richardson (Dec 19, 1902), Edgar Bergen (Feb 16, 1903), Anais Nin (Feb 21, 1903), Bix Beiderbecke (Mar 10, 1903), Lawrence Welk (Mar 11, 1903), Ward Bond (Apr 9, 1903), Dr Benjamin Spock (May 2, 1903), Bing Crosby (May 3, 1903), Bob Hope (May 29, 1903), Jeanette MacDonald (Jun 18, 1903), Lou Gehrig (Jun 19, 1903), Al Hirschfeld (Jun 21, 1903), George Orwell (Jun 25, 1903), Louis Leakey (Aug 7, 1903), Arthur Godfrey (Aug 31, 1903), Claudette Colbert (Sep 13, 1903), Roy Acuff (Sep 15, 1903), Vladimir Horowitz (Oct 1, 1903), Curly

Howard (Oct 22, 1903), Dean Jagger (Nov 7, 1903), Sally Rand (Jan 2, 1904), George Balanchine (Jan 9, 1904), Ray Bolger (Jan 10, 1904), Cary Grant (Jan 18, 1904), S.J. Perelman (Feb 1, 1904), Ted Mack (Feb 12, 1904), Adelle Davis (Feb 25, 1904), Jimmy Dorsey (Feb 29, 1904), Glenn Miller (Mar 1, 1904), Dr Seuss (Mar 2, 1904), B.F. Skinner (Mar 20, 1904), Joan Crawford (Mar 23, 1904), Joseph Campbell (Mar 26, 1904), John Gielgud (Apr 14, 1904), Salvador Dali (May 11, 1904), Fats Waller (May 21, 1904), Johnny Weissmuller (Jun 2, 1904), Dr Charles Drew (Jun 3, 1904), Frederick Loewe (Jun 10, 1904), Ralph Bellamy (Jun 17, 1904), Peter Lorre (Jun 26, 1904), Pablo Neruda (Jul 12, 1904), Ralph Bunche (Aug 7, 1904), Count Basie (Aug 21, 1904), Deng Xiaoping (Aug 22, 1904), Christopher Isherwood (Aug 26, 1904), Moss Hart (Oct 24, 1904), Alger Hiss (Nov 11, 1904), Dick Powell (Nov 14, 1904)

**Uranus Capricorn**: Dec 20, 1904 – Jan 30, 1912

Ray Milland (Jan 3, 1905), Sterling Holloway (Jan 4, 1905), Tex Ritter (Jan 12, 1905), Ayn Rand (Feb 2, 1905), Lon Chaney Jr (Feb 10, 1905), Philip Ahn (Mar 29, 1905), Joseph Cotten (May 15, 1905), Henry Fonda (May 16, 1905), Jean-Paul Sartre (Jun 21, 1905), Dag Hammarskjold (Jul 29, 1905), Myrna Loy (Aug 2, 1905), Clara Bow (Aug 25, 1905), Eddie 'Rochester' Anderson (Sep 18, 1905), Greta Garbo (Sep 18, 1905), Andy Devine (Oct 7, 1905), Jean Arthur (Oct 17, 1905), Joel McCrea (Nov 5, 1905), Tommy Dorsey (Nov 19, 1905), Howard Hughes (Dec 24, 1905 – Sun conjunct Uranus), Cliff Arquette (Dec 28, 1905), Earl 'Fatha' Hines (Dec 28, 1905), William Bendix (Jan 14, 1906), Aristotle Onassis (Jan 15, 1906), Gale Gordon (Feb 2, 1906), Clyde W. Tombaugh (Feb 4, 1906), Lou Costello (Mar 6, 1906), Henny Youngman (Mar 16, 1906), Ozzie Nelson (Mar 20, 1906), John Cameron Swayze (Apr 4, 1906), Samuel Beckett (Apr 13, 1906), Josephine Baker (Jun 3, 1906), Billy Wilder (Jun 22, 1906), John Huston (Aug 5, 1906), Dmitri Shostakovich (Sep 25, 1906), Otto Preminger (Dec 5, 1906), Agnes

Moorehead (Dec 6, 1906), Leonid Brezhnev (Dec 12, 1906), Oscar Levant (Dec 27, 1906), James Michener (Feb 3, 1907), Cesar Romero (Feb 15, 1907), Sheldon Leonard (Feb 22, 1907), Robert Young (Feb 22, 1907), Earl Scheib (Feb 28, 1907), Katharine Hepburn (May 12, 1907), Sir Laurence Olivier (May 22, 1907), John Wayne (May 26, 1907), Rosalind Russell (Jun 4, 1907), Barbara Stanwyck (Jul 16, 1907), Melvin Belli (Jul 29, 1907), Fay Wray (Sep 15, 1907), Gene Autry (Sep 29, 1907), Cab Calloway (Dec 25, 1907), George Dolenz (Jan 5, 1908), Larry 'Buster' Crabbe (Feb 7, 1908), Red Barber (Feb 17, 1908), John Mills (Feb 22, 1908), Rex Harrison (Mar 5, 1908), Louis L'Amour (Mar 22, 1908), Abraham Maslow (Apr 1, 1908), Buddy Ebsen (Apr 2, 1908), Bette Davis (Apr 5, 1908), Lionel Hampton (Apr 20, 1908), Eddie Albert (Apr 22, 1908), Edward R. Murrow (Apr 25, 1908), Eve Arden (Apr 30, 1908), Jimmy Stewart (May 20, 1908), Robert Morley (May 26, 1908), Ian Fleming (May 28, 1908), Mel Blanc (May 30, 1908), Don Ameche (May 31, 1908), Bud Collyer (Jun 18, 1908), Thurgood Marshall (Jul 2, 1908), Nelson Rockefeller (Jul 8, 1908), Milton Berle (Jul 12, 1908), Lyndon B. Johnson (Aug 27, 1908), Fred MacMurray (Aug 30, 1908), William Saroyan (Aug 31, 1908), Richard Wright (Sep 4, 1908), Greer Garson (Sep 29, 1908), Carole Lombard (Oct 6, 1908), Jacques Tati (Oct 9, 1908), John Kenneth Galbraith (Oct 15, 1908), Burgess Meredith (Nov 16, 1908), Imogene Coca (Nov 18, 1908), Alistair Cooke (Nov 20, 1908), Adam Clayton Powell Jr (Nov 29, 1908), Lew Ayres (Dec 28, 1908), Simon Wiesenthal (Dec 31, 1908), Barry Goldwater (Jan 1, 1909), Victor Borge (Jan 3, 1909), Gene Krupa (Jan 15, 1909), Ethel Merman (Jan 16, 1909), Ann Sothern (Jan 22, 1909), Carmen Miranda (Feb 9, 1909), Hugh Beaumont (Feb 16, 1909), Claire Trevor (Mar 8, 1909), Tom Ewell (Apr 29, 1909), Kate Smith (May 1, 1909), James Mason (May 15, 1909), Benny Goodman (May 30, 1909), Jessica Tandy (Jun 7, 1909), Burl Ives (Jun 14, 1909), Errol Flynn (Jun 20,

1909), Ruby Keeler (Aug 25, 1909), Elia Kazan (Sep 7, 1909), Al Capp (Sep 28, 1909), Senator Joseph McCarthy (Nov 14, 1909), James Agee (Nov 27, 1909), Douglas Fairbanks Jr (Dec 9, 1909), David Niven (Mar 1, 1910), Samuel Barber (Mar 9, 1910), Akira Kirosawa (Mar 23, 1910), Scatman Crothers (May 23, 1910), Artie Shaw (May 23, 1910), Robert Cummings (Jun 9, 1910), Jacques Cousteau (Jun 11, 1910), E.G. Marshall (Jun 18, 1910), Gloria Stuart (Jul 4, 1910), William Hanna (Jul 14, 1910), Mother Teresa (Aug 27, 1910), John Wooden (Oct 14, 1910), Rosemary DeCamp (Nov 14, 1910), Louis Prima (Dec 7, 1910), Butterfly McQueen (Jan 8, 1911), Dizzy Dean (Jan 16, 1911), Ronald Reagan (Feb 6, 1911 – Mercury conjunct Uranus opposed Neptune), Jean Harlow (Mar 3, 1911), L. Ron Hubbard (Mar 13, 1911), Joseph Barbera (Mar 24, 1911), Tennessee Williams (Mar 26, 1911), Phil Silvers (May 11, 1911), Maureen O'Sullivan (May 17, 1911), Hubert H. Humphrey (May 27, 1911), Vincent Price (May 27, 1911), Mitch Miller (Jul 4, 1911), Georges Pompidou (Jul 5, 1911), Ginger Rogers (Jul 16, 1911), Hume Cronyn (Jul 18, 1911), Marshall McLuhan (Jul 21, 1911), Lucille Ball (Aug 6, 1911), Cantinflas (Aug 12, 1911), Vaughn Monroe (Oct 7, 1911), Mahalia Jackson (Oct 26, 1911), Roy Rogers (Nov 5, 1911), Lee J. Cobb (Dec 8, 1911), Chet Huntley (Dec 10, 1911), Kenneth Patchen (Dec 13, 1911), Spike Jones (Dec 14, 1911), Stan Kenton (Dec 15, 1911), Sam Levenson (Dec 28, 1911), Danny Thomas (Jan 6, 1912), Charles Addams (Jan 7, 1912), José Ferrer (Jan 8, 1912), Jackson Pollock (Jan 28, 1912)

**Uranus Aquarius**: Jan 30, 1912 – Sep 4, 1912

Les Brown (Mar 14, 1912), Samuel 'Lightnin'' Hopkins (Mar 15, 1912), Pat Nixon (Mar 16, 1912), Wernher Von Braun (Mar 23, 1912), Sonja Henie (Apr 8, 1912), Foster Brooks (May 11, 1912), Perry Como (May 18, 1912), Sam Snead (May 27, 1912), Alan Türing (Jun 23, 1912), Woody Guthrie (Jul 14, 1912), Art Linkletter (Jul 17, 1912), Vivian Vance (Jul 26, 1912), Milton

Friedman (Jul 31, 1912), Raoul Wallenberg (Aug 4, 1912), Jane Wyatt (Aug 12, 1912), Julia Child (Aug 15, 1912), Gene Kelly (Aug 23, 1912), Durward Kirby (Aug 24, 1912)

**Uranus Capricorn:** Sep 4, 1912 – Nov 12, 1912

John Cage (Sep 5, 1912)

**Pluto Cancer:** Sep 10, 1912 – Oct 20, 1912

**Pluto Gemini:** Oct 20, 1912 – Jul 9, 1913

Minnie Pearl (Oct 25, 1912), Dale Evans (Oct 31, 1912)

**Uranus Aquarius:** Nov 12, 1912 – Nov 12, 1912

Eugene Ionesco (Nov 26, 1912), Eric Sevareid (Nov 26, 1912), Gordon Parks (Nov 30, 1912), Lady Bird Johnson (Dec 22, 1912), Loretta Young (Jan 6, 1913), Richard Nixon (Jan 9, 1913), Lloyd Bridges (Jan 15, 1913), Danny Kaye (Jan 18, 1913), Victor Mature (Jan 29, 1913), Rosa Parks (Feb 4, 1913), Mary Leakey (Feb 6, 1913), Mel Allen (Feb 14, 1913), Jimmy Hoffa (Feb 14, 1913), Jim Backus (Feb 25, 1913), William Casey (Mar 13, 1913), Macdonald Carey (Mar 15, 1913), Karl Malden (Mar 22, 1913), Frankie Laine (Mar 30, 1913), Oleg Cassini (Apr 11, 1913), Tyrone Power (May 5, 1913), Peter Cushing (May 26, 1913), Vince Lombardi (Jun 11, 1913), Ralph Edwards (Jun 13, 1913)

**Pluto Cancer:** Jul 9, 1913 – Dec 28, 1913

Gerald R. Ford (Jul 14, 1913), Richard 'Red' Skelton (Jul 18, 1913), Menachem Begin (Aug 16, 1913), Alan Ladd (Sep 3, 1913), Jesse Owens (Sep 12, 1913), Stanley Kramer (Sep 29, 1913), Burt Lancaster (Nov 2, 1913), Vivien Leigh (Nov 5, 1913), Hedy Lamarr (Nov 9, 1913), Benjamin Britten (Nov 22, 1913), Mary Martin (Dec 1, 1913), Carlo Ponti (Dec 11, 1913), Archie Moore (Dec 13, 1913)

**Pluto Gemini:** Dec 28, 1913 – May 26, 1914

Jane Wyman (Jan 4, 1914), George Reeves (Jan 5, 1914), William Burroughs (Feb 5, 1914), Gypsy Rose Lee (Feb 9, 1914), Arthur Kennedy (Feb 17, 1914), Harry Caray (Mar 1, 1914), Ralph Ellison (Mar 1, 1914), Alec Guinness (Apr 2,

1914), Frances Langford (Apr 4, 1914), Joe Louis (May 13, 1914)

**Pluto Cancer:** May 26, 1914 – Oct 7, 1937

Frankie Manning (May 26, 1914), Babe Didrikson Zaharias (Jun 26, 1914), Billy Eckstine (Jul 8, 1914), Harriet Nelson (Jul 18, 1914), Kitty Carlisle Hart (Sep 3, 1914), Clayton Moore (Sep 14, 1914), Allen Funt (Sep 16, 1914)

**Neptune Leo:** Sep 23, 1914 – Dec 14, 1914

Jack LaLanne (Sep 26, 1914), Fayard Nicholas (Oct 20, 1914), Jackie Coogan (Oct 26, 1914), Dylan Thomas (Oct 27, 1914), Jonas Salk (Oct 28, 1914), Ray Walston (Nov 2, 1914), Joe DiMaggio (Nov 25, 1914), Dorothy Lamour (Dec 10, 1914)

**Neptune Cancer:** Dec 14, 1914 – Jul 19, 1915

Morey Amsterdam (Dec 14, 1914), Richard Widmark (Dec 26, 1914), Bert Parks (Dec 30, 1914), Thomas Merton (Jan 31, 1915), Garry Moore (Jan 31, 1915), Lorne Greene (Feb 12, 1915), Zero Mostel (Feb 28, 1915), Henry Morgan (Mar 31, 1915), Muddy Waters (Apr 4, 1915), Billie Holiday (Apr 7, 1915), Harry Morgan (Apr 10, 1915), Anthony Quinn (Apr 21, 1915), Alice Faye (May 5, 1915), Orson Welles (May 6, 1915), Les Paul (Jun 9, 1915), Saul Bellow (Jun 10, 1915), Pat Buttram (Jun 19, 1915), Laverne Andrews (Jul 6, 1915)

**Neptune Leo:** Jul 19, 1915 – Mar 19, 1916

Ingrid Bergman (Aug 29, 1915), Cornel Wilde (Oct 13, 1915), Arthur Miller (Oct 17, 1915), Nathaniel Benchley (Nov 13, 1915), Eli Wallach (Dec 7, 1915), Frank Sinatra (Dec 12, 1915), Jackie Gleason (Feb 26, 1916), Harry James (Mar 15, 1916)

**Neptune Cancer:** Mar 19, 1916 – May 2, 1916

Herb Caen (Apr 3, 1916), Gregory Peck (Apr 5, 1916), Yehudi Menuhin (Apr 22, 1916), Glenn Ford (May 1, 1916)

**Neptune Leo:** May 2, 1916 – Sep 21, 1928

Harold Robbins (May 21, 1916), Olivia de Havilland (Jul 1, 1916), Van Johnson (Aug 25, 1916), Martha Raye (Aug 27, 1916), Roald Dahl (Sep 13, 1916), James Herriot (Oct 3, 1916),

Walter Cronkite (Nov 4, 1916), Daws Butler (Nov 16, 1916), Richard Fleischer (Dec 8, 1916), Kirk Douglas (Dec 9, 1916), Douglas Fraser (Dec 18, 1916), Betty Grable (Dec 18, 1916), Jesse White (Jan 4, 1917), Ernest Borgnine (Jan 24, 1917), Sidney Sheldon (Feb 11, 1917), Dom DiMaggio (Feb 12, 1917), Anthony Burgess (Feb 25, 1917), Dinah Shore (Mar 1, 1917), Desi Arnaz (Mar 2, 1917), Hans Conried (Apr 15, 1917), I.M. Pei (Apr 26, 1917), Raymond Burr (May 21, 1917), Dennis Day (May 21, 1917), John F. Kennedy (May 29, 1917), Leo Gorcey (Jun 3, 1917), Dean Martin (Jun 7, 1917), Lena Horne (Jun 30, 1917), Andrew Wyeth (Jul 12, 1917), Phyllis Diller (Jul 17, 1917), Richard Boone (Jun 18, 1917), Robert Mitchum (Aug 6, 1917), John Lee Hooker (Aug 22, 1917), Mel Ferrer (Aug 25, 1917), Isabel Sanford (Aug 29, 1917), Henry Ford II (Sep 4, 1917), Buddy Rich (Sep 30, 1917), Allen Ludden (Oct 5, 1917), June Allyson (Oct 7, 1917), Thelonious Monk (Oct 10, 1917), Arthur Schlesinger Jr (Oct 15, 1917), Dizzy Gillespie (Oct 21, 1917), Joan Fontaine (Oct 22, 1917), Indira Gandhi (Nov 19, 1917), 'Buffalo' Bob Smith (Nov 27, 1917), Arthur C. Clarke (Dec 16, 1917), Ossie Davis (Dec 18, 1917), Gene Rayburn (Dec 22, 1917), Maxene Andrews (Jan 3, 1918), Skitch Henderson (Jan 27, 1918), Ernie Harwell (Jan 25, 1918), John Forsythe (Jan 29, 1918), Joey Bishop (Feb 3, 1918), Ida Lupino (Feb 4, 1918), Robert Wadlow (Feb 22, 1918), Mickey Spillane (Mar 9, 1918), Pamela Mason (Mar 10, 1918), Mercedes McCambridge (Mar 17, 1918), Pearl Bailey (Mar 29, 1918), Sam Walton (Mar 29, 1918), Betty Ford (Apr 8, 1918), William Holden (Apr 17, 1918), Ella Fitzgerald (Apr 25, 1918), Jack Paar (May 1, 1918), Mike Wallace (May 9, 1918), Eddy Arnold (May 15, 1918), Claude Akins (May 25, 1918), Robert Preston (Jun 8, 1918), Ann Landers (Jul 4, 1918), Abigail Van Buren (Jul 4, 1918), Ingmar Bergman (Jul 14, 1918), Nelson Mandela (Jul 18, 1918), Harold 'Pee Wee' Reese (Jul 23, 1918), Leonard Bernstein (Aug 25, 1918), Ted Williams (Aug 30, 1918), Alan Jay Lerner (Aug

31, 1918), Paul Harvey (Sep 4, 1918), Phil Rizzuto (Sep 25, 1918), Jerome Robbins (Oct 11, 1918), Rita Hayworth (Oct 17, 1918), Art Carney (Nov 4, 1918), Billy Graham (Nov 7, 1918), Spiro Agnew (Nov 9, 1918), Jo Stafford (Nov 12, 1918), Madeleine L'Engle (Nov 29, 1918), Joe Williams (Dec 12, 1918), Jeff Chandler (Dec 15, 1918), José Greco (Dec 23, 1918), Anwar Sadat (Dec 25, 1918), J.D. Salinger (Jan 1, 1919), Robert Stack (Jan 13, 1919), Andy Rooney (Jan 14, 1919), Ernie Kovacs (Jan 23, 1919), Edwin Newman (Jan 25, 1919), Jackie Robinson (Jan 31, 1919), Red Buttons (Feb 5, 1919 – Sun conjunct Uranus), Zsa Zsa Gabor (Feb 6, 1919), Tennessee Ernie Ford (Feb 13, 1919), Jennifer Jones (Mar 2, 1919), Nat King Cole (Mar 17, 1919), Lawrence Ferlinghetti (Mar 24, 1919)

**Uranus Pisces**: Apr 1, 1919 – Aug 16, 1919

Howard Keel (Apr 13, 1919), Merce Cunningham (Apr 16, 1919), Celeste Holm (Apr 29, 1919), Pete Seeger (May 3, 1919), Heloise (May 4, 1919), Eva Peron (May 7, 1919), Liberace (May 16, 1919), Margot Fonteyn (May 18, 1919), George Gobel (May 20, 1919), Jay Silverheels (May 26, 1919), Robert Merrill (Jun 4, 1919), Gene De Paul (Jun 17, 1919), Louis Jourdan (Jun 19, 1919), Pauline Kael (Jun 19, 1919), Slim Pickens (Jun 29, 1919), Susan Hayward (Jun 30, 1919), Sir Edmund Hillary (Jul 20, 1919), Curt Gowdy (Jul 31, 1919), George Shearing (Aug 13, 1919), Huntz Hall (Aug 15, 1919)

**Uranus Aquarius**: Aug 16, 1919 – Jan 22, 1920

Malcolm Forbes (Aug 19, 1919), Donald Pleasence (Oct 5, 1919), Anita O'Day (Oct 18, 1919), Martin Balsam (Nov 4, 1919), Veronica Lake (Nov 14, 1919), Judge Joseph Wapner (Nov 15, 1919), Shirley Jackson (Dec 14, 1919), Isaac Asimov (Jan 2, 1920), Sun Myung Moon (Jan 6, 1920), Cardinal John O'Connor (Jan 15, 1920), Federico Fellini (Jan 20, 1920), DeForest Kelley (Jan 20, 1920)

**Uranus Pisces**: Jan 22, 1920 – Mar 31, 1927

Eddie Bracken (Feb 7, 1920), Eileen Farrell (Feb 13, 1920), Patty

Andrews (Feb 16, 1920), Bill Cullen (Feb 18, 1920), Jack Palance (Feb 18, 1920), Tony Randall (Feb 26, 1920), James Doohan (Mar 3, 1920), Hank Ketcham (Mar 14, 1920), Howard Cosell (Mar 25, 1920), Toshiro Mifune (Apr 1, 1920), Jack Webb (Apr 2, 1920), Ravi Shankar (Apr 7, 1920), Barry Nelson (Apr 16, 1920), Pope John Paul II (May 18, 1920), Helen O'Connell (May 23, 1920), Peggy Lee (May 26, 1920), David Brinkley (Jul 10, 1920), Yul Brynner (Jul 11, 1920), Isaac Stern (Jul 21, 1920), Amália Rodrigues (Jul 23, 1920), Charles Bukowski (Aug 16, 1920), Maureen O'Hara (Aug 17, 1920), Ray Bradbury (Aug 22, 1920), Charlie 'Bird' Parker (Aug 29, 1920), June Foray (Sep 18, 1920), Jack Warden (Sep 18, 1920), Mickey Rooney (Sep 23, 1920), William Conrad (Sep 27, 1920), Walter Matthau (Oct 1, 1920), Mario Puzo (Oct 15, 1920), Montgomery Clift (Oct 17, 1920), Timothy Leary (Oct 22, 1920), Nanette Fabray (Oct 27, 1920), Esther Rolle (Nov 8, 1920), Stan Musial (Nov 21, 1920), Ricardo Montalban (Nov 25, 1920), Dave Brubeck (Dec 6, 1920), David Susskind (Dec 19, 1920), Jack Lord (Dec 30, 1920), Donna Reed (Jan 27, 1921), Mario Lanza (Jan 31, 1921), Betty Friedan (Feb 4, 1921), Freddie Blassie (Feb 8, 1921), Lana Turner (Feb 8, 1921), Eva Gabor (Feb 11, 1921), Hugh Downs (Feb 14, 1921), Abe Vigoda (Feb 24, 1921), Betty Hutton (Feb 26, 1921), Gordon MacRae (Mar 12, 1921), Simone Signoret (Mar 25, 1921), Harold Nicholas (Mar 27, 1921), Dirk Bogarde (Mar 28, 1921), Gale Storm (Apr 5, 1921), Chuck Connors (Apr 10, 1921), Peter Ustinov (Apr 16, 1921), Sugar Ray Robinson (May 3, 1921), Nelson Riddle (Jun 1, 1921), Erroll Garner (Jun 15, 1921), Jane Russell (Jun 21, 1921), Joseph Papp (Jun 22, 1921), Nancy Reagan (Jul 6, 1921), Jake LaMotta (Jul 10, 1921), John Glenn (Jul 18, 1921), Alex Haley (Aug 11, 1921), Gene Roddenberry (Aug 19, 1921), Jacqueline Susann (Aug 20, 1921), Ben Bradlee (Aug 26, 1921), Jim McKay (Sep 24, 1921), Deborah Kerr (Sep 30, 1921), James Whitmore (Oct 1, 1921), Yves Montand (Oct

13, 1921), Tom Poston (Oct 17, 1921), Jesse Helms (Oct 18, 1921), Bill Mauldin (Oct 29, 1921), Charles Bronson (Nov 3, 1921), Brian Keith (Nov 14, 1921), Rodney Dangerfield (Nov 22, 1921), Steve Allen (Dec 26, 1921), Johnny Otis (Dec 28, 1921), Jean-Pierre Rampal (Jan 7, 1922), Betty White (Jan 17, 1922), Guy Madison (Jan 19, 1922), Paul Scofield (Jan 21, 1922), Dick Martin (Jan 30, 1922), Kathryn Grayson (Feb 9, 1922), Helen Gurley Brown (Feb 18, 1922), Margaret Leighton (Feb 26, 1922), James Noble (Mar 5, 1922), Jack Kerouac (Mar 12, 1922), Carl Reiner (Mar 20, 1922), Leon Schotter (Apr 15, 1922), Jack Klugman (Apr 27, 1922), Darren McGavin (May 7, 1922), Nancy Walker (May 10, 1922), Christopher Lee (May 27, 1922), Denholm Elliott (May 31, 1922), Gene Barry (Jun 4, 1922), Judy Garland (Jun 10, 1922), Eleanor Parker (Jun 26, 1922), Dan Rowan (Jul 2, 1922), William Schallert (Jul 6, 1922), Pierre Cardin (Jul 7, 1922), George McGovern (Jul 19, 1922), Kay Starr (Jul 21, 1922), Blake Edwards (Jul 26, 1922), Jason Robards Jr (Jul 26, 1922), Norman Lear (Jul 27, 1922), Rory Calhoun (Aug 8, 1922), Rudi Gernreich (Aug 8, 1922), Shelley Winters (Aug 18, 1922), Yvonne DeCarlo (Sep 1, 1922), Vittorio Gassman (Sep 1, 1922), Sid Caesar (Sep 8, 1922), Jackie Cooper (Sep 15, 1922), Arthur Penn (Sep 27, 1922), Jack Anderson (Oct 19, 1922), Barbara Bel Geddes (Oct 31, 1922), Al Hirt (Nov 7, 1922), Kurt Vonnegut Jr (Nov 11, 1922), Oskar Werner (Nov 13, 1922), Charles Schulz (Nov 26, 1922), Redd Foxx (Dec 9, 1922), Don Hewitt (Dec 14, 1922), George Roy Hill (Dec 20, 1922), Paul Winchell (Dec 21, 1922), Barbara Billingsley (Dec 22, 1922), Ava Gardner (Dec 24, 1922), Larry Storch (Jan 8, 1923), Jean Stapleton (Jan 19, 1923), Anne Jeffreys (Jan 26, 1923), Carol Channing (Jan 31, 1923), Norman Mailer (Jan 31, 1923), James Dickey (Feb 2, 1923), Keefe Brasselle (Feb 7, 1923), Brendan Behan (Feb 9, 1923), Franco Zeffirelli (Feb 12, 1923), Chuck Yeager (Feb 13, 1923), Charles Durning (Feb 28, 1923), Ed McMahon (Mar 6, 1923), Cyd Charisse (Mar 8, 1923),

Marcel Marceau (Mar 22, 1923), Doc Watson (Mar 23, 1923), Ann Miller (Apr 12, 1923), Harry Reasoner (Apr 17, 1923), Beatrice Arthur (May 13, 1923), James Arness (May 26, 1923), Henry Kissinger (May 27, 1923), Dale Robertson (Jul 14, 1923), Bob Dole (Jul 22, 1923), Esther Williams (Aug 8, 1923), Rhonda Fleming (Aug 10, 1923), Chris Schenkel (Aug 21, 1923), Monty Hall (Aug 25, 1923), Richard Attenborough (Aug 29, 1923), Rocky Marciano (Sep 1, 1923), Glynis Johns (Oct 5, 1923), Melina Mercouri (Oct 18, 1923), Roy Lichtenstein (Oct 27, 1923), Alan Shepard Jr (Nov 18, 1923), Efrem Zimbalist Jr (Nov 30, 1923), Maria Callas (Dec 2, 1923), Ted Knight (Dec 7, 1923), Bob Barker (Dec 12, 1923), Bob Dorough (Dec 12, 1923), Robert N. Cronk (Jan 1, 1924), Ron Moody (Jan 8, 1924), Telly Savalas (Jan 21, 1924), Audrey Meadows (Feb 8, 1924), Lee Marvin (Feb 19, 1924), Sidney Poitier (Feb 20, 1924), Gloria Vanderbilt (Feb 20, 1924), Sarah Vaughan (Mar 27, 1924), Marlon Brando (Apr 3, 1924), Doris Day (Apr 3, 1924), Henry Mancini (Apr 16, 1924), Nina Foch (Apr 20, 1924), Terry Southern (May 1, 1924), Theodore Bikel (May 2, 1924), Peggy Cass (May 21, 1924), Dennis Weaver (Jun 4, 1924), George Bush (Jun 12, 1924), Chet Atkins (Jun 20, 1924), Audie Murphy (Jun 20, 1924), Sidney Lumet (Jun 25, 1924), Eva Marie Saint (Jul 4, 1924), Bess Myerson (Jul 16, 1924), Don Knotts (Jul 21, 1924), Estelle Getty (Jul 25, 1924), James Baldwin (Aug 2, 1924), Carroll O'Connor (Aug 2, 1924), Phyllis Schlafly (Aug 15, 1924), Jack Weston (Aug 21, 1924), Buddy Hackett (Aug 31, 1924), Lauren Bacall (Sep 16, 1924), Sheila MacRae (Sep 24, 1924), Marcello Mastroianni (Sep 28, 1924), Truman Capote (Sep 30, 1924), Jimmy Carter (Oct 1, 1924), Charlton Heston (Oct 4, 1924), Edward D. Wood Jr (Oct 10, 1924), Nipsey Russell (Oct 13, 1924), Lee Iacocca (Oct 15, 1924), Billy Barty (Oct 25, 1924), Ruby Dee (Oct 27, 1924), Wally Cox (Dec 6, 1924), Rod Serling (Dec 25, 1924), Gwen Verdon (Jan 13, 1925), Benny Hill (Jan 21, 1925), Maria

Tallchief (Jan 24, 1925), Paul Newman (Jan 26, 1925), Dorothy Malone (Jan 30, 1925), Jack Lemmon (Feb 8, 1925), Hal Holbrook (Feb 17, 1925), George Kennedy (Feb 18, 1925), Robert Altman (Feb 20, 1925), Sam Peckinpah (Feb 21, 1925), Leo Buscaglia (Mar 31, 1925), Jan Merlin (Apr 3, 1925), Rod Steiger (Apr 14, 1925), Hugh O'Brian (Apr 19, 1925), Roscoe Lee Browne (May 2, 1925), Yogi Berra (May 12, 1925), Malcolm X (May 19, 1925), Jeanne Crain (May 25, 1925), Tony Curtis (Jun 3, 1925), Barbara Bush (Jun 8, 1925), Pierre Salinger (Jun 14, 1925), Maureen Stapleton (Jun 21, 1925), June Lockhart (Jun 25, 1925), Merv Griffin (Jul 6, 1925), Bill Haley (Jul 6, 1925), Mike Douglas (Aug 11, 1925), Russell Baker (Aug 14, 1925), Mike Connors (Aug 15, 1925), Rose Marie (Aug 15, 1925), Fess Parker (Aug 16, 1925), Donald O'Connor (Aug 28, 1925), Peter Sellers (Sep 8, 1925), Cliff Robertson (Sep 9, 1925), Mel Torme (Sep 13, 1925), B.B. King (Sep 16, 1925), Arnold Stang (Sep 28, 1925), Gore Vidal (Oct 3, 1925), Elmore Leonard (Oct 11, 1925), Lenny Bruce (Oct 13, 1925), Margaret Thatcher (Oct 13, 1925), Angela Lansbury (Oct 16, 1925), Art Buchwald (Oct 20, 1925), Joyce Randolph (Oct 21, 1925), Johnny Carson (Oct 23, 1925), Richard Burton (Nov 10, 1925), Jonathan Winters (Nov 11, 1925), Rock Hudson (Nov 17, 1925), Robert F. Kennedy (Nov 20, 1925), Johnny Mandel (Nov 23, 1925), William F. Buckley, Jr. (Nov 24, 1925), Sammy Davis Jr (Dec 8, 1925), Dina Merrill (Dec 9, 1925), Dick Van Dyke (Dec 13, 1925), George Martin (Jan 3, 1926), Soupy Sales (Jan 8, 1926), Grant Tinker (Jan 11, 1926), Ray Price (Jan 12, 1926), Patricia Neal (Jan 20, 1926), Shelley Berman (Feb 3, 1926), Leslie Nielsen (Feb 11, 1926), Joe Garagiola (Feb 12, 1926), Pete Rozelle (Mar 1, 1926), Alan Greenspan (Mar 6, 1926), Irene Papas (Mar 9, 1926), Ralph Abernathy (Mar 11, 1926), Jerry Lewis (Mar 16, 1926), Peter Graves (Mar 18, 1926), Anne McCaffrey (Apr 1, 1926), Roger Corman (Apr 5, 1926), Shecky Greene (Apr 8, 1926), Hugh Hefner (Apr 9, 1926), Don Adams

(Apr 13, 1926), Elizabeth II, Queen of the United Kingdom (Apr 21, 1926), Cloris Leachman (Apr 30, 1926), Ann B. Davis (May 5, 1926), Don Rickles (May 8, 1926), Miles Davis (May 25, 1926), Andy Griffith (Jun 1, 1926), Marilyn Monroe (Jun 1, 1926), Colleen Dewhurst (Jun 3, 1926), Allen Ginsberg (Jun 3, 1926), Paul Lynde (Jun 13, 1926), Mel Brooks (Jun 28, 1926), Fred Gwynne (Jul 10, 1926), Harry Dean Stanton (Jul 14, 1926), Norman Jewison (Jul 21, 1926), Tony Bennett (Aug 3, 1926), Stan Freberg (Aug 7, 1926), John Derek (Aug 12, 1926), Fidel Castro (Aug 13, 1926), Jiang Zemin (Aug 17, 1926), John Coltrane (Sep 23, 1926), Julie London (Sep 26, 1926), Jayne Meadows (Sep 27, 1926), Richard Jaeckel (Oct 10, 1926), Chuck Berry (Oct 18, 1926), Y.A. Tittle (Oct 24, 1926), Joan Sutherland (Nov 7, 1926), Kaye Ballard (Nov 20, 1926), Richard Crenna (Nov 30, 1926), Joe Paterno (Dec 21, 1926), Gisele MacKenzie (Jan 10, 1927), Johnnie Ray (Jan 10, 1927), Eartha Kitt (Jan 17, 1927), Leontyne Price (Feb 10, 1927), Harvey Korman (Feb 15, 1927), Erma Bombeck (Feb 21, 1927), Harry Belafonte (Mar 1, 1927), George Plimpton (Mar 18, 1927)

**Uranus Aries**: Mar 31, 1927 – Nov 4, 1927

Cesar Chavez (Mar 31, 1927), William Daniels (Mar 31, 1927), Coretta Scott King (Apr 27, 1927), Pat Carroll (May 5, 1927), Mort Sahl (May 11, 1927), Robert Ludlum (May 25, 1927), Bob Fosse (Jun 23, 1927), Bob 'Captain Kangaroo' Keeshan (Jun 27, 1927), Ken Russell (Jul 3, 1927), Gina Lollobrigida (Jul 4, 1927), Neil Simon (Jul 4, 1927), Janet Leigh (Jul 6, 1927), Doc Severinsen (Jul 7, 1927), Ed Ames (Jul 9, 1927), John Chancellor (Jul 14, 1927), Carl 'Alfalfa' Switzer (Aug 7, 1927), Robert Shaw (Aug 9, 1927), Rosalynn Carter (Aug 18, 1927), Peter Falk (Sep 16, 1927), Tommy Lasorda (Sep 22, 1927), R.D. Laing (Oct 7, 1927), Roger Moore (Oct 14, 1927), George C. Scott (Oct 18, 1927)

**Uranus Pisces**: Nov 4, 1927 – Jan 13, 1928

Patti Page (Nov 8, 1927), Estelle Parsons (Nov 20, 1927), Joseph Campanella (Nov 21, 1927), Vin Scully (Nov 29, 1927), Christopher Plummer (Dec 13, 1927), Alan King (Dec 26, 1927), Walter Mondale (Jan 5, 1928), William Peter Blatty (Jan 7, 1928)

**Uranus Aries:** Jan 13, 1928 – Jun 6, 1934

Vidal Sassoon (Jan 17, 1928), Jeanne Moreau (Jan 23, 1928), Roger Mudd (Feb 9, 1928), Fats Domino (Feb 26, 1928), Ariel Sharon (Feb 27, 1928), James Earl Ray (Mar 10, 1928), Edward Albee (Mar 12, 1928), Frank Borman (Mar 14, 1928), Patrick McGoohan (Mar 19, 1928), Fred 'Mr' Rogers (Mar 20, 1928), Gordie Howe (Mar 31, 1928), Maya Angelou (Apr 4, 1928), James Garner (Apr 7, 1928), Ethel Kennedy (Apr 11, 1928), Aaron Spelling (Apr 22, 1928), Shirley Temple Black (Apr 23, 1928), Rosemary Clooney (May 23, 1928), Dr Ruth Westheimer (Jun 4, 1928), Tony Richardson (Jun 5, 1928), Maurice Sendak (Jun 10, 1928), Vic Damone (Jun 12, 1928), Warren Oates (Jul 5, 1928), Orson Bean (Jul 22, 1928), Stanley Kubrick (Jul 26, 1928), Andy Warhol (Aug 6, 1928), Jimmy Dean (Aug 10, 1928), Eddie Fisher (Aug 10, 1928), Arlene Dahl (Aug 11, 1928), Ann Blyth (Aug 16, 1928), Dick O'Neill (Aug 29, 1928), James Coburn (Aug 31, 1928), Roddy McDowall (Sep 17, 1928), Adam West (Sep 19, 1928), Dr Joyce Brothers (Sep 20, 1928)

**Neptune Virgo:** Sep 21, 1928 – Feb 19, 1929

George Peppard (Oct 1, 1928), George 'Spanky' McFarland (Oct 2, 1928), Alvin Toffler (Oct 4, 1928), Dick Van Patten (Dec 9, 1928), Dan Blocker (Dec 10, 1928), Bo Diddley (Dec 30, 1928), Vic Tayback (Jan 6, 1929), Dr Martin Luther King Jr (Jan 15, 1929), Jules Feiffer (Jan 26, 1929), Jean Simmons (Jan 31, 1929)

**Neptune Leo:** Feb 19, 1929 – Jul 24, 1929

Roger Bannister (Mar 23, 1929), André Previn (Apr 6, 1929), Max Von Sydow (Apr 10, 1929), Edie Adams (Apr 16, 1929), Audrey Hepburn (May 4, 1929), Burt Bacharach (May 12,

1929), Beverly Sills (May 25, 1929), Jerry Stiller (Jun 8, 1929), Anne Frank (Jun 12, 1929), June Carter (Jun 23, 1929), Dick Button (Jul 18, 1929)

**Neptune Virgo:** Jul 24, 1929 – Oct 3, 1942

Jacqueline Kennedy Onassis (Jul 28, 1929), Pat Harrington Jr (Aug 13, 1929), X.J. Kennedy (Aug 21, 1929), Yasser Arafat (Aug 24, 1929), Bob Newhart (Sep 5, 1929), Arnold Palmer (Sep 10, 1929), Anne Meara (Sep 20, 1929), Grace Kelly (Nov 12, 1929), Ed Asner (Nov 15, 1929), Berry Gordy, Jr. (Nov 28, 1929), Dick Clark (Nov 30, 1929), William Safire (Dec 17, 1929), Mary Higgins Clark (Dec 24, 1929), Rod Taylor (Jan 11, 1930), Glenn Yarborough (Jan 12, 1930), Edwin 'Buzz' Aldrin (Jan 20, 1930), Gene Hackman (Jan 30, 1930), Robert Wagner (Feb 10, 1930), Gahan Wilson (Feb 18, 1930), Joanne Woodward (Feb 27, 1930), Gavin MacLeod (Feb 28, 1930), Lord Snowdon (Mar 7, 1930), Stephen Sondheim (Mar 22, 1930), Steve McQueen (Mar 24, 1930), Sandra Day O'Connor (Mar 26, 1930), David Janssen (Mar 27, 1930), John Astin (Mar 30, 1930), Rolf Harris (Mar 30, 1930), Peter Marshall (Mar 30, 1930), Tiny Tim (Apr 12, 1930), Herbie Mann (Apr 16, 1930), Paul Mazursky (Apr 25, 1930), Pat Summerall (May 10, 1930), Pernell Roberts (May 18, 1930), Clint Eastwood (May 31, 1930), H. Ross Perot (Jun 27, 1930), Robert Evans (Jun 29, 1930), George Steinbrenner (Jul 4, 1930), Polly Bergen (Jul 14, 1930), Neil Armstrong (Aug 5, 1930), Don Ho (Aug 13, 1930), Robert Culp (Aug 16, 1930), Frank Gifford (Aug 16, 1930), Vera Miles (Aug 23, 1930), Sean Connery (Aug 25, 1930 – Sun conjunct Neptune, Jupiter conjunct Pluto), Ben Gazzara (Aug 28, 1930), Warren Buffett (Aug 30, 1930), Mitzi Gaynor (Sep 4, 1930), Charles (Sep 23, 1930), Shel Silverstein (Sep 25, 1930), Jimmy Breslin (Oct 17, 1930), Doris Roberts (Nov 4, 1930), G. Gordon Liddy (Nov 30, 1930), Jean Luc Godard (Dec 3, 1930), Andy Williams (Dec 3, 1930), Maximilian Schell (Dec 8, 1930), Buck Henry (Dec 9, 1930), Bob Guccione (Dec 17, 1930),

Odetta (Dec 31, 1930), Robert Duvall (Jan 5, 1931), James Earl Jones (Jan 17, 1931), Tippi Hedren (Jan 19, 1931), Dean Jones (Jan 25, 1931), Ernie Banks (Jan 31, 1931), Boris Yeltsin (Feb 1, 1931), Rip Torn (Feb 6, 1931), Mamie Van Doren (Feb 6, 1931), James Dean (Feb 8, 1931), Claire Bloom (Feb 15, 1931), Toni Morrison (Feb 18, 1931), Mikhail Gorbachev (Mar 2, 1931), Rupert Murdoch (Mar 11, 1931), Hal Linden (Mar 20, 1931), William Shatner (Mar 22, 1931), Leonard Nimoy (Mar 26, 1931), Richard Alpert/Ram Dass (Apr 6, 1931), Willie Mays (May 6, 1931), Robert Morse (May 18, 1931), Carroll Baker (May 28, 1931), Martin Landau (Jun 20, 1931), Leslie Caron (Jul 1, 1931), Roone Arledge (Jul 8, 1931), Tab Hunter (Jul 11, 1931), Jerry Van Dyke (Jul 27, 1931), William Goldman (Aug 12, 1931), Willie Shoemaker (Aug 19, 1931), Anne Bancroft (Sep 17, 1931), Larry Hagman (Sep 21, 1931), Anthony Newley (Sep 24, 1931), Barbara Walters (Sep 25, 1931), Anita Ekberg (Sep 29, 1931), Angie Dickinson (Sep 30, 1931), Bishop Desmond Tutu (Oct 7, 1931), John Le Carré (Oct 19, 1931), Mickey Mantle (Oct 20, 1931), Dan Rather (Oct 31, 1931), Ike Turner (Nov 5, 1931), Mike Nichols (Nov 6, 1931), Morley Safer (Nov 8, 1931), Rita Moreno (Dec 11, 1931), Dabney Coleman (Jan 3, 1932), Piper Laurie (Jan 22, 1932), John Williams (Feb 8, 1932), Vic Morrow (Feb 14, 1932), Milos Forman (Feb 18, 1932), Edward M. Kennedy (Feb 22, 1932), Johnny Cash (Feb 26, 1932), Elizabeth Taylor (Feb 27, 1932), Miriam Makeba (Mar 4, 1932), Andrew Young (Mar 12, 1932), John Updike (Mar 18, 1932), Debbie Reynolds (Apr 1, 1932), Anthony Perkins (Apr 4, 1932), Omar Sharif (Apr 10, 1932), Meadowlark Lemon (Apr 25, 1932), Casey Kasem (Apr 27, 1932), Paul Ehrlich (May 29, 1932), Jim Nabors (Jun 12, 1932), Mario Cuomo (Jun 15, 1932), Della Reese (Jul 6, 1932), Roosevelt Grier (Jul 14, 1932), Peter O'Toole (Aug 2, 1932), Eydie Gorme (Aug 16, 1932), Melvin Van Peebles (Aug 21, 1932), Mark Russell (Aug 23, 1932), Patsy Cline (Sep 8, 1932),

Glenn Gould (Sep 25, 1932), Richard Harris (Oct 1, 1932), Dick Gregory (Oct 12, 1932), Robert Reed (Oct 19, 1932), Louis Malle (Oct 30, 1932), Petula Clark (Nov 15, 1932), Richard Dawson (Nov 20, 1932), Robert Vaughn (Nov 22, 1932), Diane Ladd (Nov 29, 1932), Little Richard (Dec 5, 1932), Ellen Burstyn (Dec 7, 1932), Charlie Rich (Dec 14, 1932), Charles Osgood (Jan 8, 1933), Chita Rivera (Jan 23, 1933), Corazon Aquino (Jan 25, 1933), Susan Sontag (Jan 28, 1933), Louis Rukeyser (Jan 30, 1933), Kim Novak (Feb 13, 1933), Yoko Ono (Feb 18, 1933), Nina Simone (Feb 21, 1933), Michael Caine (Mar 14, 1933), Quincy Jones (Mar 14, 1933), J.P. McCarthy (Mar 22, 1933), Wayne Rogers (Apr 7, 1933), Jean Paul Belmondo (Apr 9, 1933), Elizabeth Montgomery (Apr 15, 1933), Jayne Mansfield (Apr 19, 1933), Carol Burnett (Apr 26, 1933), Willie Nelson (Apr 30, 1933), James Brown (May 3, 1933), Johnny Unitas (May 7, 1933), Louis Farrakhan (May 11, 1933), Joan Collins (May 23, 1933), Joan Rivers (Jun 8, 1933), F. Lee Bailey (Jun 10, 1933), Jerzy Kosinski (Jun 14, 1933), Danny Aiello (Jun 20, 1933), Edd 'Kookie' Byrnes (Jul 30, 1933), Dom DeLuise (Aug 1, 1933), Rocky Colavito (Aug 10, 1933), Reverend Jerry Falwell (Aug 11, 1933), Roman Polanski (Aug 18, 1933), Regis Philbin (Aug 25, 1933), Conway Twitty (Sep 1, 1933), Robert Blake (Sep 18, 1933), David McCallum (Sep 19, 1933), Ken Berry (Nov 3, 1933), Michael Dukakis (Nov 3, 1933), Larry King (Nov 19, 1933), Robert Goulet (Nov 26, 1933), John Mayall (Nov 29, 1933), Flip Wilson (Dec 8, 1933), Tim Conway (Dec 15, 1933), Cicely Tyson (Dec 19, 1933), Shari Lewis (Jan 17, 1934), Arte Johnson (Jan 20, 1934), Bill Bixby (Jan 22, 1934), Tammy Grimes (Jan 30, 1934), Les Dawson (Feb 2, 1934), Henry 'Hank' Aaron (Feb 5, 1934), Tina Louise (Feb 11, 1934), Bill Russell (Feb 12, 1934), George Segal (Feb 13, 1934), Florence Henderson (Feb 14, 1934), Alan Bates (Feb 17, 1934), Bobby Unser (Feb 20, 1934), Ralph Nader (Feb 27, 1934), Willard Scott (Mar 7, 1934), Yuri Gagarin (Mar 9, 1934),

Sam Donaldson (Mar 11, 1934), Gloria Steinem (Mar 25, 1934), Alan Arkin (Mar 26, 1934), Shirley Jones (Mar 31, 1934), Jane Goodall (Apr 3, 1934), Shirley MacLaine (Apr 24, 1934), Dwayne Hickman (May 18, 1934), Peter Nero (May 22, 1934), Pat Boone (Jun 1, 1934), Bill Moyers (Jun 5, 1934)

**Uranus Taurus:** Jun 6, 1934 – Oct 10, 1934

Jackie Mason (Jun 9, 1934), Harry Blackstone Jr (Jun 30, 1934), Jamie Farr (Jul 1, 1934), Jean Marsh (Jul 1, 1934), Giorgio Armani (Jul 11, 1934), Van Cliburn (Jul 12, 1934), Donald Sutherland (Jul 17, 1934), Louise Fletcher (Jul 22, 1934), Norman Schwarzkopf (Aug 22, 1934), Barbara Eden (Aug 23, 1934), Carol Lawrence (Sep 5, 1934), Charles Kuralt (Sep 10, 1934), Roger Maris (Sep 10, 1934), Sophia Loren (Sep 20, 1934), Leonard Cohen (Sep 21, 1934), Greg Morris (Sep 27, 1934), Brigitte Bardot (Sep 28, 1934)

**Uranus Aries:** Oct 10, 1934 – Mar 28, 1935

Carl Sagan (Nov 9, 1934), Dame Judy Dench (Dec 9, 1934), Al Kaline (Dec 19, 1934), Maggie Smith (Dec 28, 1934), Russ Tamblyn (Dec 30, 1934), Floyd Patterson (Jan 4, 1935), Elvis Presley (Jan 8, 1935), Bob Denver (Jan 9, 1935), A.J. Foyt (Jan 16, 1935), Sam Cooke (Jan 22, 1935), Bob Uecker (Jan 26, 1935), Sonny Bono (Feb 16, 1935), Sally Jessy Raphael (Feb 25, 1935), Robert Conrad (Mar 1, 1935), Judd Hirsch (Mar 15, 1935), Phyllis Newman (Mar 19, 1935)

**Uranus Taurus:** Mar 28, 1935 – Aug 7, 1941

Herb Alpert (Mar 31, 1935), Richard Chamberlain (Mar 31, 1935), Lyle Waggoner (Apr 13, 1935), Loretta Lynn (Apr 14, 1935), Bobby Vinton (Apr 16, 1935), Dudley Moore (Apr 19, 1935), Charles Grodin (Apr 21, 1935), Gene Wilder (Jun 11, 1935), Christo (Jun 13, 1935), the Dalai Lama (Jul 6, 1935), Steve Lawrence (Jul 8, 1935), Jack Kemp (Jul 13, 1935), Alex Karras (Jul 15, 1935), Diahann Carroll (Jul 17, 1935), Barbara Harris (Jul 25, 1935), Geraldine Ferraro (Aug 26, 1935), Eldridge Cleaver (Aug 31, 1935), Frank Robinson (Aug 31,

1935), Seiji Ozawa (Sep 1, 1935), Eileen Brennan (Sep 3, 1935), Ken Kesey (Sep 17, 1935), Henry Gibson (Sep 21, 1935), Jerry Lee Lewis (Sep 29, 1935), Z.Z. Hill (Sep 30, 1935), Johnny Mathis (Sep 30, 1935), Julie Andrews (Oct 1, 1935), Luciano Pavarotti (Oct 12, 1935), Peter Boyle (Oct 18, 1935), Gary Player (Nov 1, 1935), Roy Scheider (Nov 10, 1935), Bibi Andersson (Nov 11, 1935), King Hussein of Jordan (Nov 14, 1935), Woody Allen (Dec 1, 1935), Lee Remick (Dec 14, 1935), Phil Donahue (Dec 21, 1935), Sandy Koufax (Dec 30, 1935), Roger Miller (Jan 2, 1936), Troy Donahue (Jan 27, 1936), Alan Alda (Jan 28, 1936), Burt Reynolds (Feb 11, 1936), Jim Brown (Feb 17, 1936), Barbara Jordan (Feb 21, 1936), Jack Lousma (Feb 29, 1936), Dean Stockwell (Mar 5, 1936), Marion Barry (Mar 6, 1936), Mickey Gilley (Mar 9, 1936), F.W. de Klerk (Mar 18, 1936), Ursula Andress (Mar 19, 1936), John Madden (Apr 10, 1936), Glen Campbell (Apr 22, 1936), Roy Orbison (Apr 23, 1936), Jill Ireland (Apr 24, 1936), Zubin Mehta (Apr 29, 1936), Engelbert Humperdinck (May 2, 1936), Albert Finney (May 9, 1936), Glenda Jackson (May 9, 1936), Gary Owens (May 10, 1936), Tom Snyder (May 12, 1936), Bobby Darin (May 14, 1936), Anna Maria Alberghetti (May 15, 1936), Dennis Hopper (May 17, 1936), Louis Gossett Jr (May 27, 1936), Keir Dullea (May 30, 1936), Bruce Dern (Jun 4, 1936), Chad Everett (Jun 11, 1936), Kris Kristofferson (Jun 22, 1936), Don Drysdale (Jul 23, 1936), Elizabeth Dole (Jul 29, 1936), Buddy Guy (Jul 30, 1936), Yves Saint Laurent (Aug 1, 1936), Wilt Chamberlain (Aug 21, 1936), John McCain (Aug 29, 1936), Buddy Holly (Sep 7, 1936), Jim Henson (Sep 24, 1936), Juliet Prowse (Sep 25, 1936), Stella Stevens (Oct 1, 1936), Rona Barrett (Oct 8, 1936), David Nelson (Oct 24, 1936), Charlie Daniels (Oct 28, 1936), Michael Landon (Oct 31, 1936), Mary Travers (Nov 9, 1936), Dick Cavett (Nov 19, 1936), Abbie Hoffman (Nov 30, 1936), Lou Rawls (Dec 1, 1936), David Ossman (Dec 6, 1936), David Carradine (Dec 8, 1936), Mary Tyler Moore (Dec 29,

1936), Dyan Cannon (Jan 4, 1937), Shirley Bassey (Jan 8, 1937), Margaret O'Brien (Jan 15, 1937), Dorothy Provine (Jan 20, 1937), Joseph Wambaugh (Jan 22, 1937), Vanessa Redgrave (Jan 30, 1937), Boris Spassky (Jan 30, 1937), Suzanne Pleshette (Jan 31, 1937), Don Everly (Feb 1, 1937), Tom Smothers (Feb 2, 1937), Nancy Wilson (Feb 20, 1937), Tom Courtenay (Feb 25, 1937), Lois Lowry (Mar 20, 1937), Warren Beatty (Mar 30, 1937), Colin Powell (Apr 5, 1937), Merle Haggard (Apr 6, 1937), Billy Dee Williams (Apr 6, 1937), Jack Nicholson (Apr 22, 1937), Sandy Dennis (Apr 27, 1937), Saddam Hussein (Apr 28, 1937), Frankie Valli (May 3, 1937), George Carlin (May 12, 1937), Madeleine Albright (May 15, 1937), Trini Lopez (May 15, 1937), Brooks Robinson (May 18, 1937), Morgan Freeman (Jun 1, 1937), Sally Kellerman (Jun 2, 1937), Waylon Jennings (Jun 15, 1937), Erich Segal (Jun 16, 1937), Richard Petty (Jul 2, 1937), Tom Stoppard (Jul 3, 1937), Ned Beatty (Jul 6, 1937), Bill Cosby (Jul 12, 1937), Dustin Hoffman (Aug 8, 1937), Robert Redford (Aug 18, 1937), Jo Anne Worley (Sep 6, 1937), Linda Lavin (Oct 15, 1937), Peter Max (Oct 19, 1937), Claude Lelouch (Oct 30, 1937), Loretta Swit (Nov 4, 1937), Robert Guillaume (Nov 30, 1937), Jane Fonda (Dec 21, 1937), Noel Paul Stookey (Dec 30, 1937), Anthony Hopkins (Dec 31, 1937), Paul Revere (Jan 7, 1938), Jack Jones (Jan 14, 1938), Sherman Hemsley (Feb 1, 1938), Judy Blume (Feb 12, 1938), James Farentino (Feb 24, 1938), Paula Prentiss (Mar 4, 1938), Rudolf Nureyev (Mar 17, 1938), Charlie Pride (Mar 18, 1938), Ali McGraw (Apr 1, 1938), Kofi Annan (Apr 8, 1938), Duane Eddy (Apr 26, 1938), Richard Benjamin (May 22, 1938), Susan Strasberg (May 22, 1938), Tommy Chong (May 24, 1938), Peter Yarrow (May 31, 1938), Joyce Carol Oates (Jun 16, 1938), Paul Verhoeven (Jul 18, 1938), Diana Rigg (Jul 20, 1938), Natalie Wood (Jul 20, 1938), Peter Jennings (Jul 29, 1938)

**Pluto Leo:** Aug 3, 1938 – Feb 7, 1939

Connie Stevens (Aug 8, 1938), Kenny Rogers (Aug 21, 1938),

Elliott Gould (Aug 29, 1938), Nicol Williamson (Sep 14, 1938), Rex Reed (Oct 2, 1938), Evel Knievel (Oct 17, 1938), Christopher Lloyd (Oct 22, 1938), Pat Buchanan (Nov 2, 1938), Gordon Lightfoot (Nov 17, 1938), Ted Turner (Nov 19, 1938), Marlo Thomas (Nov 21, 1938), Rich Little (Nov 26, 1938), Connie Francis (Dec 12, 1938), Jon Voight (Dec 29, 1938), Jim Bakker (Jan 2, 1939), Bobby Hull (Jan 3, 1939), Yvette Mimieux (Jan 8, 1939), Sal Mineo (Jan 10, 1939), Maury Povich (Jan 17, 1939), Phil Everly (Jan 19, 1939), Wolfman Jack (Jan 21, 1939), Mike Farrell (Feb 6, 1939)

**Pluto Cancer**: Feb 7, 1939 – Jun 14, 1939

Roberta Flack (Feb 10, 1939), Ray Manzarek (Feb 12, 1939), Peter Fonda (Feb 23, 1939), Tommy Tune (Feb 28, 1939), Samantha Eggar (Mar 5, 1939), Neil Sedaka (Mar 13, 1939), James Caan (Mar 26, 1939), Marvin Gaye (Apr 2, 1939), Francis Coppola (Apr 7, 1939), David Frost (Apr 7, 1939), Michael Learned (Apr 9, 1939), Claudia Cardinale (Apr 15, 1939), Dusty Springfield (Apr 16, 1939), Judy Collins (May 1, 1939), Harvey Keitel (May 13, 1939), James Fox (May 19, 1939), Brent Musburger (May 26, 1939), Al Unser (May 29, 1939), Michael J. Pollard (May 30, 1939)

**Pluto Leo**: Jun 14, 1939 – Oct 20, 1956

Hunter S. Thompson (Jul 18, 1939), Terrence Stamp (Jul 22, 1939), Peter Bogdanovich (Jul 30, 1939), George Hamilton (Aug 12, 1939), Carl Yastrzemski (Aug 22, 1939), Lily Tomlin (Sep 1, 1939), Frankie Avalon (Sep 18, 1939), Paul Hogan (Oct 8, 1939), Ralph Lauren (Oct 14, 1939), Mike Ditka (Oct 18, 1939), Lee Harvey Oswald (Oct 18, 1939), Tony Roberts (Oct 22, 1939), F. Murray Abraham (Oct 24, 1939), John Cleese (Oct 27, 1939), Grace Slick (Oct 30, 1939), Brenda Vaccaro (Nov 18, 1939), Dick Smothers (Nov 20, 1939), Tina Turner (Nov 26, 1939), Peter Bergman (Nov 29, 1939), Lee Trevino (Dec 1, 1939), James Galway (Dec 8, 1939), Liv Ullmann (Dec 16, 1939), John Amos (Dec 27, 1939), Del Shannon (Dec 30, 1939),

Jack Nicklaus (Jan 21, 1940), John Hurt (Jan 22, 1940), Fran Tarkenton (Feb 3, 1940), Tom Brokaw (Feb 6, 1940), Ted Koppel (Feb 8, 1940), Nick Nolte (Feb 8, 1940), Smokey Robinson (Feb 19, 1940), Mario Andretti (Feb 28, 1940), Raul Julia (Mar 9, 1940), Chuck Norris (Mar 10, 1940), Al Jarreau (Mar 12, 1940), Phil Lesh (Mar 15, 1940), Bernardo Bertolucci (Mar 16, 1940), Anita Bryant (Mar 25, 1940), Astrud Gilberto (Mar 30, 1940), Herbie Hancock (Apr 12, 1940), Lee Majors (Apr 23, 1940), Al Pacino (Apr 25, 1940), Burt Young (Apr 30, 1940), Peter Benchley (May 8, 1940), Rick Nelson (May 8, 1940), James L. Brooks (May 9, 1940), Tom Jones (Jun 7, 1940), Nancy Sinatra (Jun 8, 1940), Mariette Hartley (Jun 21, 1940), Ringo Starr (Jul 7, 1940), Patrick Stewart (Jul 13, 1940), Alex Trebek (Jul 22, 1940), Don Imus (Jul 23, 1940), Martin Sheen (Aug 3, 1940), Jill St. John (Aug 19, 1940), Valerie Harper (Aug 22, 1940), Raquel Welch (Sep 5, 1940), Brian DePalma (Sep 11, 1940), Linda Gray (Sep 12, 1940), Merlin Olsen (Sep 15, 1940), Paul Williams (Sep 19, 1940), John Lennon (Oct 9, 1940), Sir Cliff Richard (Oct 14, 1940), Pelé (Oct 23, 1940), Bobby Knight (Oct 25, 1940), Elke Sommer (Nov 5, 1940), Sam Waterston (Nov 15, 1940), Bruce Lee (Nov 27, 1940), Chuck Mangione (Nov 29, 1940), Richard Pryor (Dec 1, 1940), Frank Zappa (Dec 21, 1940), Phil Spector (Dec 26, 1940), Don Francisco (Dec 28, 1940), Joan Baez (Jan 9, 1941), Susannah York (Jan 9, 1941), Faye Dunaway (Jan 14, 1941), Bobby Goldsboro (Jan 18, 1941), Placido Domingo (Jan 21, 1941), Neil Diamond (Jan 24, 1941), Aaron Neville (Jan 24, 1941), Dick Cheney (Jan 30, 1941), Richard Gephardt (Jan 31, 1941), Segio Mendes (Feb 11, 1941), Buffy Sainte-Marie (Feb 20, 1941), Willie Stargell (Mar 6, 1941), Barbara Feldon (Mar 12, 1941), Paul Kantner (Mar 17, 1941), Wilson Pickett (Mar 18, 1941), Julie Christie (Apr 14, 1941), Pete Rose (Apr 14, 1941), Ryan O'Neal (Apr 20, 1941), Ann-Margret (Apr 28, 1941), Ritchie Valens (May 13, 1941), Nora Ephron (May 19, 1941), Paul Winfield (May 22, 1941), Bob

Dylan (May 24, 1941), Johnny Paycheck (May 31, 1941), Charlie Watts (Jun 2, 1941), Marv Albert (Jun 12, 1941), Chick Corea (Jun 12, 1941), Ed Bradley (Jun 22, 1941), Martha Reeves (Jul 18, 1941), Vikki Carr (Jul 19, 1941), Paul Anka (Jul 30, 1941), Martha Stewart (Aug 3, 1941)

**Uranus Gemini**: Aug 7, 1941 – Oct 5, 1941

Lynne Cheney (Aug 14, 1941), David Crosby (Aug 14, 1941), Robin Leach (Aug 29, 1941), Otis Redding (Sep 9, 1941), Linda McCartney (Sep 24, 1941), Chubby Checker (Oct 3, 1941), Anne Rice (Oct 4, 1941)

**Uranus Taurus**: Oct 5, 1941 – May 15, 1942

Jesse Jackson (Oct 8, 1941), Paul Simon (Oct 13, 1941), Helen Reddy (Oct 25, 1941), Art Garfunkel (Nov 5, 1941), Tom Fogerty (Nov 9, 1941), Eddie Rabbit (Nov 27, 1941), Beau Bridges (Dec 9, 1941), Dionne Warwick (Dec 12, 1941), John Davidson (Dec 13, 1941), Lesley Stahl (Dec 16, 1941), Sarah Miles (Dec 31, 1941), Stephen Hawking (Jan 8, 1942), Muhammad Ali (Jan 17, 1942), Michael Crawford (Jan 19, 1942), Katharine Ross (Jan 29, 1942), Marty Balin (Jan 30, 1942), Graham Nash (Feb 2, 1942), Roger Staubach (Feb 5, 1942), Carole King (Feb 9, 1942), Peter Tork (Feb 13, 1942), Joe Lieberman (Feb 24, 1942), Brian Jones (Feb 28, 1942), Tammy Faye Bakker (Mar 7, 1942), Charles W. Swan (Mar 11, 1942), Aretha Franklin (Mar 25, 1942), Erica Jong (Mar 26, 1942), Michael York (Mar 27, 1942), Wayne Newton (Apr 3, 1942), Sandra Dee (Apr 23, 1942), Barbra Streisand (Apr 24, 1942), Bobby Rydell (Apr 26, 1942), Tammy Wynette (May 5, 1942)

**Uranus Gemini**: May 15, 1942 – Aug 30, 1948

Curtis Mayfield (Jun 3, 1942), Roger Ebert (Jun 18, 1942), Sir Paul McCartney (Jun 18, 1942), Brian Wilson (Jun 20, 1942), Mick Fleetwood (Jun 24, 1942), Michele Lee (Jun 24, 1942), Karen Black (Jul 1, 1942), Vincente Fox (Jul 2, 1942), Harrison Ford (Jul 13, 1942), Jerry Garcia (Aug 1, 1942), Garrison Keillor (Aug 7, 1942), Isaac Hayes (Aug 20, 1942), Richard

Roundtree (Sep 7, 1942), Bela Karolyi (Sep 13, 1942), Madeline Kahn (Sep 29, 1942)

**Neptune Libra**: Oct 3, 1942 – Apr 17, 1943

Britt Ekland (Oct 6, 1942), Penny Marshall (Oct 15, 1942), Judge Judy Sheindlin (Oct 21, 1942), Annette Funicello (Oct 22, 1942), Michael Crichton (Oct 23, 1942), Larry Flynt (Nov 1, 1942), Stefanie Powers (Nov 2, 1942), Martin Scorsese (Nov 17, 1942), Linda Evans (Nov 18, 1942), Calvin Klein (Nov 19, 1942), Jimi Hendrix (Nov 27, 1942), Harry Chapin (Dec 7, 1942), Dick Butkus (Dec 9, 1942), Donna Mills (Dec 11, 1942), Dave Clark (Dec 15, 1942), Michael Nesmith (Dec 30, 1942), Don Novello (Jan 1, 1943), Janis Joplin (Jan 19, 1943), Fabian (Feb 6, 1943), Joe Pesci (Feb 9, 1943), David Geffen (Feb 21, 1943), George Harrison (Feb 25, 1943), Lynn Redgrave (Mar 8, 1943), Bobby Fischer (Mar 9, 1943), George Benson (Mar 22, 1943), Paul Michael Glaser (Mar 25, 1943), Bob Woodward (Mar 26, 1943), John Major (Mar 29, 1943), Christopher Walken (Mar 31, 1943)

**Neptune Virgo**: Apr 17, 1943 – Aug 2, 1943

Leslie Uggams (May 25, 1943), Joe Namath (May 31, 1943), Malcolm McDowell (Jun 13, 1943), Newt Gingrich (Jun 17, 1943), Geraldo Rivera (Jul 4, 1943), Arthur Ashe (Jul 10, 1943), Christine McVie (Jul 12, 1943), Bobby Sherman (Jul 22, 1943), Mick Jagger (Jul 26, 1943), Bill Bradley (Jul 28, 1943)

**Neptune Libra**: Aug 2, 1943 – Dec 24, 1955

Robert De Niro (Aug 17, 1943), Martin Mull (Aug 18, 1943), Tuesday Weld (Aug 27, 1943), David Soul (Aug 28, 1943), Jean-Claude Killy (Aug 30, 1943), Valerie Perrine (Sep 3, 1943), Roger Waters (Sep 9, 1943), Lola Falana (Sep 11, 1943), Maria Muldaur (Sep 12, 1943), 'Mama' Cass Elliott (Sep 19, 1943), Julio Iglesias (Sep 23, 1943), Lech Walesa (Sep 29, 1943), Chevy Chase (Oct 8, 1943), R.L. Stine (Oct 8, 1943), Catherine Deneuve (Oct 22, 1943), Sam Shepard (Nov 5, 1943), Joni Mitchell (Nov 7, 1943), Lauren Hutton (Nov 17, 1943),

Veronica Hamel (Nov 20, 1943), Billie Jean King (Nov 22, 1943), Randy Newman (Nov 28, 1943), Jim Morrison (Dec 8, 1943), John Kerry (Dec 11, 1943), Steven Bochco (Dec 16, 1943), Keith Richards (Dec 18, 1943), Harry Shearer (Dec 23, 1943), Cokie Roberts (Dec 27, 1943), John Denver (Dec 31, 1943), Ben Kingsley (Dec 31, 1943), Bonnie Franklin (Jan 6, 1944), Jimmy Page (Jan 9, 1944), Joe Frazier (Jan 12, 1944), Ronnie Milsap (Jan 16, 1944), Shelley Fabares (Jan 19, 1944), Rutger Hauer (Jan 23, 1944), Angela Davis (Jan 26, 1944), Nick Mason (Jan 27, 1944), Charlie Musselwhite (Jan 31, 1944), Michael Tucker (Feb 6, 1944), Alice Walker (Feb 9, 1944), Stockard Channing (Feb 13, 1944), Jerry Springer (Feb 13, 1944), Carl Bernstein (Feb 14, 1944), John Sandford (Feb 23, 1944), Johnny Winter (Feb 23, 1944), Roger Daltrey (Mar 1, 1944), Lou Reed (Mar 2, 1944), Sly Stone (Mar 15, 1944), John Sebastian (Mar 17, 1944), Timothy Dalton (Mar 21, 1944), Diana Ross (Mar 26, 1944), Ken Howard (Mar 28, 1944), Tony Orlando (Apr 3, 1944), Jack Casady (Apr 13, 1944), Jill Clayburgh (Apr 30, 1944), George Lucas (May 14, 1944), Joe Cocker (May 20, 1944), Patti LaBelle (May 24, 1944), Frank Oz (May 25, 1944), Rudolph Giuliani (May 28, 1944), Gladys Knight (May 28, 1944), Marvin Hamlisch (Jun 2, 1944), Michelle Phillips (Jun 4, 1944), Boz Scaggs (Jun 8, 1944), Ray Davies (Jun 21, 1944), Jeff Beck (Jun 24, 1944), Gary Busey (Jun 29, 1944), Erno Rubik (Jul 13, 1944), Bobbie Gentry (Jul 27, 1944), Geraldine Chaplin (Jul 31, 1944), Sam Elliott (Aug 9, 1944), Linda Ellerbee (Aug 15, 1944), Frank 'Tug' McGraw (Aug 30, 1944), Swoosie Kurtz (Sep 6, 1944), Barry White (Sep 12, 1944), Jacqueline Bisset (Sep 13, 1944), Michael Douglas (Sep 25, 1944), Anne Robinson (Sep 26, 1944), Roy Uwe Ludwig Horn (Oct 3, 1944), John Entwistle (Oct 9, 1944), Jon Anderson (Oct 25, 1944), Dennis Franz (Oct 28, 1944), Tim Rice (Nov 10, 1944), Al Michaels (Nov 12, 1944), Danny DeVito (Nov 17, 1944), Lorne Michaels (Nov 17, 1944), Tom

Seaver (Nov 17, 1944), John Densmore (Dec 1, 1944), Dennis Wilson (Dec 4, 1944), Brenda Lee (Dec 11, 1944), Richard Leakey (Dec 19, 1944), Alvin Lee (Dec 19, 1944), Tim Reid (Dec 19, 1944), Stephen Stills (Jan 3, 1945), Rod Stewart (Jan 10, 1945), Tom Selleck (Jan 29, 1945), David Brenner (Feb 4, 1945), Bob Marley (Feb 6, 1945), Mia Farrow (Feb 9, 1945), Rob Reiner (Mar 6, 1945), Micky Dolenz (Mar 8, 1945), Robin Trower (Mar 9, 1945), Pat Riley (Mar 20, 1945), Eric Clapton (Mar 30, 1945), Gabe Kaplan (Mar 31, 1945), Linda Hunt (Apr 2, 1945), Tony Dow (Apr 13, 1945), Ritchie Blackmore (Apr 14, 1945), Doug Clifford (Apr 24, 1945), Stu Cook (Apr 25, 1945), Rita Coolidge (May 1, 1945), Bianca Jagger (May 2, 1945), Bob Seger (May 6, 1945), Pete Townshend (May 19, 1945), Priscilla Presley (May 24, 1945), John Fogerty (May 28, 1945), Art Bell (Jun 17, 1945), Anne Murray (Jun 20, 1945), Carly Simon (Jun 25, 1945), Deborah Harry (Jul 1, 1945), Burt Ward (Jul 6, 1945), Jim Davis (Jul 28, 1945), Rick Wright (Jul 28, 1945), Steve Martin (Aug 14, 1945), Van Morrison (Aug 31, 1945), Itzhak Perlman (Aug 31, 1945), José Feliciano (Sep 10, 1945), Paul Petersen (Sep 23, 1945), Rod Carew (Oct 1, 1945), Don McLean (Oct 2, 1945), Jim Palmer (Oct 15, 1945), John Lithgow (Oct 19, 1945), Jeannie C. Riley (Oct 19, 1945), Henry Winkler (Oct 30, 1945), Neil Young (Nov 12, 1945), Goldie Hawn (Nov 21, 1945), Bette Midler (Dec 1, 1945), Diane Sawyer (Dec 22, 1945), Gary Sandy (Dec 25, 1945), John Walsh (Dec 26, 1945), Davy Jones (Dec 30, 1945), John Paul Jones (Jan 3, 1946), Diane Keaton (Jan 5, 1946), Robby Krieger (Jan 8, 1946), Naomi Judd (Jan 11, 1946), Dolly Parton (Jan 19, 1946), David Lynch (Jan 20, 1946), Gene Siskel (Jan 26, 1946), Gregory Hines (Feb 14, 1946), Sandy Duncan (Feb 20, 1946), Tyne Daly (Feb 21, 1946), Alan Rickman (Feb 21, 1946), Dan Millman (Feb 22, 1946), Michael Warren (Mar 5, 1946), David Gilmour (Mar 6, 1946), Liza Minnelli (Mar 12, 1946), Bonnie Bedelia (Mar 25, 1946), Craig T. Nelson (Apr 4, 1946), Ed O'Neill (Apr 12, 1946), Al

Green (Apr 13, 1946), Hayley Mills (Apr 18, 1946), Tim Curry (Apr 19, 1946), Lesley Gore (May 2, 1946), Candice Bergen (May 9, 1946), Donovan (May 10, 1946), Reggie Jackson (May 18, 1946), André the Giant (May 19, 1946), Cher (May 20, 1946), Jenny Jones (Jun 7, 1946), Donald Trump (Jun 14, 1946), Barry Manilow (Jun 17, 1946), Gilda Radner (Jun 28, 1946), George W. Bush (Jul 6, 1946), Sylvester Stallone (Jul 6, 1946), Cheech Marin (Jul 13, 1946), Linda Ronstadt (Jul 15, 1946), Kim Carnes (Jul 20, 1946), Kenneth Starr (Jul 21, 1946), Helen Mirren (Jul 26, 1946), Loni Anderson (Aug 5, 1946), Susan St James (Aug 14, 1946), Jimmy Webb (Aug 15, 1946), Lesley Ann Warren (Aug 16, 1946), Bill Clinton (Aug 19, 1946), Connie Chung (Aug 20, 1946), Rollie Fingers (Aug 25, 1946), Barry Gibb (Sep 1, 1946), Freddie Mercury (Sep 5, 1946), Billy Preston (Sep 9, 1946), Tommy Lee Jones (Sep 15, 1946), Oliver Stone (Sep 15, 1946), Susan Sarandon (Oct 4, 1946), Charles Dance (Oct 10, 1946), Ben Vereen (Oct 10, 1946), Richard Carpenter (Oct 15, 1946), Suzanne Somers (Oct 16, 1946), Laura W. Bush (Nov 4, 1946), Sally Field (Nov 6, 1946), Duane Allman (Nov 20, 1946), Joe Dante (Nov 28, 1946), Gianni Versace (Dec 2, 1946), Emerson Fittipaldi (Dec 12, 1946), Patty Duke (Dec 14, 1946), Benny Andersson (Dec 16, 1946), Steven Spielberg (Dec 18, 1946), Robert Urich (Dec 19, 1946), Uri Geller (Dec 20, 1946), Jimmy Buffett (Dec 25, 1946), Edgar Winter (Dec 28, 1946), Marianne Faithfull (Dec 29, 1946), Patti Smith (Dec 30, 1946), Don Bendell (Jan 8, 1947), David Bowie (Jan 8, 1947), Jill Eikenberry (Jan 21, 1947), Dr Laura Schlessinger (Jan 23, 1947), Warren Zevon (Jan 24, 1947), Steve Marriott (Jan 30, 1947), Nolan Ryan (Jan 31, 1947), Farrah Fawcett (Feb 2, 1947), Dave Davies (Feb 3, 1947), Dan Quayle (Feb 4, 1947), Edward James Olmos (Feb 24, 1947), Alan Thicke (Mar 1, 1947), Kim Campbell (Mar 10, 1947), Bob Greene (Mar 10, 1947), Billy Crystal (Mar 14, 1947), Glenn Close (Mar 19, 1947), Elton John (Mar 25, 1947), Emmylou

Harris (Apr 2, 1947), Tom Clancy (Apr 12, 1947), David Letterman (Apr 12, 1947), Kareem Abdul-Jabbar (Apr 16, 1947), James Woods (Apr 18, 1947), Iggy Pop (Apr 21, 1947), Doug Henning (May 3, 1947), Bob Edwards (May 16, 1947), Salman Rushdie (Jun 19, 1947), Meredith Baxter (Jun 21, 1947), Michael Gross (Jun 21, 1947), Richard Lewis (Jun 29, 1947), O.J. Simpson (Jul 9, 1947), Arlo Guthrie (Jul 10, 1947), Camilla Parker Bowles (Jul 17, 1947), Brian May (Jul 19, 1947), Carlos Santana (Jul 20, 1947), Albert Brooks (Jul 22, 1947), Danny Glover (Jul 22, 1947), Don Henley (Jul 22, 1947), Betty Thomas (Jul 27, 1947), Arnold Schwarzenegger (Jul 30, 1947), Ian Anderson (Aug 10, 1947), Danielle Steel (Aug 14, 1947), Cindy Williams (Aug 22, 1947), Barbara Bach (Aug 27, 1947), James Hunt (Aug 29, 1947), Peggy Lipton (Aug 30, 1947), Jane Curtin (Sep 6, 1947), Sam Neill (Sep 14, 1947), Stephen King (Sep 21, 1947), Mary Kay Place (Sep 23, 1947), Cheryl Tiegs (Sep 25, 1947), Meat Loaf (Sep 27, 1947), Chris Wallace (Oct 12, 1947), Sammy Hagar (Oct 13, 1947), Laura Nyro (Oct 18, 1947), Kevin Kline (Oct 24, 1947), Hillary Rodham Clinton (Oct 26, 1947), Pat Sajak (Oct 26, 1947), Jaclyn Smith (Oct 26, 1947), Richard Dreyfuss (Oct 29, 1947), Deidre Hall (Oct 31, 1947), Peter Noone (Nov 5, 1947), John Larroquette (Nov 25, 1947), David Mamet (Nov 30, 1947), Jim Messina (Dec 5, 1947), Johnny Bench (Dec 7, 1947), Gregg Allman (Dec 8, 1947), Carlton Fisk (Dec 26, 1947), Ted Danson (Dec 29, 1947), Kenny Loggins (Jan 7, 1948), John Carpenter (Jan 16, 1948), Mikhail Baryshnikov (Jan 27, 1948), Alice Cooper (Feb 4, 1948), Christopher Guest (Feb 5, 1948), Barbara Hershey (Feb 5, 1948), Jennifer O'Neill (Feb 20, 1948), Bernadette Peters (Feb 28, 1948), James Taylor (Mar 12, 1948), Andrew Lloyd Webber (Mar 22, 1948), Steven Tyler (Mar 26, 1948), Dianne Wiest (Mar 28, 1948), Al Gore (Mar 31, 1948), Rhea Perlman (Mar 31, 1948), Steve Winwood (May 12, 1948), Stevie Nicks (May 26, 1948), John Bonham (May 31, 1948), Jerry Mathers (Jun 2, 1948), Phylicia Rashad

(Jun 19, 1948), Todd Rundgren (Jun 22, 1948), Kathy Bates (Jun 28, 1948), Richard Simmons (Jul 12, 1948), Cat Stevens/Yusuf Islam (Jul 21, 1948), Peggy Fleming (Jul 27, 1948), Sally Struthers (Jul 28, 1948), Jean Reno (Jul 30, 1948), Tipper Gore (Aug 19, 1948), Robert Plant (Aug 20, 1948)

**Uranus Cancer:** Aug 30, 1948 – Nov 12, 1948

Christa McAuliffe (Sep 2, 1948), Nell Carter (Sep 13, 1948), John Ritter (Sep 17, 1948), Jeremy Irons (Sep 19, 1948), Phil Hartman (Sep 24, 1948), Olivia Newton-John (Sep 26, 1948), Bryant Gumbel (Sep 29, 1948), Donna Karan (Oct 2, 1948), Jackson Browne (Oct 9, 1948), Margot Kidder (Oct 17, 1948), George Wendt (Oct 17, 1948), Kate Jackson (Oct 29, 1948), Lulu (Nov 3, 1948), Glenn Frey (Nov 6, 1948)

**Uranus Gemini:** Nov 12, 1948 – Jun 10, 1949

Prince Charles (Nov 14, 1948), Cathy Lee Crosby (Dec 2, 1948), Ozzy Osbourne (Dec 3, 1948), Ted Nugent (Dec 13, 1948), Samuel L. Jackson (Dec 21, 1948), Steve Garvey (Dec 22, 1948), Susan Lucci (Dec 23, 1948), Barbara Mandrell (Dec 25, 1948), Gerard Depardieu (Dec 27, 1948), Donna Summer (Dec 31, 1948), George Foreman (Jan 10, 1949), Andy Kaufman (Jan 17, 1949), Robert Palmer (Jan 19, 1949), Steve Perry (Jan 22, 1949), John Belushi (Jan 24, 1949), Ivana Trump (Feb 20, 1949), Erik Estrada (Mar 16, 1949), Patrick Duffy (Mar 17, 1949), Vicki Lawrence (Mar 26, 1949), Paloma Picasso (Apr 19, 1949), Jessica Lange (Apr 20, 1949), Billy Joel (May 9, 1949), Philip Michael Thomas (May 26, 1949), Hank Williams Jr (May 26, 1949), Ken Follett (Jun 5, 1949)

**Uranus Cancer:** Jun 10, 1949 – Aug 24, 1955

Lionel Richie (Jun 20, 1949), Meryl Streep (Jun 22, 1949), Lindsay Wagner (Jun 22, 1949), Phyllis George (Jun 25, 1949), Jimmie Walker (Jun 25, 1949), Shelley Duvall (Jul 7, 1949), Tommy Mottola (Jul 14, 1949), Alan Menken (Jul 22, 1949), Michael Richards (Jul 24, 1949), Roger Taylor (Jul 26, 1949), Maureen McGovern (Jul 27, 1949), Marilyn Quayle (Jul 29,

1949), Keith Carradine (Aug 8, 1949), Shelley Long (Aug 23, 1949), Rick Springfield (Aug 23, 1949), Gene Simmons (Aug 25, 1949), Richard Gere (Aug 31, 1949), Tom Watson (Sep 4, 1949), Gloria Gaynor (Sep 7, 1949), Ed Begley Jr (Sep 16, 1949), Lesley 'Twiggy' Lawson (Sep 19, 1949), Bruce Springsteen (Sep 23, 1949), Mike Schmidt (Sep 27, 1949), Lindsey Buckingham (Oct 3, 1949), Sigourney Weaver (Oct 8, 1949), Benjamin Netanyahu (Oct 21, 1949), Bruce Jenner (Oct 28, 1949), Bonnie Raitt (Nov 8, 1949), Alexander Godunov (Nov 28, 1949), Paul Shaffer (Nov 28, 1949), Garry Shandling (Nov 29, 1949), Jeff Bridges (Dec 4, 1949), Tom Waits (Dec 7, 1949), Teri Garr (Dec 11, 1949), Don Johnson (Dec 15, 1949), Maurice Gibb (Dec 22, 1949), Robin Gibb (Dec 22, 1949), Sissy Spacek (Dec 25, 1949), Victoria Principal (Jan 3, 1950), Debbie Allen (Jan 16, 1950), Ann Jillian (Jan 29, 1950), Morgan Fairchild (Feb 3, 1950), Natalie Cole (Feb 6, 1950), Mark Spitz (Feb 10, 1950), Peter Gabriel (Feb 13, 1950), John Hughes (Feb 18, 1950), Cybill Shepherd (Feb 18, 1950), Julius 'Dr J' Erving (Feb 22, 1950), Karen Carpenter (Mar 2, 1950), Bobby McFerrin (Mar 11, 1950), William H. Macy (Mar 13, 1950), Brad Dourif (Mar 18, 1950), William Hurt (Mar 20, 1950), Teddy Pendergrass (Mar 26, 1950), Martin Short (Mar 26, 1950), Bud Cort (Mar 29, 1950), David Cassidy (Apr 12, 1950), Peter Frampton (Apr 22, 1950), Jay Leno (Apr 28, 1950), Stevie Wonder (May 13, 1950), Gregory Harrison (May 31, 1950), Suzi Quatro (Jun 3, 1950), Judge Lance Ito (Aug 2, 1950), Ann Wilson (Jun 19, 1950), John Landis (Aug 3, 1950), Steve Wozniak (Aug 11, 1950), Gary Larson (Aug 14, 1950), Dr Phil McGraw (Sep 1, 1950), Cathy Guisewite (Sep 5, 1950), Joan Lunden (Sep 19, 1950), Bill Murray (Sep 21, 1950), Randy Quaid (Oct 1, 1950), Tom Petty (Oct 20, 1950), John Candy (Oct 31, 1950), Jane Pauley (Oct 31, 1950), Markie Post (Nov 4, 1950), Ed Harris (Nov 28, 1950), Leonard Maltin (Dec 18, 1950), Crystal Gayle (Jan 9, 1951), Rush Limbaugh (Jan 12, 1951), Charo (Jan 15, 1951), Yakov

Smirnoff (Jan 24, 1951), Phil Collins (Jan 30, 1951), Melissa Manchester (Feb 15, 1951), Jane Seymour (Feb 15, 1951), Patricia Richardson (Feb 23, 1951), Kurt Russell (Mar 17, 1951), Janis Ian (Apr 7, 1951), Olivia Hussey (Apr 17, 1951), Tony Danza (Apr 21, 1951), Dale Earnhardt (Apr 29, 1951), Christopher Cross (May 3, 1951), Robert Zemeckis (May 14, 1951), Joey Ramone (May 19, 1951), Sally Ride (May 26, 1951), Deniece Williams (Jun 3, 1951), Joe Piscopo (Jun 17, 1951), Julia Duffy (Jun 27, 1951), Huey Lewis (Jul 5, 1951), Geoffrey Rush (Jul 6, 1951), Anjelica Huston (Jul 8, 1951), Cheryl Ladd (Jul 12, 1951), Jesse Ventura (Jul 15, 1951), Lynda Carter (Jul 24, 1951), Jay North (Aug 3, 1951), Dan Fogelberg (Aug 13, 1951), Timothy Bottoms (Aug 30, 1951), Mark Harmon (Sep 2, 1951), Julie Kavner (Sep 7, 1951), Michael Keaton (Sep 9, 1951), Cassandra 'Elvira' Peterson (Sep 17, 1951), Mark Hamill (Sep 25, 1951), Sting (Oct 2, 1951), Karen Allen (Oct 5, 1951), John Cougar Mellencamp (Oct 7, 1951), Pam Dawber (Oct 18, 1951), Mary Hart (Nov 8, 1951), Lou Ferrigno (Nov 9, 1951), Marc Summers (Nov 11, 1951), Morgan Brittany (Dec 5, 1951), Ben Crenshaw (Jan 11, 1952), Laraine Newman (Mar 2, 1952), Douglas Adams (Mar 11, 1952), Bob Costas (Mar 22, 1952), Marilu Henner (Apr 6, 1952), Steven Seagal (Apr 10, 1952), David Byrne (May 14, 1952), Mr. T (May 21, 1952), Marvin Hagler (May 23, 1952), Liam Neeson (Jun 7, 1952), Isabella Rossellini (Jun 18, 1952), John Goodman (Jun 20, 1952), Dan Aykroyd (Jul 1, 1952), Alan Autry (Jul 3, 1952), Christopher G. Moore (Jul 8, 1952), Marianne Williamson (Jul 8, 1952), John Tesh (Jul 9, 1952), David Hasselhoff (Jul 17, 1952), Phoebe Snow (Jul 17, 1952), Robin Williams (Jul 21, 1952), Robin Quivers (Aug 8, 1952), Paul 'Pee-wee Herman' Reubens (Aug 27, 1952), Jimmy Connors (Sep 2, 1952), Christopher Reeve (Sep 25, 1952), Sharon Osbourne (Oct 9, 1952), Harry Anderson (Oct 14, 1952), Vladimir Putin (Oct 7, 1952), Jeff Goldblum (Oct 22, 1952), Roseanne (Nov 3, 1952), Mandy

Patinkin (Nov 30, 1952), Cathy Rigby (Dec 12, 1952), Pamela Sue Martin (Jan 5, 1953), Pat Benatar (Jan 10, 1953), Desi Arnaz Jr (Jan 19, 1953), Lucinda Williams (Jan 26, 1953), Michael Bolton (Feb 26, 1953), Chaka Khan (Mar 23, 1953), Louie Anderson (Mar 24, 1953), Tony Blair (May 6, 1953), George Brett (May 15, 1953), Pierce Brosnan (May 16, 1953), Danny Elfman (May 29, 1953), Tim Allen (Jun 13, 1953), Cyndi Lauper (Jun 22, 1953), Leon Spinks (Jul 11, 1953), Hollywood Hulk Hogan (Aug 11, 1953), Kathie Lee Gifford (Aug 16, 1953), Robert Parrish (Aug 30, 1953), Amy Irving (Sep 10, 1953), Kate Capshaw (Nov 3, 1953), Dennis Miller (Nov 3, 1953), Kim Basinger (Dec 8, 1953), John Malkovich (Dec 9, 1953), Howard Stern (Jan 12, 1954), Oprah Winfrey (Jan 29, 1954), Christie Brinkley (Feb 2, 1954), Matt Groening (Feb 15, 1954), Rene Russo (Feb 17, 1954), John Travolta (Feb 18, 1954), Patty Hearst (Feb 20, 1954), Ron Howard (Mar 1, 1954), Jackie Chan (Apr 7, 1954), Dennis Quaid (Apr 9, 1954), Jerry Seinfeld (Apr 29, 1954), Jim Belushi (Jun 15, 1954), Kathleen Turner (Jun 19, 1954), Freddie Prinze (Jun 22, 1954), Walter Payton (Jul 25, 1954), James Cameron (Aug 16, 1954), Patrick Swayze (Aug 18, 1954), Al Roker (Aug 20, 1954), Elvis Costello (Aug 25, 1954), Stevie Ray Vaughan (Oct 3, 1954), Bob Geldof (Oct 5, 1954), Adam Ant (Nov 3, 1954), Yanni (Nov 14, 1954), Bruce Hornsby (Nov 23, 1954), Jermaine Jackson (Dec 11, 1954), Chris Evert (Dec 21, 1954), Annie Lennox (Dec 25, 1954), Ozzie Smith (Dec 26, 1954), Denzel Washington (Dec 28, 1954), Rowan Atkinson (Jan 6, 1955), Kirstie Alley (Jan 12, 1955), Kevin Costner (Jan 18, 1955), Eddie Van Halen (Jan 26, 1955), Charles Shaughnessy (Feb 9, 1955), Greg Norman (Feb 10, 1955), Arsenio Hall (Feb 12, 1955), Jeff Daniels (Feb 19, 1955), Margaux Hemingway (Feb 19, 1955), Kelsey Grammer (Feb 21, 1955), Steven Jobs (Feb 24, 1955), Gilbert Gottfried (Feb 28, 1955), Bruce Willis (Mar 19, 1955), Lena Olin (Mar 22, 1955), Reba McEntire (Mar 28, 1955), Dana Carvey (Apr 2, 1955),

Ellen Barkin (Apr 16, 1955), Tom Bergeron (May 6, 1955), Olga Korbut (May 16, 1955), Debra Winger (May 16, 1955), Bill Paxton (May 17, 1955), Rosanne Cash (May 24, 1955), Sandra Bernhard (Jun 6, 1955), Jimmy Smits (Jul 9, 1955), Willem Dafoe (Jul 22, 1955), Billy Bob Thornton (Aug 4, 1955)

**Uranus Leo**: Aug 24, 1955 – Jan 28, 1956

Robin Yount (Sep 16, 1955), Lorraine Bracco (Oct 2, 1955), YoYo Ma (Oct 7, 1955), David Lee Roth (Oct 10, 1955), Bill Gates (Oct 28, 1955), Maria Shriver (Nov 6, 1955), Whoopi Goldberg (Nov 13, 1955), Howie Mandel (Nov 29, 1955), Billy Idol (Nov 30, 1955)

**Neptune Scorpio**: Dec 24, 1955 – Mar 12, 1956

Mel Gibson (Jan 3, 1956)

**Uranus Cancer**: Jan 28, 1956 – Jun 10, 1956

Eddie Murray (Feb 24, 1956)

**Neptune Libra**: Mar 12, 1956 – Oct 19, 1956

Andy Garcia (Apr 12, 1956), Eric Roberts (Apr 18, 1956), Pia Zadora (May 4, 1956), Sugar Ray Leonard (May 17, 1956), Bob Saget (May 17, 1956), LaToya Jackson (May 29, 1956), Kenny G (Jun 5, 1956), Bjorn Borg (Jun 6, 1956)

**Uranus Leo**: Jun 10, 1956 – Nov 1, 1961; Jan 10, 1962 – Aug 10, 1962

Joe Montana (Jun 11, 1956), Chris Isaak (Jun 26, 1956), Montel Williams (Jul 3, 1956), Tom Hanks (Jul 9, 1956), Dorothy Hamill (Jul 26, 1956), Delta Burke (Jul 30, 1956), Adam Arkin (Aug 19, 1956), Kim Cattrall (Aug 21, 1956), David Copperfield (Sep 16, 1956), Linda Hamilton (Sep 26, 1956), Martina Navratilova (Oct 18, 1956)

**Neptune Scorpio**: Oct 19, 1956 – Jun 15, 1957

**Pluto Virgo**: Oct 20, 1956 – Jan 15, 1957

Carrie Fisher (Oct 21, 1956), Sinbad (Nov 10, 1956), Bo Derek (Nov 20, 1956), Larry Bird (Dec 7, 1956), Nancy Lopez (Jan 6, 1957), Katie Couric (Jan 7, 1957)

**Pluto Leo**: Jan 15, 1957 – Aug 19, 1957

Geena Davis (Jan 21, 1957), Princess Caroline of Monaco (Jan 23, 1957), Vanna White (Feb 18, 1957), Osama bin Laden (Mar 10, 1957), Spike Lee (Mar 20, 1957), Paul Reiser (Mar 30, 1957), Daniel Day-Lewis (Apr 29, 1957), Michelle Pfeiffer (Apr 29, 1957), Sid Vicious (May 10, 1957), Scott Adams, creator of Dilbert (Jun 8, 1957)

**Neptune Libra:** Jun 15, 1957 – Aug 6, 1957

Frances McDormand (Jun 23, 1957), Jon Lovitz (Jul 21, 1957)

**Neptune Scorpio:** Aug 6, 1957 – Jan 4, 1970; May 3, 1970 – Nov 6, 1970

Melanie Griffith (Aug 9, 1957)

**Pluto Virgo:** Aug 19, 1957 – Apr 11, 1958

Gloria Estefan (Sep 1, 1957), Rachel Ward (Sep 12, 1957), Gary Cole (Sep 20, 1957), Fran Drescher (Sep 30, 1957), Bernie Mac (Oct 5, 1957), Chris Carter (Oct 13, 1957), Lyle Lovett (Nov 1, 1957), Caroline Kennedy (Nov 27, 1957), Donny Osmond (Dec 9, 1957), Sheila E. (Dec 12, 1957), Ray Romano (Dec 21, 1957), Matt Lauer (Dec 30, 1957), Anita Baker (Jan 26, 1958), Ellen DeGeneres (Jan 26, 1958), Brett Butler (Jan 30, 1958), IceT (Feb 16, 1958), Andy Gibb (Mar 5, 1958), Sharon Stone (Mar 10, 1958), Holly Hunter (Mar 20, 1958), Gary Oldman (Mar 21, 1958), Alec Baldwin (Apr 3, 1958)

**Pluto Leo:** Apr 11, 1958 – Jun 10, 1958

Andie MacDowell (Apr 21, 1958), Drew Carey (May 23, 1958), Annette Bening (May 29, 1958), Prince (Jun 7, 1958), Keenen Ivory Wayans (Jun 8, 1958)

**Pluto Virgo:** Jun 10, 1958 – Oct 5, 1971; Apr 17, 1972 – Jul 30, 1972

Kevin Bacon (Jul 8, 1958), Angela Bassett (Aug 16, 1958), Madonna (Aug 16, 1958), Steve Guttenberg (Aug 24, 1958), Tim Burton (Aug 25, 1958), Scott Hamilton (Aug 28, 1958), Michael Jackson (Aug 29, 1958), Shaun Cassidy (Sep 27, 1958), Tanya Tucker (Oct 10, 1958), Tim Robbins (Oct 16, 1958), Viggo Mortensen (Oct 20, 1958), Jamie Lee Curtis (Nov 22, 1958), Rickey Henderson (Dec 25, 1958), Sade (Jan 16, 1959), Linda

Blair (Jan 22, 1959), Cris Collinsworth (Jan 27, 1959), Lawrence Taylor (Feb 4, 1959), John McEnroe (Feb 16, 1959), Ira Glass (Mar 3, 1959), Tom Arnold (Mar 6, 1959), David Hyde Pierce (Apr 3, 1959), Emma Thompson (Apr 15, 1959), Sheena Easton (Apr 27, 1959), Morrissey (May 22, 1959), Suzanne Vega (Jul 11, 1959), Kevin Spacey (Jul 26, 1959), Victoria Jackson (Aug 2, 1959), Rosanna Arquette (Aug 10, 1959), Earvin 'Magic' Johnson (Aug 14, 1959), Jason Alexander (Sep 23, 1959), Marie Osmond (Oct 13, 1959), Sarah Ferguson (Oct 15, 1959), 'Weird' Al Yankovic (Oct 23, 1959), Bryan Adams (Nov 5, 1959), MacKenzie Phillips (Nov 10, 1959), Judd Nelson (Nov 28, 1959), Florence Griffith Joyner (Dec 21, 1959), Tracey Ullman (Dec 30, 1959), Val Kilmer (Dec 31, 1959), Greg Louganis (Jan 29, 1960), Meg Tilly (Feb 14, 1960), Ivan Lendl (Mar 7, 1960), Marcus Allen (Mar 26, 1960), Valerie Bertinelli (Apr 23, 1960), John Elway (Jun 28, 1960), David Duchovny (Aug 7, 1960), Antonio Banderas (Aug 10, 1960), Timothy Hutton (Aug 16, 1960), Sean Penn (Aug 17, 1960), Cal Ripken Jr (Aug 24, 1960), Branford Marsalis (Aug 26, 1960), Damon Wayans (Sep 4, 1960), Hugh Grant (Sep 9, 1960), Joan Jett (Sep 22, 1960), Jean-Claude Van Damme (Oct 18, 1960), RuPaul (Nov 17, 1960), Amy Grant (Nov 25, 1960), John F. Kennedy Jr (Nov 25, 1960), Daryl Hannah (Dec 3, 1960), Julianne Moore (Dec 3, 1960), Kenneth Branagh (Dec 10, 1960), Gabrielle Carteris (Jan 2, 1961), Julia Louis-Dreyfus (Jan 13, 1961), Wayne Gretzky (Jan 26, 1961), George Stephanopoulos (Feb 10, 1961), Fabio (Mar 15, 1961), Eddie Murphy (Apr 3, 1961), Don Mattingly (Apr 20, 1961), Isiah Thomas (Apr 30, 1961), George Clooney (May 6, 1961), Dennis Rodman (May 13, 1961), Tim Roth (May 14, 1961), Enya (May 17, 1961), Melissa Etheridge (May 29, 1961), Lea Thompson (May 31, 1961), Michael J. Fox (Jun 9, 1961), Boy George (Jun 14, 1961), Greg LeMond (Jun 26, 1961), Princess Diana (Jul 1, 1961), Carl Lewis (Jul 1, 1961), Michelle Wright (Jul 1, 1961),

Woody Harrelson (Jul 23, 1961), Barack Obama (Aug 4, 1961), Billy Ray Cyrus (Aug 25, 1961), Dan Marino (Sep 15, 1961), Jennifer Tilly (Sep 16, 1961), James Gandolfini (Sep 18, 1961), Heather Locklear (Sep 25, 1961), Eric Stoltz (Sep 30, 1961), Steve Young (Oct 11, 1961), Wynton Marsalis (Oct 18, 1961)

**Uranus Virgo:** Nov 1, 1961 – Jan 10, 1962

k.d. lang (Nov 2, 1961), Nadia Comaneci (Nov 12, 1961), Meg Ryan (Nov 19, 1961), Mariel Hemingway (Nov 22, 1961), Kim Delaney (Nov 29, 1961)

**Uranus Leo:** Jan 10, 1962 – Aug 10, 1962

Jim Carrey (Jan 17, 1962), Jennifer Jason Leigh (Feb 5, 1962), Axl Rose (Feb 6, 1962), Garth Brooks (Feb 7, 1962), Cliff Burton (Feb 10, 1962), Steve 'Crocodile Hunter' Irwin (Feb 22, 1962), Jon Bon Jovi (Mar 2, 1962), Jackie Joyner-Kersee (Mar 3, 1962), Herschel Walker (Mar 3, 1962), Darryl Strawberry (Mar 12, 1962), Matthew Broderick (Mar 21, 1962), Rosie O'Donnell (Mar 21, 1962), M.C. Hammer (Mar 30, 1962), Al Unser Jr (Apr 19, 1962), Emilio Estevez (May 12, 1962), Ally Sheedy (Jun 13, 1962), Paula Abdul (Jun 19, 1962), Tom Cruise (Jul 3, 1962), Wesley Snipes (Jul 31, 1962), Roger Clemens (Aug 4, 1962), Patrick Ewing (Aug 5, 1962)

**Uranus Virgo:** Aug 10, 1962 – Sep 28, 1968; May 20, 1969 – Jun 24, 1969

James Marsters (Aug 20, 1962), Craig Kilborn (Aug 24, 1962), Kristy McNichol (Sep 11, 1962), Rob Morrow (Sep 21, 1962), Nia Vardalos (Sep 24, 1962), Tommy Lee (Oct 3, 1962), Joan Cusack (Oct 11, 1962), Jerry Rice (Oct 13, 1962), Evander Holyfield (Oct 19, 1962), Demi Moore (Nov 11, 1962), Jodie Foster (Nov 19, 1962), Bo Jackson (Nov 30, 1962), Tracy Austin (Dec 12, 1962), Sheryl Crow (Feb 11, 1963), Michael Jordan (Feb 17, 1963), Seal (Feb 19, 1963), Charles Barkley (Feb 20, 1963), Russell Wong (Mar 1, 1963), Kathy Ireland (Mar 8, 1963), Vanessa Williams (Mar 18, 1963), Quentin Tarantino (Mar 27, 1963), Julian Lennon (Apr 8, 1963), Garry Kasparov

(Apr 13, 1963), Conan O'Brien (Apr 18, 1963), Jet Li (Apr 26, 1963), Mike Myers (May 25, 1963), Johnny Depp (Jun 9, 1963), Helen Hunt (Jun 15, 1963), Lisa Kudrow (Jul 30, 1963), Whitney Houston (Aug 9, 1963), John Stamos (Aug 19, 1963), Tori Amos (Aug 22, 1963), Mark McGwire (Oct 1, 1963), Elisabeth Shue (Oct 6, 1963), Brian Boitano (Oct 22, 1963), Tatum O'Neal (Nov 5, 1963), Brad Pitt (Dec 18, 1963), Jennifer Beals (Dec 19, 1963), Nicolas Cage (Jan 7, 1964), Bridget Fonda (Jan 27, 1964), Chris Farley (Feb 15, 1964), Matt Dillon (Feb 18, 1964), Prince Edward (Mar 10, 1964), Will Clark (Mar 13, 1964), Rob Lowe (Mar 17, 1964), Bonnie Blair (Mar 18, 1964), Elle Macpherson (Mar 29, 1964), Ian Ziering (Mar 30, 1964), Russell Crowe (Apr 7, 1964), Melissa Gilbert (May 8, 1964), Lenny Kravitz (May 26, 1964), Wynonna Judd (May 30, 1964), Courteney Cox (Jun 15, 1964), José Canseco (Jul 2, 1964), Courtney Love (Jul 9, 1964), Barry Bonds (Jul 24, 1964), Sandra Bullock (Jul 26, 1964), Keanu Reeves (Sep 2, 1964), Rosie Perez (Sep 6, 1964), Trisha Yearwood (Sep 19, 1964), Janeane Garofalo (Sep 28, 1964), Dana Plato (Nov 7, 1964), Calista Flockhart (Nov 11, 1964), Robin Givens (Nov 27, 1964), Marisa Tomei (Dec 4, 1964), Brandon Lee (Feb 1, 1965), Dr Dre (Feb 18, 1965), Booker T (Mar 1, 1965), Sarah Jessica Parker (Mar 25, 1965), Robert Downey Jr (Apr 4, 1965), Martin Lawrence (Apr 16, 1965), Todd Bridges (May 27, 1965), Brooke Shields (May 31, 1965), Elizabeth Hurley (Jun 10, 1965), Dan Jansen (Jun 17, 1965), J.K. Rowling (Jul 31, 1965), Shania Twain (Aug 28, 1965), Charlie Sheen (Sep 3, 1965), Scottie Pippen (Sep 25, 1965), Mario Lemieux (Oct 5, 1965), Jon Stewart (Nov 28, 1965), Ben Stiller (Nov 30, 1965), Chris Rock (Feb 7, 1966), Cindy Crawford (Feb 20, 1966), Janet Jackson (May 16, 1966), John Cusack (Jun 28, 1966), Mike Tyson (Jun 30, 1966), Adam Sandler (Sep 9, 1966), Luke Perry (Oct 11, 1966), David Schwimmer (Nov 12, 1966), Daisy Fuentes (Nov 17, 1966), Troy Aikman (Nov 21, 1966), Sinead O'Connor (Dec

8, 1966), Kiefer Sutherland (Dec 21, 1966), Dave Matthews (Jan 9, 1967), Laura Dern (Feb 10, 1967), Kurt Cobain (Feb 20, 1967), Andrew Shue (Feb 20, 1967), Liz Phair (Apr 17, 1967), Tim McGraw (May 1, 1967), Nicole Kidman (Jun 20, 1967), Pamela Anderson (Jul 1, 1967), Vin Diesel (Jul 18, 1967), Matt LeBlanc (Jul 25, 1967), Deion Sanders (Aug 9, 1967), Harry Connick Jr (Sep 11, 1967), Faith Hill (Sep 21, 1967), Mira Sorvino (Sep 28, 1967), Moon Unit Zappa (Sep 28, 1967), Julia Roberts (Oct 28, 1967), Anna Nicole Smith (Nov 28, 1967), Cuba Gooding Jr (Jan 2, 1968), LL Cool J (Jan 14, 1968), Mary Lou Retton (Jan 24, 1968), Sarah McLachlan (Jan 28, 1968), Lisa Marie Presley (Feb 1, 1968), Gary Coleman (Feb 8, 1968), Molly Ringwald (Feb 18, 1968), Jeri Ryan (Feb 22, 1968), Lucy Lawless (Mar 29, 1968), Celine Dion (Mar 30, 1968), Ashley Judd (Apr 19, 1968), Tony Hawk (May 12, 1968), Yasmine Bleeth (Jun 14, 1968), Barry Sanders (Jul 16, 1968), Gillian Anderson (Aug 9, 1968), Halle Berry (Aug 14, 1968), Salma Hayek (Sep 2, 1968), Mike Piazza (Sep 4, 1968), Ricki Lake (Sep 21, 1968), Will Smith (Sep 25, 1968)

**Uranus Libra**: Sep 28, 1968 – May 20, 1969; Jun 24, 1969 – Nov 21, 1974; May 1, 1975 – Sep 8, 1975

Monica Bellucci (Sep 30, 1968), Jay Underwood (Oct 1, 1968), Toni Braxton (Oct 7, 1968), Thom Yorke (Oct 7, 1968), Hugh Jackman (Oct 12, 1968), Shaggy (Oct 22, 1968), Parker Posey (Nov 8, 1968), Sammy Sosa (Nov 12, 1968), Jon Knight (Nov 29, 1968), Lucy Liu (Dec 2, 1968), Brendan Fraser (Dec 3, 1968), Kurt Angle (Dec 9, 1968), Verne 'Mini-Me' Troyer (Jan 1, 1969), Christy Turlington (Jan 2, 1969), Michael Schumacher (Jan 3, 1969), Marilyn Manson (Jan 5, 1969), Ami Dolenz (Jan 8, 1969), R. Kelly (Jan 8, 1969), Stephen Hendry (Jan 13, 1969), Jason Bateman (Jan 14, 1969), Wendy Moniz (Jan 19, 1969), Junior Seau (Jan 19, 1969), Brendan Shanahan (Jan 23, 1969), Masaharu Fukuyama (Feb 6, 1969), Jennifer Aniston (Feb 11, 1969), Chastity Bono (Mar 4, 1969), Ari Meyers (Apr 6, 1969),

Renée Zellweger (Apr 25, 1969), Robert M. Hensel (May 8, 1969), Kim Fields (May 12, 1969), Cate Blanchett (May 14, 1969), Danny Wood (May 14, 1969), Emmitt Smith (May 15, 1969), Tracey Gold (May 16, 1969)

**Uranus Virgo:** May 20, 1969 – Jun 24, 1969

**Uranus Libra:** Jun 24, 1969 – Nov 21, 1974; May 1, 1975 – Sep 8, 1975

Cree Summer (Jul 7, 1969), Triple H (Jul 27, 1969), Donnie Wahlberg (Aug 17, 1969), Edward Norton (Aug 18, 1969), Erik 'Everlast' Schrody (Aug 18, 1969), Christian Slater (Aug 18, 1969), Matthew Perry (Aug 19, 1969), Jason Priestley (Aug 28, 1969), Dweezil Zappa (Sep 5, 1969), Catherine Zeta Jones (Sep 25, 1969), Gwen Stefani (Oct 3, 1969), Brett Favre (Oct 10, 1969), Martie Seidel (Oct 12, 1969), Nancy Kerrigan (Oct 13, 1969), Vanessa Marcil (Oct 15, 1969), Reginald 'Fieldy' Arvizu (Nov 2, 1969), Matthew McConaughey (Nov 4, 1969), Ken Griffey Jr (Nov 21, 1969), Andrew J. Howard (Dec 6, 1969), Jakob Dylan (Dec 9, 1969), Jack Noseworthy (Dec 21, 1969)

**Neptune Sagittarius:** Jan 4, 1970 – May 3, 1970

Kirk Franklin (Jan 26, 1970), Jennifer L.B. Leese (Jan 27, 1970), Heather Graham (Jan 29, 1970), Queen Latifah (Mar 18, 1970), Sharon Corr (Mar 24, 1970), Mase (Mar 24, 1970), Mariah Carey (Mar 27, 1970), Nick Hexum (Apr 12, 1970), Rick Schroder (Apr 13, 1970), Luis Miguel Basteri (Apr 19, 1970), Scott Bairstow (Apr 23, 1970), Tionne 'T-Boz' Watkins (Apr 26, 1970), André Agassi (Apr 29, 1970), Master P (Apr 29, 1970), Uma Thurman (Apr 29, 1970)

**Neptune Scorpio:** May 3, 1970 – Nov 6, 1970

Jordan Knight (May 17, 1970), Naomi Campbell (May 22, 1970), Joseph Fiennes (May 27, 1970), James 'Munky' Shaffer (Jun 6, 1970), Rivers Cuomo (Jun 13, 1970), Brian 'Head' Welch (Jun 19, 1970), Chris O'Donnell (Jun 26, 1970), Steve Burton (Jun 28, 1970), Charisma Carpenter (Jul 23, 1970), Jennifer Lopez (Jul 24, 1970), M. Night Shyamalan (Aug 6,

1970), Christopher Cuomo (Aug 9, 1970), Arion Salazar (Aug 9, 1970), Pete Sampras (Aug 12, 1970), Kevin Cadogan (Aug 14, 1970), Jim Courier (Aug 17, 1970), Malcolm-Jamal Warner (Aug 18, 1970), River Phoenix (Aug 23, 1970), Claudia Schiffer (Aug 25, 1970), Deborah Gibson (Aug 31, 1970), Ione Skye (Sep 4, 1970), Mark Brunell (Sep 17, 1970), Amy Jo Johnson (Oct 6, 1970), Matt Damon (Oct 8, 1970), Kirk Cameron (Oct 12, 1970), Sean 'P. Diddy' Combs (Nov 4, 1970), Javy Lopez (Nov 5, 1970)

**Neptune Sagittarius**: Nov 6, 1970 – Jan 19, 1984; Jun 23, 1984 – Nov 21, 1984

Ethan Hawke (Nov 6, 1970), Chris Jericho (Nov 9, 1970), Peta Wilson (Nov 11, 1970), Tonya Harding (Nov 12, 1970), Brooke Langton (Nov 27, 1970), Julie Condra (Dec 1, 1970), Jay-Z (Dec 4, 1970), David Kersh (Dec 9, 1970), Jennifer Connelly (Dec 12, 1970), Earl 'DMX' Simmons (Dec 18, 1970), Rob Van Dam (Dec 18, 1970), Taye Diggs (Jan 2, 1971), Joey Lauren Adams (Jan 6, 1971), David Yost (Jan 7, 1971), Mary J. Blige (Jan 11, 1971), Kid Rock (Jan 17, 1971), Jonathan Davis (Jan 18, 1971), Shawn Wayans (Jan 19, 1971), Gary Barlow (Jan 20, 1971), China Kantner (Jan 25, 1971), Minnie Driver (Jan 31, 1971), Renée O'Connor (Feb 15, 1971), Lea Salonga (Feb 22, 1971), Sean Astin (Feb 25, 1971), Rozonda 'Chilli' Thomas (Feb 27, 1971), Emmanuel Lewis (Mar 9, 1971), Sheryl Swoopes (Mar 25, 1971), Juliandra Gillen (Mar 28, 1971), Pavel Bure (Mar 31, 1971), Ewan McGregor (Mar 31, 1971), Picabo Street (Apr 3, 1971), Austin Peck (Apr 9, 1971), Nicholas Brendon (Apr 12, 1971), Shannen Doherty (Apr 12, 1971), Selena Quintanilla (Apr 16, 1971), Carolyn Dawn Johnson (Apr 30, 1971), David Boreanaz (May 16, 1971), Lisa 'Left Eye' Lopes (May 27, 1971), Joel Tobeck (Jun 2, 1971), Noah Wyle (Jun 4, 1971), 'Marky' Mark Wahlberg (Jun 5, 1971), Tupac Shakur (Jun 16, 1971), Nathan Morris (Jun 18, 1971), Kurt Warner (Jun 22, 1971), Missy Elliott (Jul 1, 1971), Kristi Yamaguchi (Jul 12, 1971), Corey Feldman (Jul 16, 1971), Tom Green (Jul 30, 1971), Jeff

Gordon (Aug 4, 1971), Fred Durst (Aug 20, 1971), Carla Gugino (Aug 29, 1971), Henry Thomas (Sep 8, 1971), Lance Armstrong (Sep 18, 1971), Jada Pinkett Smith (Sep 18, 1971), Alfonso Ribeiro (Sep 21, 1971), Jenna Elfman (Sep 30, 1971), Kevin Richardson (Oct 3, 1971)

**Pluto Libra**: Oct 5, 1971 – Apr 17, 1972

Chris Kirkpatrick (Oct 17, 1971), Winona Ryder (Oct 29, 1971), Christina Applegate (Nov 25, 1971), Michael McCary (Dec 16, 1971), Tyson Beckford (Dec 19, 1971), Amy Locane (Dec 19, 1971), Corey Haim (Dec 23, 1971), Ricky Martin (Dec 24, 1971), Dido (Dec 25, 1971), Amanda Peet (Jan 11, 1972), Drew Bledsoe (Feb 14, 1972), Billie Joe Armstrong (Feb 17, 1972), Denise Richards (Feb 17, 1972), Michael Chang (Feb 22, 1972), Erykah Badu (Feb 26, 1972), Antonio Sabato Jr (Feb 29, 1972), Shaquille O'Neal (Mar 6, 1972), Mark Hoppus (Mar 15, 1972), Mia Hamm (Mar 17, 1972), Elvis Stojko (Mar 22, 1972), Jennie Garth (Apr 3, 1972)

**Pluto Virgo**: Apr 17, 1972 – Jul 30, 1972

Jennifer Garner (Apr 17, 1972), Carmen Electra (Apr 20, 1972), Chipper Jones (Apr 24, 1972), Dwayne 'The Rock' Johnson (May 2, 1972), Darren Hayes (May 8, 1972), David Charvet (May 15, 1972), Busta Rhymes (May 20, 1972), Notorious B.I.G. (May 21, 1972), Wayne Brady (Jun 2, 1972), Karl Urban (Jun 7, 1972), Selma Blair (Jun 23, 1972), Marlon Wayans (Jul 23, 1972)

**Pluto Libra**: Jul 30, 1972 – Nov 5, 1983; May 18, 1984 – Aug 28, 1984

Brad Hargreaves (Jul 30, 1972), Geri Estelle Halliwell (Aug 6, 1972), Ben Affleck (Aug 15, 1972), Emily Robison (Aug 16, 1972), Cameron Diaz (Aug 30, 1972), Chris Tucker (Aug 31, 1972), Liam Gallagher (Sep 21, 1972), David Silveria (Sep 21, 1972), Shawn Stockman (Sep 26, 1972), Gwyneth Paltrow (Sep 28, 1972), Grant Hill (Oct 5, 1972), Eminem (Oct 17, 1972), Wyclef Jean (Oct 17, 1972), Snoop Dogg (Oct 20, 1972), Jenny

McCarthy (Nov 1, 1972), Rebecca Romijn-Stamos (Nov 6, 1972), Jason and Jeremy London (Nov 7, 1972), Bucky Lasek (Dec 3, 1972), Alyssa Milano (Dec 19, 1972), Jude Law (Dec 29, 1972), Joe McIntyre (Dec 31, 1972), Oscar De La Hoya (Feb 4, 1973), Justin Jeffre (Feb 25, 1973), Eric Lindros (Feb 28, 1973), Caroline Corr (Mar 17, 1973), David Blaine (Apr 4, 1973), Jeff Timmons (Apr 30, 1973), Tina Yothers (May 5, 1973), Tori Spelling (May 16, 1973), Juliette Lewis (Jun 21, 1973), Carson Daly (Jun 22, 1973), Kathleen Robertson (Jul 8, 1973), Brian Austin Green (Jul 15, 1973), Daniel Jones (Jul 22, 1973), Rufus Wainwright (Jul 22, 1973), Nomar Garciapara (Jul 23, 1973), Monica Lewinsky (Jul 23, 1973), Kate Beckinsale (Jul 26, 1973), Wanya Morris (Jul 29, 1973), Tempestt Bledsoe (Aug 1, 1973), Howie Dorough (Aug 22, 1973), Dave Chappelle (Aug 24, 1973), Lisa Ling (Aug 30, 1973), Jason David Frank (Sep 4, 1973), Rose McGowan (Sep 5, 1973), Greg Rusedski (Sep 6, 1973), Paul Walker (Sep 12, 1973), Neve Campbell (Oct 3, 1973), Steve Burns (Oct 9, 1973), Nick Lachey (Nov 9, 1973), Monica Seles (Dec 2, 1973), Holly Marie Combs (Dec 3, 1973), Tyra Banks (Dec 4, 1973), Christie Clark (Dec 13, 1973), Melanie Jayne Chisholm (Jan 12, 1974), Kate Moss (Jan 16, 1974), Tiffani-Amber Thiessen (Jan 23, 1974), Christian Bale (Jan 30, 1974), Seth Green (Feb 8, 1974), Robbie Williams (Feb 13, 1974), Jerry O'Connell (Feb 17, 1974), Bryan White (Feb 17, 1974), Mark-Paul Gosselaar (Mar 1, 1974), Kevin Connolly (Mar 5, 1974), Alyson Hannigan (Mar 24, 1974), Victoria Addams (Apr 17, 1974), Penelope Cruz (Apr 28, 1974), Andrea Corr (May 17, 1974), Fairuza Balk (May 21, 1974), Jewel (May 23, 1974), Alanis Morissette (Jun 1, 1974), Derek Jeter (Jun 26, 1974), Jeremy Castle (Aug 2, 1974), Rich Cronin (Aug 30, 1974), Ryan Phillippe (Sep 10, 1974), Jimmy Fallon (Sep 19, 1974), Matt Hardy (Sep 23, 1974), Dale Earnhardt Jr (Oct 10, 1974), Natalie Maines (Oct 14, 1974), Joaquin Phoenix (Oct 28, 1974), Leonardo DiCaprio (Nov 11, 1974)

**Uranus Scorpio:** Nov 21, 1974 – May 1, 1975

Emjay (Dec 9, 1974), Rey Mysterio Jr (Dec 12, 1974), Ryan Seacrest (Dec 24, 1974), Danica McKellar (Jan 3, 1975), Sara Gilbert (Jan 29, 1975), Big Boi (Feb 1, 1975), Natalie Imbruglia (Feb 4, 1975), Brian Littrell (Feb 20, 1975), Drew Barrymore (Feb 22, 1975), Niki Taylor (Mar 5, 1975),

**Uranus Libra:** May 1, 1975 – Sep 8, 1975

Enrique Iglesias (May 8, 1975), Lauryn Hill (May 25, 1975), André 3000 (May 27, 1975), Melanie Janine Brown (May 29, 1975), Angelina Jolie (Jun 4, 1975), Staci Keanan (Jun 6, 1975), Allen Iverson (Jun 7, 1975), Tobey Maguire (Jun 27, 1975), Ralf Schumacher (Jun 30, 1975), Alex Rodriguez (Jul 27, 1975), Kajol (Aug 5, 1975), Charlize Theron (Aug 7, 1975), Dante Basco (Aug 29, 1975)

**Uranus Scorpio:** Sep 8, 1975 – Feb 17, 1981; Mar 20, 1981 – Nov 16, 1981

Brad Fischetti (Sep 11, 1975), India Arie (Oct 3, 1975), Kate Winslet (Oct 5, 1975), Marion Jones (Oct 12, 1975), Kellie Martin (Oct 16, 1975), Tara Reid (Nov 8, 1975), Travis Barker (Nov 14, 1975), Mayim Bialik (Dec 12, 1975), Tom DeLonge (Dec 13, 1975), Milla Jovovich (Dec 17, 1975), Heather O'Rourke (Dec 27, 1975), Tiger Woods (Dec 30, 1975), Emma Lee Bunton (Jan 21, 1976), Lance Berkman (Feb 10, 1976), Brandon Boyd (Feb 15, 1976), Ja Rule (Feb 29, 1976), Freddie Prinze Jr (Mar 8, 1976), Chester Bennington (Mar 20, 1976), Reese Witherspoon (Mar 22, 1976), Keri Russell (Mar 23, 1976), Peyton Manning (Mar 24, 1976), Amy Smart (Mar 25, 1976), Jennifer Capriati (Mar 29, 1976), Matt Doran (Mar 30, 1976), Candace Cameron (Apr 6, 1976), Jonathan Brandis (Apr 13, 1976), Melissa Joan Hart (Apr 18, 1976), Joey Lawrence (Apr 20, 1976), Kelly Monaco (May 23, 1976), Colin Farrell (May 31, 1976), 50 Cent (Jul 6, 1976), Fred Savage (Jul 9, 1976), J.C. Chasez (Aug 8, 1976), Drew Lachey (Aug 8, 1976), Erin Hershey (Sep 2, 1976), Tina Barrett (Sep 16, 1976), Alison

Sweeney (Sep 19, 1976), Kip Pardue (Sep 23, 1976), Alicia Silverstone (Oct 4, 1976), Bob Burnquist (Oct 10, 1976), Omar Gooding (Oct 19, 1976), Jeremy Miller (Oct 21, 1976), Donovan McNabb (Nov 25, 1976), Jaleel White (Nov 27, 1976), Orlando Bloom (Jan 13, 1977), Joey Fatone Jr (Jan 28, 1977), Shakira (Feb 2, 1977), David 'Phoenix' Farrell (Feb 8, 1977), Mike Shinoda (Feb 11, 1977), Donovan Patton (Mar 1, 1977), Paul Cattermole (Mar 7, 1977), James Van Der Beek (Mar 8, 1977), Shannon Miller (Mar 10, 1977), Joe Hahn (Mar 15, 1977), Devin Lima (Mar 18, 1977), Sarah Michelle Gellar (Apr 14, 1977), Amanda Borden (May 10, 1977), Liv Tyler (Jul 1, 1977), Brock Lesnar (Jul 12, 1977), Edward Furlong (Aug 2, 1977), Tom Brady (Aug 3, 1977), Nicole Bobek (Aug 23, 1977), Jeff Hardy (Aug 31, 1977), Ludacris (Sep 11, 1977), Fiona Apple (Sep 13, 1977), Oksana Baiul (Nov 16, 1977), Laura Wilkinson (Nov 17, 1977), Kerri Strug (Nov 19, 1977), Brad Delson (Dec 1, 1977), Laila Ali (Dec 30, 1977), A.J. McLean (Jan 9, 1978), Ashton Kutcher (Feb 7, 1978), Jen Frost (Feb 22, 1978), Jensen Ackles (Mar 1, 1978), Rachel Stevens (Apr 9, 1978), Kyle Howard (Apr 13, 1978), Kim Elizabeth (Apr 22, 1978), Kenan Thompson (May 10, 1978), Jason Biggs (May 12, 1978), Shane West (Jun 10, 1978), Joshua Jackson (Jun 11, 1978), Zoë Saldana (Jun 19, 1978), Tia and Tamera Mowry (Jul 6, 1978), Josh Hartnett (Jul 21, 1978), Louise Brown (Jul 25, 1978), Kobe Bryant (Aug 23, 1978), Kel Mitchell (Aug 25, 1978), Mason Betha (Aug 27, 1978), Devon Sawa (Sep 7, 1978), Benjamin McKenzie (Sep 12, 1978), Ruben Studdard (Sep 12, 1978), Ayumi Hamasaki (Oct 2, 1978), Jodi Lyn O'Keefe (Oct 10, 1978), Nelly (Nov 2, 1978), Sisqo (Nov 9, 1978), Katherine Heigl (Nov 24, 1978), Clay Aiken (Nov 30, 1978), Nelly Furtado (Dec 2, 1978), Katie Holmes (Dec 18, 1978), Aaliyah (Jan 16, 1979), Rob Bourdon (Jan 20, 1979), Tatyana Ali (Jan 24, 1979), Andrew Keegan (Jan 29, 1979), Josh Keaton (Feb 8, 1979), Mena Suvari (Feb 9, 1979), Ziyi Zhang (Feb 9, 1979), Brandy (Feb 11, 1979), Jennifer Love

Hewitt (Feb 21, 1979), Norah Jones (Mar 30, 1979), Heath Ledger (Apr 4, 1979), Keshia Knight Pulliam (Apr 9, 1979), Claire Danes (Apr 12, 1979), Kate Hudson (Apr 19, 1979), Daniel Johns (Apr 22, 1979), Jo O'Meara (Apr 29, 1979), Lance Bass (May 4, 1979), Jesse Bradford (May 28, 1979), Shane Filan (Jul 5, 1979), Chad Brannon (Aug 31, 1979), Pink (Sep 8, 1979), Ariana Richards (Sep 11, 1979), Erik-Michael Estrada (Sep 23, 1979), Rachael Leigh Cook (Oct 4, 1979), Shawn Ashmore (Oct 7, 1979), Mya (Oct 10, 1979), Stacy Keibler (Oct 14, 1979), Usher (Oct 14, 1979), Ben Gillies (Oct 24, 1979), Chris Joannou (Nov 10, 1979), Trevor Penick (Nov 16, 1979), Scott Robinson (Nov 22, 1979), Rider Strong (Dec 11, 1979), Michael Owen (Dec 14, 1979), Kristanna Loken (Dec 19, 1979), Jenson Button (Jan 19, 1980), Nick Carter (Jan 28, 1980), Matt Lawrence (Feb 11, 1980), Christina Ricci (Feb 12, 1980), Tommy McCarthy (Feb 23, 1980), Chelsea Clinton (Feb 27, 1980), Adam Brody (Apr 8, 1980), Jacob Underwood (Apr 25, 1980), Venus Williams (Jun 17, 1980), Eric Stretch (Jun 22, 1980), Michelle Kwan (Jul 7, 1980), Jessica Simpson (Jul 10, 1980), Michelle Williams (Jul 23, 1980), Dominique Swain (Aug 12, 1980), Vanessa Carlton (Aug 16, 1980), Macaulay Culkin (Aug 26, 1980), Dan Miller (Sep 4, 1980), Michelle Williams (Sep 9, 1980), Yao Ming (Sep 12, 1980), Ben Savage (Sep 13, 1980), Martina Hingis (Sep 30, 1980), Ashanti (Oct 13, 1980), Nick Cannon (Oct 17, 1980), Monica (Oct 24, 1980), Ben Foster (Oct 29, 1980), Ryan Gosling (Nov 12, 1980), Isaac Hanson (Nov 17, 1980), Anna Chlumsky (Dec 3, 1980), Ric Felix (Dec 2, 1980), Christina Aguilera (Dec 18, 1980), Izabella Miko (Jan 21, 1981), Willa Ford (Jan 22, 1981), Alicia Keys (Jan 25, 1981), Elijah Wood (Jan 28, 1981), Jonny Lang (Jan 29, 1981), Justin Timberlake (Jan 31, 1981), Kelly Rowland (Feb 11, 1981)

**Uranus Sagittarius**: Feb 17, 1981 – Mar 20, 1981

Joseph Gordon-Levitt (Feb 17, 1981), Paris Hilton (Feb 17, 1981), Josh Groban (Feb 27, 1981), LeToya Luckett (Mar 11,

1981)

**Uranus Scorpio**: Mar 20, 1981 – Nov 16, 1981

Julia Stiles (Mar 28, 1981), Hannah Spearitt (Apr 1, 1981), Lil McClarnon (Apr 10, 1981), Hayden Christensen (Apr 19, 1981), Jessica Alba (Apr 28, 1981), Craig David (May 5, 1981), Danielle Fishel (May 5, 1981), Jamie-Lynn Sigler (May 15, 1981), Anna Kournikova (Jun 7, 1981), Larisa Oleynik (Jun 7, 1981), Natalie Portman (Jun 9, 1981), Hoku Ho (Jun 10, 1981), Eric Lively (Jul 31, 1981), Ashley Angel (Aug 1, 1981), Vanessa Amorosi (Aug 8, 1981), Bradley McIntosh (Aug 8, 1981), Beyoncé Knowles (Sep 4, 1981), Jonathan Taylor Thomas (Sep 8, 1981), Serena Williams (Sep 26, 1981), Dominique Moceanu (Sep 30, 1981), Zachery Ty Bryan (Oct 9, 1981), LaTavia Roberson (Nov 1, 1981), Rachel Bilson (Nov 13, 1981),

**Uranus Sagittarius**: Nov 16, 1981 – Feb 15 1988; May 27, 1988 – Dec 2, 1988

Britney Spears (Dec 2, 1981), Brian Bonsall (Dec 3, 1981), Lila McCann (Dec 4, 1981), Jodie Sweetin (Jan 19, 1982), Adam Lambert (Jan 29, 1982), Jessica Biel (Mar 3, 1982), Landon Donovan (Mar 4, 1982), Thora Birch (Mar 11, 1982), Hideaki Takizawa (Mar 29, 1982), Riley Smith (Apr 12, 1982), Kelly Clarkson (Apr 24, 1982), Jon Lee (Apr 26, 1982), Kirsten Dunst (Apr 30, 1982), Danny Zavatsky (Jun 1, 1982), Tara Lipinski (Jun 10, 1982), Leelee Sobieski (Jun 10, 1982), Prince William (Jun 21, 1982), Tash Hamilton (Jul 17, 1982), Anna Paquin (Jul 24, 1982), Brad Renfro (Jul 25, 1982), Devon Aoki (Aug 10, 1982), LeAnn Rimes (Aug 28, 1982), Andy Roddick (Aug 30, 1982), Alexis Bledel (Sep 16, 1982), Wade Robson (Sep 17, 1982), Christina Milian (Sep 26, 1982), Kieran Culkin (Sep 30, 1982), Lacey Chabert (Sep 30, 1982), Eric von Detten (Oct 3, 1982), Taylor Hanson (Mar 14, 1983), Sean Biggerstaff (Mar 15, 1983), Scott Moffatt (Mar 30, 1983), Ryan Merriman (Apr 10, 1983), Holly Valance (May 11, 1983), Kim Clijsters (Jun 8, 1983), Lee Ryan (Jun 17, 1983), Michelle Branch (Jul 2, 1983),

Marie Serneholt (Jul 11, 1983), Joseph Mazzello (Sep 21, 1983), Amit Paul (Oct 29, 1983)

**Pluto Scorpio**: Nov 5, 1983 – May 18, 1984

Mischa Mandel (Nov 20, 1983)

**Neptune Capricorn**: Jan 19, 1984 – Jun 23, 1984

Trever O'Brien (Jan 19, 1984), Lee Thompson Young (Feb 1, 1984), Bob Moffatt (Mar 8, 1984), Clint Moffatt (Mar 8, 1984), Dave Moffatt (Mar 8, 1984), Christy Carlson Romano (Mar 20, 1984), Kirsten Storms (Apr 8, 1984), Mandy Moore (Apr 10, 1984)

**Pluto Libra**: May 18, 1984 – Aug 28, 1984

**Neptune Sagittarius**: Jun 23, 1984 – Nov 21, 1984

Dhani Lennevald (Jul 24, 1984)

**Pluto Scorpio**: Aug 28, 1984 – Jan 17, 1995; Apr 21, 1995 – Nov 10, 1995

Adam Lamberg (Sep 14, 1984), Prince Harry (Sep 15, 1984), Kevin Zegers (Sep 19, 1984), Avril Lavigne (Sep 27, 1984), Sara Lumholdt (Oct 25, 1984), Kelly Osbourne (Oct 27, 1984),

**Neptune Capricorn**: Nov 21, 1984 – Jan 29, 1998; Aug 23, 1998 – Nov 28, 1998

LeBron James (Dec 30, 1984), Brandon 'Bug' Hall (Feb 4, 1985), Tina Majorino (Feb 7, 1985), David Gallagher (Feb 9, 1985), Keira Knightley (Mar 22, 1985), Greg Raposo (May 3, 1985), Raz-B (Jun 13, 1985), J-Boog (Aug 11, 1985), Jeff Licon (Aug 29, 1985), Madeline Zima (Sep 16, 1985), Michelle Trachtenberg (Oct 11, 1985), Zac Hanson (Oct 22, 1985), Masiela Lusha (Oct 23, 1985), Jack Osbourne (Nov 8, 1985), Omarion (Nov 12, 1985), Lil Fizz (Nov 26, 1985), Kaley Cuoco (Nov 30, 1985), Frankie Muniz (Dec 5, 1985), Raven (Dec 10, 1985), Mason Gamble (Jan 16, 1986), Mischa Barton (Jan 24, 1986), Charlotte Church (Feb 21, 1986), Miko Hughes (Feb 22, 1986), Margo Harshman (Mar 4, 1986), Eli Marienthal (Mar 6, 1986), Amanda Bynes (Apr 3, 1986), Joseph Cross (May 28, 1986), Joey Zimmerman (Jun 10, 1986), Shia LaBeouf (Jun 11,

1986), Mary-Kate and Ashley Olsen (Jun 13, 1986), Drake Bell (Jun 27, 1986), Lindsay Lohan (Jul 2, 1986), Lauren Collins (Aug 29, 1986), A.J. Trauth (Sep 14, 1986), Alexz Johnson (Nov 4, 1986), Vanessa Zima (Dec 17, 1986), Robyn Richards (Jan 22, 1987), Chelsea Brummet (Jan 28, 1987), Bow Wow (Mar 9, 1987), Tahj Mowry (May 17, 1987), Ashlie Brillaut (May 21, 1987), Lalaine (Jun 3, 1987), Scott Terra (Jun 25, 1987), Matthew O'Leary (Jul 6, 1987), Tom Felton (Sep 22, 1987), Hilary Duff (Sep 28, 1987), Kaci (Oct 3, 1987), Aaron Carter (Dec 7, 1987), Hallee Hirsh (Dec 16, 1987), Andy Lawrence (Jan 12, 1988)

**Uranus Capricorn**: Feb 15 1988 – May 27, 1988; Dec 2, 1988 – Apr 1, 1995; Jun 9, 1995 – Jan 12, 1996

Haley Joel Osment (Apr 10, 1988), Alex D. Linz (Jan 3, 1989), Yvonne Zima (Jan 17, 1989), Khleo Thomas (Jan 30, 1989), Jeremy Sumpter (Feb 5, 1989), Jake Lloyd (Mar 5, 1989), Daniel Radcliffe (Jul 23, 1989), Lil' Romeo (Aug 19, 1989), Michelle Wie (Oct 11, 1989), Emma Watson (Apr 15, 1990), Steven Anthony Lawrence (Jul 9, 1990), JonBenet Ramsey (Aug 6, 1990), Carly Schroeder (Oct 18, 1990), Jonathan Lipnicki (Oct 22, 1990), Jamie Lynn Spears (Apr 4, 1991), Madylin Sweeten (Jun 27, 1991), Emily Roeske (Jul 15, 1991), Steffani Brass (Feb 16, 1992), Rachel Appleton (May 19, 1992), Daryl Sabara (Jun 14, 1992), Hallie Eisenberg (Aug 2, 1992), Cole and Dylan Sprouse (Aug 4, 1992), Skye Bartusiak (Sep 28, 1992)

**Pluto Sagittarius**: Jan 17, 1995 – Apr 21, 1995; Nov 10, 1995 – Jan 26, 2008; Jun 14, 2008 – Nov 27, 2008

**Uranus Aquarius**: Apr 1, 1995 – Jun 9, 1995

**Uranus Capricorn**: Jun 9, 1995 – Jan 12, 1996

Austin Majors (Nov 23, 1995)

**Uranus Aquarius**: Jan 12, 1996 – Mar 10, 2003; Sep 15, 2003 – Dec 30, 2003

**Neptune Aquarius**: Jan 29, 1998 – Aug 23, 1998; Nov 28, 1998 – Apr 4, 2011; Aug 5, 2011 – Feb 3, 2012

**Uranus Pisces**: Mar 10, 2003 – Sep 15, 2003; Dec 30, 2003 – May 28, 2010; Aug 14, 2010 – Mar 12, 2011

# Bibliography

Allen, Frederick Lewis, *Only Yesterday: An Informal History of the 1920s* (New York: Harper & Row, 1964)

Durant, Will and Ariel, *The History of Civilization*, I–XI (New York: Simon & Schuster, 1975)

Fraser, Rebecca, *The Story of Britain: From the Romans to the Present: A Narrative History* (New York: W.W. Norton & Co., 2005)

Grun, Bernard, *The Timetables of History: A Historical Linkage of People and Events*, 4th edn (New York: Simon & Schuster, 2005)

'Io Edition' (library of famous charts included), Astrology Software for Mac OSX, Time Cycles Research, 1 Apr 2009 <http://timecycles.com/edition.html>

McNeill, William H., *A World History* (New York: OUP, 1967)

Michelsen, Neil F., *Tables of Planetary Phenomena* (ACS Publications, 1990)

Morison, Samuel Eliot, *The Oxford History of the American People* (New York: OUP, 1965)

Palmer, R.R. and Joel Colton, *A History of the Modern World* (New York: Alfred A. Knopf, 1965)

Stipp, John L., C. Warren Hollister, Allen W. Dirrim, *The Rise and Development of Western Civilization* (New York: John Wiley & Sons, 1972)

Strauss, William and Neil Howe, *Generations: The History of America's Future, 1584 to 2069* (New York: Quill, 1991)

Thomson, David, *Europe since Napoleon* (New York: Alfred A. Knopf, 1957)

Zinn, Howard, *A People's History of the United States: 1492 to Present* (New York: Harper Perennial, 1995)